William Holman Hunt

With John Everett Millais and Dante Gabriel Rossetti, William Holman Hunt is a key figure in the Pre-Raphaelite Brotherhood, that Victorian rebellion against what they considered the frivolity of contemporary artists. His most famous painting, 'The Light of the World', is a representative image of the religious and moral aspirations of the movement.

Born in 1827 of humble origins, Hunt started work as a clerk at the age of twelve but began to paint in his spare time, winning a place at the Royal Academy Schools when he was seventeen. It was there that he met Millais, and found intellectual support in the writings of Ruskin. The painstaking technique of Hunt's style demanded months of prolonged labour to finish one picture, some taking between five and ten years to complete. No wonder he complained that 'I work and work until I feel my brain as dry as an old bit of cork.'

With his mane of red hair and exuberant beard, Hunt looked suitably like an Old Testament prophet, and his major canvases, calculated to appeal to wide audiences, seemed part of the man. Sin and guilt, retribution and redemption, were recurring themes in his work. Like Rossetti, he fell victim to a *femme fatale*, a resplendent model called Annie Miller, whom he attempted to reform and then marry, failing in both objectives. Hunt eventually married Fanny Waugh, and, several years after her death, married her sister Edith, a union still forbidden under English law.

Hunt made several journeys to Egypt and Palestine in order to achieve the utmost accuracy for his biblical scenes; he became absorbed in Jewish customs and history. Despite the taint of illegality which clouded much of his later life, the rewards of his final forty years were to compensate for the hardship of the first. An elaborate and highly wrought picture, 'The Finding of Christ in the Temple', was sold in the early 1860s for the then stupendous sum of £5,500, and later works fetched even higher sums. He died in 1910.

The sincerity of Hunt's aims and the lapses of his behaviour continue to intrigue us. He is an archetypal Victorian figure, as this memoir by his grand-daughter reveals.

The Lively Arts
General Editor: Robert Ottaway

A Mingled Chime · Sir Thomas Beecham
Dance to the Piper · Agnes de Mille
A Life in the Theatre · Tyrone Guthrie
My Grandfather, His Wives and Loves · Diana Holman-Hunt
Groucho and Me · Groucho Marx
Fun in a Chinese Laundry · Josef von Sternberg

Forthcoming titles include

Around Theatres · Max Beerbohm
Memoirs Vol. I · Alexandre Benois
The Movies, Mr Griffith and Me · Lillian Gish
Chaliapin · Maxim Gorky
Renoir, My Father · Jean Renoir
Liszt · Sir Sacheverell Sitwell

MY GRANDFATHER

HIS WIVES AND LOVES

*

DIANA HOLMAN-HUNT

COLUMBUS BOOKS
LONDON

This trade paperback edition
published in Great Britain in 1987 by
Columbus Books Limited
19-23 Ludgate Hill
London, EC4M 7PD
Reprinted 1987

First published in 1969 by Hamish Hamilton Ltd

British Library Cataloguing in Publication Data

Holman-Hunt, Diana
My grandfather, his wives and loves——
(The Lively arts).
1. Hunt, William Holman 2. Symbolism in art
——England
I. Title II. Series
759.2   ND497.H9

ISBN 0–86287–379–7

Printed and bound by The Guernsey Press
Guernsey, CI

ACKNOWLEDGMENTS

First of all I should like to express my gratitude to Mrs Elizabeth Burt for lending me her large collection of letters. Those from F.G. Stephens to Hunt were of particular value to dovetail with the Hunt letters to F.G. Stephens in the Iggulden Collection which the Bodleian Library kindly gave me permission to use.

I should also like to thank the Pierpont Morgan Library, New York, for allowing me to use extracts from their J.E. Millais letters to Hunt and the Henry E. Huntington Library and Art Gallery, San Marino, California, for letting me quote from a Hunt letter to Walter Deverell. Miss Jean F. Preston, the Assistant Curator of Manuscripts, was especially helpful in deciphering various passages, which had been illegible hitherto.

I am also indebted to the Princeton University Library for permission to publish some of Hunt's letters to J.H. Bradley, which they now own. Mrs Stabile Smith, granddaughter of J.H. Bradley, was most kind in letting me copy these for Evelyn Waugh some years before they were sold.

I much appreciate Evelyn Waugh's literary executors' allowing me to include in the Prologue extracts from his letters written to me when he 'aspired to write a life of Hunt. . . .' and to the *Spectator* for allowing me to reprint his The Only *Pre-Raphaelite*.

I should like to thank Sir Ralph Millais for permission to include many letters from J.E. Millais to Hunt, now in the possession of Mrs Elizabeth Burt; also Raoul Millais for lending me interesting letters and giving me useful information.

I am extremely grateful to Miss Mary Bennett of the Walker Art Gallery, Liverpool, for answering my innumerable queries as to the whereabouts of certain pictures with such good will and for providing a mine of information about the period; also to Mr Ian Lowe of the Ashmolean Museum and Mr Richard Ormond of the National Portrait Gallery, and Dr Cannon Brooks of the City Museum and Art Galleries, Birmingham, who have been most helpful in assisting me to trace and choose illustrations.

Mr David Piper of the Fitzwilliam Museum, Cambridge, and Mr Wilfrid Blunt of the Watts Museum, Guildford, and Sir Colin Anderson have all advised on different points and put me on the right track for further investigation. I am also grateful for permission to reproduce Holman Hunt's 'The Awakening Conscience', the property of the Trustees of Sir Colin and Lady Anderson.

Mr Ian Robertson, lately Keeper of the Department of Western Art at the Ashmolean, and Mr John Bryson both encouraged me to write this book when I became increasingly aware of the size of the task that faced me, and, two years ago, had it not been for Rosalie Mander's keen interest in the project I might well have lost heart.

The practical enthusiasm of Mr E.R. Beecher of the Conservation Department of the Victoria and Albert Museum was of the greatest assistance: it was through him that I learned how to decipher heavily censored illegible words and passages in many letters.

The Arts Council has been most co-operative in producing photographs for my illustrations and the Photo Process Co. has come to my aid at short notice on several occasions.

My distant cousin Mrs Mary White has solved many puzzles in the Waugh family tree. I much appreciated her long informative letters on family affairs. Miss Frances Reynolds of the Bridport Museum has made brave efforts to track down illustrated letters from Hunt to his eldest son, my half-uncle Cyril.

I doubt if I could have written this book in less than four years without help from Bridget Lakin of the Society of Genealogists. I am extremely grateful for her professional and efficient research into the backgrounds of major and minor characters.

I have been fortunate in having many good friends, who have a personal interest in the Pre-Raphaelites and the Victorian period. I should like to thank Virginia Surtees in particular for her kindness and forbearance in answering my anxious enquiries on practical problems so promptly by letter and for suffering my telephone calls at all hours with good humour.

I have frequently asked Mary Lutyens, James Laver and Jeremy Maas for advice or information and feel full of gratitude to them all.

Concerning the actual writing of my book, I am again indebted. When I had almost completed my research, Peter Leslie was a great help in aiding me to sort out a mass of material into chronological order and in devising a filing system for subjects and characters. His advice on certain chapters was most welcome. My brother-in-law, Guy Strutt, has taken a sympathetic interest in my work and made many constructive criticisms. Christopher Busby of Curtis Brown Ltd has shown great generosity in giving up much of his free time to help me with my final corrections.

Last, but by no means least, I should like to thank my part-time secretary, Diana Porter, for her efficiency and devotion over the last two years.

Finally, I gratefully acknowledge permission to use quotations from the following publishers and copyright owners:

The Clarendon Press, *Letters of Dante Gabriel Rossetti*, edited by Doughty and Wahl, Oxford, 1965.

Hamish Hamilton Ltd, 'The Spell of Rossetti', *Time Was: Reminiscences*, by W. Graham Robertson, London, 1931.

Weidenfeld and Nicolson Ltd, *Age of Optimism*, by James Laver, London, 1966.

The Bodley Head Ltd, *The Wife of Rossetti, Her Life and Death*, by Violet Hunt, London, 1932.

The Oxford University Press, *A Victorian Romantic: Dante Gabriel Rossetti*, by Oswald Doughty, London, 1949; second edition 1960.

Chapman and Hall Ltd, *Thomas Woolner, R.A., Sculptor and Poet: His Life in Letters*, by Amy Woolner, London, 1917.

Allen and Unwin Ltd, *Vindication of Ruskin*, by J.H. Whitehouse, London, 1950.

Prologue

I HAD ONLY met my cousin, Evelyn Waugh, three or four times before the war and the last time was in 1949, in Gloucestershire. I was staying with friends who had recently changed the spelling of their name to disguise its Jewish origin. Like me they were great admirers of Evelyn's work. He lived quite near, and when they heard that he was my relation (I had foolishly boasted of this) they persuaded me to invite him and his wife to luncheon at their house.

Throughout the visit, in spite of my warning frowns, he insisted on addressing them by name with embarrassing frequency, stressing its origin with a strong Semitic pronunciation. His wife, Laura, was very quiet.

Shortly afterwards, Laura telephoned me to say that her father-in-law, Arthur Waugh the publisher, who knew my grandmother, and her brother-in-law Alec were staying with them: they wanted to meet me.

I was introduced by Evelyn as 'Diana Holman-Hunt, Mrs Bergner'—he should have said Bergne—'she's just *being* divorced.' I had married in my teens and was now in my early twenties: I had little self-confidence and felt this injustice keenly. Being a compulsive writer, I have kept a journal since I was a child: I noted my indignation.

Because Evelyn was such a brilliant literary figure I felt that anything I said to him was idiotic. Unfortunately, I was unaware that he had written a paper on Pre-Raphaelitism and published a life of Rossetti.[1] I thought that his interest in my grandfather and his Pre-Raphaelite brother-in-law, Thomas Woolner, was due only to their marriages to the Waugh sisters.

---

[1] Evelyn Waugh, *Rossetti: His Life and Works*, Duckworth, London, 1928.

13

I was at first surprised, then puzzled and suspicious, to hear him enthuse about my grandfather's work. Surely, like most contemporary intellectuals, he must find it awful? Throughout the thirties and forties, I had become used to hearing that unfashionable Pre-Raphaelitism, and crazy Surrealism, were but 'withered branches on the tree of art', which lead nowhere. There was no future for literal painters, mere illustrators.

When asked which of my grandfather's pictures I liked or disliked my replies were therefore wary. Pressed for my opinions, I admitted that I quite liked the background for *The Light of the World*, but wished that some pretty girl, like my great-aunt Alice Woolner, had been standing at the door instead of what Carlyle had called 'that papistical fancy figure'. I ventured that the model who posed for *April Love*, perhaps with a baby in her arms, would have pleased me more.

Cautiously sipping my second glass of sherry, I added how shocked I had been as a child that my grandfather had bullied his grandmother (who had had twenty-one children) into sacrificing the precious family tablecloth—an heirloom, richly embroidered—for cutting up and hanging on the lay figure. After all, the drapery in this picture was painted so stiffly that he might just as well have used paper.

Arthur Waugh referred to my grandfather's conviction that Christ was fair-skinned and red-haired.

I said what a pity it was that my father had been given all those horrid red curls as the Christ child in *The Triumph of the Innocents*. How much prettier was the small replica where Papa was painted as he was, with short mouse-coloured hair. He had told me that his earliest recollection was of being smacked because he shivered—he was naked and cold : the studio stove had gone out.

Evelyn returned to the subject of Pre-Raphaelite backgrounds. Before Rossetti painted *Found* he had searched desperately for 'an eligible wall . . . not too far countrified to represent a city wall, some moss but no prodigality of grass, weeds, etc'. I could have capped this by saying that Lear wrote to my grandfather, whom he addressed as Daddy or Pa, although he was the elder, begging him to 'send some grass—a longish tuft, not to eat—but to paint from in the 4 ground' (his spelling was original).

Talking of grass, Alec said how odd it was that they all had

14

such a passion for sheep: this might account for many painters of the day wishing to emigrate to Australia. Not only Woolner, but one of Hunt's brothers and my great-uncle, George Waugh, had sought their fortunes there only to return disappointed to England.

Grass having led so suitably to sheep, I was able to refer to the time when Millais painted a whole flock from two severed woolly heads produced by a London butcher.

At this point Evelyn, fixing me with a piercing look, said how cruel my grandfather had been, to starve three goats to death in the desert.

I had never heard this accusation before and protested that my grandmother had always assured me to the contrary—how kind he had been to animals and how much he loved birds. According to Millais' diary[2] they were both horrified to find English village boys stoning sparrows with their legs tied together having thrown them in a pond. I admitted that my grandfather trapped birds to paint from, but had, as Millais wrote in his journal, 'afterwards decorated their heads with green, and sent them on their way rejoicing'.

Under slight pressure I was bound to agree at last that in their search for realism, the Brothers were somewhat ruthless.

I wish I had known then what I know now from a Rossetti letter. When he was painting the calf in a net for *Found*, about which there was much controversy later, he wrote, 'he kicks and fights all the time he remains tied up' and 'appears to be so melancholy that he punctually attempts suicide by hanging himself at 3.30 p.m. daily. At these times I have to cut him down and then shake him up and lick him like blazes. There is a pleasure in it, my dear fellow: the Smithfield drovers are a kind of opium-eaters at it, but a moderate practitioner might perhaps sustain an argument'.

I was unaccustomed to alcohol and had it not been for the wine at luncheon I doubt if I would have made any conversation at all, but they all led me on and seemed amused when I told them that my grandfather had boiled a horse in the garden at home much to the annoyance and asphyxiation of the neighbours

[2] J. G. Millais, *Millais: The Life and Letters of Sir John Everett Millais*, Methuen, London, 1899.

—he had needed the skeleton to study from as a model.

As I said goodbye I was amazed when Evelyn, beetling his brows, asked rather pompously, but with apparent sincerity, 'Do you write these things down? I find your views and reminiscences extremely interesting.'

When I got back to the house where I was staying my hosts were convinced that he had meant this sarcastically. At once I lost confidence and vowed not to see this alarming, clever man again, however keen my friends were to meet him on the slender excuse of our relationship.

We lost touch until just after the war when I had remarried and become Mrs David Cuthbert and lived at Beaufront in Northumberland. My husband told me that Evelyn, who was a great friend of his step-sister and her husband, the Actons, had come up to him in White's Club and said, 'I hear you have married my *beautiful* cousin.' After this, each time David and Evelyn met they were very friendly, but when David told me that he had invited Evelyn to stay I felt, in spite of reassurances, sick with apprehension. However, he didn't come—to my relief then, but regret now.

When my husband died and once more my life was turned upside down, Evelyn wrote, 'I mourned David's death, as did his numberless friends . . . Is there any chance of luring you to visit us? We have no engagements—Sundays or weekdays are the same to us, if you could spare a night or two . . . Do come. Your affectionate cousin, Evelyn.'

Shortly after this, I produced a book called *My Grandmothers and I*,[3] an autobiographical venture. To my astonishment, it proved a bestseller, perhaps partly due to a review, or rather an article, which Evelyn wrote about it in the *Spectator*.[4]

I wrote to thank him. He replied, again urging me to come and stay at Combe Florey. 'Your book is enchanting. . . . Were the yellow coins sovereigns or *faery* gold? . . . My curiosity about your grandfather and "Grand" is insatiable. How bad your handwriting is! . . .'

I was now 'Dear Coz' and his letters usually ended with

[3] Diana Holman-Hunt, *My Grandmothers and I*, Hamish Hamilton, London, 1960.
[4] Evelyn Waugh, 'The Only Pre-Raphaelite', *Spectator*, London, 14 October 1960, reprinted here as Appendix II, p. 292.

'Cousinly love'. There was something engaging about his frequent 'thanks awfully for your most interesting letter'. I no longer felt afraid of him. He wanted to know all that I could tell him about my grandparents. The things that I had left unexplained in my book intrigued him because, he said, 'I aspire to write a life of Hunt but I would not be able to start work for two years and by that time I may have lost my reason.' In this letter he added, 'P.S. I was in London for a day and popped in on the Max Ernst exhibition with great enjoyment.' His taste in painting was clearly consistent.

I was anxious to give such a biographer any clues I could of my grandfather's personal life. For example, some art historians have given elaborate reasons for his quarrel with Rossetti. The truth was that the latter had stolen from him for a time the notorious beauty, Annie Miller. Grant Allen saw the making of a novel in the whole affair, saying that 'she was the one Pre-Raphaelite heroine whose rôle had been sedulously concealed, out of consideration for these two great men'. References to her in the Pre-Raphaelite memoirs are scanty, although at the time her name was a byword.

Also Evelyn wanted to know about 'the mysterious ten years between two Waughs', the interval between my grandfather's marriages to Fanny and Edith and Edith's estrangement from their sister, who married Woolner. 'I shall never tire of your stories of Grand: please recollect all you can,' Evelyn had written on a postcard.

At last I boarded the train for Taunton. I was still suffering from the shock of my husband's death and the second one of having written a successful book. I had about three hours to think over such things as might be of interest to Evelyn. In my book there were a number of discrepancies and obscurities because I had disciplined myself to describe everything as it had seemed through the eyes of the child I then was.

As Evelyn said, my Holman-Hunt grandmother would have been extravagantly original in any age. I thought that she was an interesting eccentric because her character was made up of two violently contrasting sides. To depict her in sharp silhouette I had concentrated on black and white and used very little grey. I had not wanted to confuse the average reader, but it was the grey that Evelyn wished to see.

17

While the train rattled on, I hoped that I should succeed in explaining her inconsistencies. Certainly, she was ruled by lofty moral principles, and inspired by extreme idolatry of her husband. She was the dedicated custodian of his good name for posterity. Like many Victorian widows she devoted her life to canonizing him. She wept copiously and regularly over the stone which covered his ashes in St Paul's and to the end defended his claim to have been the originator of Pre-Raphaelitism, training me, as the only family member of the third generation, to remember all his achievements. Any weaknesses or personal foibles were ruthlessly suppressed. She spoke favourably of Ruskin and Millais, but did all she could to prejudice me against Rossetti, and of course Whistler.

She was unaware that the image she tried to impose on my mind was that of a boring prig. Yet she didn't wholly succeed. At an early age, various sly hints from my father and my half-uncle Cyril had made me sceptical. I felt sure that after all Grandpa Holman was more human than she, or perhaps he, would have me and others believe.

By the time I was twelve years old I knew that he had not decided to become a religious painter for religious reasons, but because the subject of Christianity appealed to him historically and satisfied not only his passion for the Orient, but his obsession with the intense study of natural appearances, and the representation of detail in different lights. The Bible and the Holy Land enabled him to apply these to a popular theme. 'While his French contemporaries, the Impressionists, sought to record a glimpse, he recorded months of intense scrutiny.'

When my grandmother hurried me past the Renoirs and Monets in the Louvre during a memorable visit to Paris I wondered that I was allowed to look at the Turners in the Tate. Why were they all right? Perhaps just because Grandpa Holman remembered him as 'that shabby man' he was brushed with a little sanctity in her eyes.

And yet surely my grandfather and the Impressionists were obsessed with light at the same date?

His intense concentration on the effect of sunlight on the fleece of a sheep, reflected light on a face, moonlight combined with lamplight and the entirely different light in the East, was

18

his main interest in painting for painting's sake, regardless of the subjects.[5]

My grandmother would have been horrified had I expressed such a view then. She held that 'art for art's sake was a *sin*: art must have a message'.

The older and more suspicious I grew, the more boring her eulogies of my grandfather became. When I asked questions about people or events which interested me, she would answer stuffily, 'Beloved Holman so rightly disapproved of tittle tattle.' I supposed that loving her, and knowing what she expected, compelled him to fulfil his rôle as Holy Hunt in the niche which she and the public created for him. I think that she was the only woman he really tried to please and didn't try to reform or change. Why should he? She worshipped him: it was restful and flattering. She was strong mentally and physically and it was she who succeeded in changing him.

There is no doubt that in Victorian England she suffered at first much criticism as a deceased wife's sister, especially from the Waughs. The Queen however was sympathetic—according to gossip one of her daughters wanted to do the same.

To what lengths these Victorians went in their longing for respectability! Millais' dying wish that his wife should be received by the Queen was typical.

Certainly, my grandmother was obsessed with thrift and insisted on the practice of self-discipline and self-denial, stressing the need of the subjugation of the body to the spirit. My grandfather was nearly fifty and she twenty-nine when they married. His health had suffered from the rigours of travel in the East. She had been in love with him since she was fifteen, when she had seen him over the banisters—a suitor courting her elder sister Fanny. She often told me that she had never loved any

[5] 'I think that there was always something abnormal about his eyesight and that perhaps this was why he finally lost it: he was not only obsessed by light but even made an attempt to depict *supernatural light*. To this end, he tested the "character of intensified moonlight" using a lens and found to his surprise "that the focus transmitted was not of silvery tone, but of warm sunlight" giving both a real and unreal effect. At least one contemporary critic understood him and wrote: "The eye, when dazzled by effects of light, sees colours which do not exist outwardly and physically, but only inwardly and within the mind's consciousness." In fact, what some might now call "psychedelic" colours.'

other man. Her two children were born within the first five years of their marriage. I suspect that the marriage was platonic after this.

She was extremely vain and would only grudgingly admit that other beautiful women, like her sisters, Fanny and Alice Waugh, and Mrs William Morris, had any looks at all, saying, 'I know I should not divulge it, but her eyes were too small' or, 'she was rather C.'

She was attracted by bearded men and declared, 'A handsome beard is so *manly*.' She often referred to my grandfather's vigorous but unconventional dancing. Evelyn was intrigued by the stories of his dancing solo in the desert or with his shotgun as a partner. I thought I understood. It is only when one is old that one cannot dance alone.

I knew that he would ask me for an explanation of the 'faery gold', which I had found in a chest by accident. I had only described in my book how, when I pulled out the drawer, its bottom collapsed and showered coins all over the floor. My grandmother and I had shovelled them into a pillow case, and slid it downstairs on a tea tray.

After all these years I could think of only one explanation. John Woodward, of the Birmingham Art Gallery, had once told me that she had been prosecuted during the First World War for breaking the currency laws and withdrawing a lot of money —thousands of sovereigns—from the bank. Perhaps the gold was part of this haul.

I reached Taunton at last. Laura met me at the station and we climbed into a bus-like vehicle, which she explained was used to take the chrysanthemums to market and was big enough for all their children. She drove very fast. When we arrived, I was flattered to see Evelyn waiting in the cold at the door, with his arms outstretched: 'Welcome, dear Coz.'

His manner and gesture were wonderfully courteous and old-fashioned. 'What a splendid coat,' he went on, helping me off with it in the hall. I explained that it had belonged to my husband's uncle, old General Cuthbert, and was the leather lining of a military coat, fifty years old or more.

'Splendid, splendid, it suits you perfectly and fits you too. A general? You are a tall woman: he was a man of middle height, no doubt.'

I was led into a comfortable room with a blazing fire, and shabby hide buttoned sofas and library chairs. The walls were covered with Victorian portraits and narrative pictures.

He announced that we were going to have over two hours to ourselves before dinner and that this was the time for drinking and discussion. What did I drink? Whisky?

I said that I never drank whisky, but that gin and something would be excellent. He clapped his hands and in a loud voice commanded, 'A bottle of gin for Cousin Diana!'

A fair-haired girl ran in, said 'How d'you do', and ran out; she returned immediately with a new bottle of Booth's and a tumbler. These she put on the table at my elbow. Evelyn settled down in his chair. Nervously, I protested that I couldn't drink the gin neat. He looked quite put out and said, 'I hope you aren't going to ask for a lot of those new-fangled minerals and vermouths.'

I said anything would do.

'If you want ice, we will send my daughter to scrape some off a puddle in the drive; we have no frigidaire, as I believe they are called, no money for such luxuries.' He then launched into a grumbling saga of financial worries, copyrights and film rights sold long ago for ridiculous sums, holes in the roof, and so on. The fair-haired girl was hovering at the door. 'Mrs Cuthbert is not satisfied with a bottle of gin.' He sounded irritable. 'See what she wants. Time is passing: we are getting nowhere.'

Already, I noticed that I was dear Coz or Cousin Diana or Mrs Cuthbert depending on how I was regarded. Feeling a great nuisance, I said I would be quite happy with tap water, not daring to ask if there was any lemon in the house.

'Tap water for Cousin Diana . . .'

At last, the door was shut and we settled down.

He said, 'I never drink until this hour—except in London, of course.'

'You don't find that it helps you to work?'

He looked shocked. 'Never!'

There was a silence except for the splash of gin and water into my tumbler. The fire was hot.

I told him all I could about the gold and some of the things I had remembered in the train. We both referred to my grandfather as Hunt.

Evelyn clearly regarded him as a dark horse and relished the thought of his prolonged love-affair with Annie Miller. He was sure that Hunt and Millais had picked her up at Ewell. He thought that she had sat for the shepherdess in *The Hireling Shepherd*. Millais had described in his diary how, smoking their pipes and leaning on a stile, they had waited for girls returning from work in the nearby fields.

I knew from family papers that a girl called Emma Watkins, not Annie Miller, was the model in *The Hireling Shepherd*. It had always amused me that 'her brother was a seller of groundsel'. For what purpose, I wondered?

Evelyn was not convinced. Hunt had threatened Dickens with a libel action over a sketch in *Household Words* which seemed to refer to his seduction of the shepherdess from Ewell. The story had been particularly offensive to Hunt because, when it was published, he was engaged to marry Annie Miller.

In those days I didn't know much about Emma Watkins or Annie Miller. We were both confused about these girls. I promised to investigate further.

Now Evelyn was enjoying his drink. 'Ramble on. I shall not interrupt, but, later, if I can contribute anything of interest, I will.'

I said I didn't know much about the Waughs. It was only during the dreaded hour set aside each day for me to practise the 'pianoforte' that I sometimes succeeded in extracting a little information about my Waugh grandmother's early life. The drawing-room was terribly cold during the week: even in winter; a fire was only lit on Sundays when she was 'At Home'.

'Are you musical?' Evelyn interrupted.

I explained that I had found it best to pretend I was because the practice hour at school was the only time one could go to the lavatory without waiting in a queue.

He said this seemed fair enough.

When I practised at Melbury Road my grandmother would sometimes enter clutching her sewing and draw up a chair beside me. Her discourse always began with the same phrase, 'My seven sisters and I practised the pianoforte every day except, of course, on Sundays.' Modestly excluding herself, she would add, 'They were known as the seven beautiful Miss Waughs—just as *my* grandmother was one of the beautiful Miss Pasfields—she was painted by Opie . . .' She would continue in this vein, telling me that she, Edith, was the tenth child, the youngest: 'I began practising scales and arpeggios before breakfast—Alice took over punctually at nine.' The elder sisters, Mary, Fanny and Margaret, were the most accomplished, but it was not until the evening that their turn came. They used to change into silk dresses as soon as their parents, together with a few privileged friends who joined the family circle, were free to enjoy their talents. The younger children were Emily, Eve, Isabelle, George, Edith and Alice, who would be already banished to bed, but she sometimes crept down to sit on the knee of her father, the eminent Scottish divine, or to pass round the sugarplums and sweetmeats, making her bob to the guests. Then Father would announce, 'From dawn to dusk, this brave instrument is never silent. Day after day, hour after hour, my eight daughters pound the ivory keys.'

The idea of *eight* beautiful daughters always appealed to me.

By the time my grandfather married Fanny Waugh she was thirty—'on the shelf' in those days (she had even considered taking the veil). Edith had to wait for another ten years, 'through endless vicissitudes', before she was to marry the man whom she had always craved. Of course when I was a child she had never told me of the Deceased Wife's Sister Act or the Table of Affinities. My other grandfather referred to the marriage as 'All's fair in love and Waugh—WAUGH!'

At this point, I topped up my glass with gin.

Evelyn said he was quite sure that there were only three Waugh sisters. I repeated that there were eight. He seemed not to hear and by now I knew better than to insist. He even re-iterated this error in his autobiography.

He did, however, agree that there were two brothers. One went to America: nothing was recalled about him. The other was always referred to as 'poor-great-uncle-George'. He was drowned near Dartmouth, in sight of F. G. Stephens' farmhouse. I owned an oil portrait of him by my grandfather in a hand-some tortoiseshell and ebony frame which I promised to sell to Evelyn. My grandmother was always reticent about George. I couldn't tell whether it was because, like the rest of the family, he never forgave her marriage or perhaps because she considered him a black sheep.

After a reflective pause Evelyn said that in some matters he could see that I had been deliberately misled. Obviously my grandmother was so obsessed with respectability that she had applied her sanctifying process to her family background.

He revealed that Dr Alexander Waugh, the Scottish divine whose tedious and pious sermons had been published in very small print, was in fact her grandfather. His son was a doctor of *medicine*.

I was amazed. No one had ever divulged a word of this.

As if I were very naïve, Evelyn explained that formerly there was much prejudice amongst the upper and professional classes against anyone 'in trade'. This was why my grandmother, with her passion for conventionality, had fostered this image of her background in my mind and concealed the fact that her father had given up his practice and 'set up shop' at a fashionable address in Regent Street.

According to Evelyn, Dr George Waugh had a very good head for business; appreciating a freedom and leisure rarely enjoyed by a doctor he became druggist to the Queen and was involved in many highly lucrative schemes for the cheap importation of drugs.

For some years the family lived over the shop. It was there that my grandmother and great-aunts entertained the young bloods from the various clubs, and such students as he tolerated from the Royal Academy Schools. Presumably these included Millais, Hunt and Woolner. Small wonder that the shop and his prescriptions were popular! Regular patients and customers flocked to Dr Waugh to cure their hangovers and other ills. There were many quacks about and after all he saved his patients money. So well did the business prosper that in a few years he was able to buy a 'desirable residence' in Kensington and another at Leatherhead.

Evelyn gave me a wicked look. 'Now I wonder if, once Hunt became so involved with the Middle East, they made some deals, and he brought back drugs from Syria?'

My eyes were popping with astonishment; but there was no time now to digest these revelations. It was a thought that opium or hashish may have been concealed in the packing of *The Scapegoat* and *The Finding of Christ in the Temple*.

Laura came to escort me to my room. I was not to change: it was too late. Evelyn asked me whether I would prefer claret or burgundy for dinner. Before my arrival he had brought up a choice from the cellar. While I was upstairs he would decant the bottle. I protested that although my husband had been a connoisseur of wine and a lover of port I was unable to appreciate either. After three glasses of tepid gin and water, and all the excitement of our talk, I did not want to drink any more.

At once I fell from favour and the fair-haired daughter was informed in disgusted tones, 'Mrs Cuthbert will continue to drink tap-water!'

Laura then took me up to my room, which I looked forward to exploring thoroughly later. There was a fascinating nineteenth-century painted washing stand, and a Rossetti nude over the fireplace called *The Spirit of the Rainbow*.

The dining-room was rather cold and Evelyn's manner had cooled somewhat once we left the glow of the fire. Perhaps I had dreamt it all about the chemist's shop. I felt tired and a little drunk.

'This is said to be a pheasant shot by my son, Bron,' he announced, 'and not at all good. Rather a tough bird, or perhaps not well cooked.' He glared and my heart sank: he was in one of his famous irritable moods.

In desperation I chattered to Laura, who seemed unperturbed. I said that after Evelyn's revelations, I had to transport the Waugh sisters from a Scottish manse to a chemist's shop in Regent Street. Turning to Evelyn I asked, 'But what about the conservatory?' My grandmother had always told me that Hunt had at long last declared his love for her in the conservatory. Perhaps on the top floor in Regent Street there was a glass dome where the Doctor conducted sinister experiments in horticulture —by now I visualised not only aspidistras but marijuana.

'The conservatory,' Evelyn pontificated, 'was in Kensington or Leatherhead—and now the *pièce de resistance* of this meal is *crêpes suzette* for which I am responsible.'

I expressed suitable delight, wondering if he would rise and *flamber* it before our eyes. But no. He had bought it in a tin from Fortnum and Mason.

When we returned to the warm room, I said that I already pictured the huge glass bottles of coloured liquid in the windows of the chemist's shop and, behind the counters, rows of mahogany drawers labelled in gold. I wondered if, as a girl, young

Edith helped to make up prescriptions, pounding away with pestle and mortar and screwing up conversation peppermints for customers.

Evelyn thought not and that my great-grandfather, his great-uncle, had been far too prosperous to employ his daughters in the shop. 'I repeat,' he said, 'they were hidden away with their mother upstairs—a legend except for the privileged few—the beautiful Miss Waughs.'

Settled by the fire, he became once more extremely affable although I didn't accept a liqueur. I felt that I shouldn't ask to go to bed until after Laura rejoined us—I was afraid that she was washing up. Suddenly she appeared and sat down in a shabby armchair. She started stitching away at a patchwork quilt without the least hesitation as to which scrap would go with what. I had made a patchwork quilt myself and was impressed by her confidence.

Evelyn showed me his collection of pictures, and we gossiped all three for a while. Then Laura suggested bed, realising that I was exhausted.

Evelyn was most considerate, and helped me choose suitable books from the library to take upstairs. I remember that Stanley's South African Diary, profusely illustrated, was one. They both kissed me goodnight, and he said gravely, 'No novels, dear Coz; so-called fiction will distress you for a while. In the Burlington, you will find quite an interesting article by Nancy [Mitford].'

The next morning, Laura brought me a tempting breakfast on a tray. When I came downstairs Evelyn was about. Instead of saying that he hoped I had slept well he asked, 'Did you sleep at all?'

On my way home I resolved to do all the research I could to help him with his book on Hunt. I had access to, and owned the copyright of, masses of family papers, which I had not yet read.

Many Waugh relations wrote to me, including an elderly lady, my cousin Mary, who had laboriously copied out the Waugh family tree. Originally it had taken one of my innumerable Australian cousins seven years to make and consisted of

nineteen enormous sheets. At first I found it most confusing:
I had 160 Waugh second cousins, many of whom had married
their cousins, and in each generation there seemed to be countless
Alexanders and Georges. Fortunately, however, Cousin Mary
had added her 'own notes to make it more interesting'. From
these I discovered that my 'great-grandfather, George Waugh,
when he was thirty, was left a legacy of £30,000 by a rich uncle
. . . he did not have much to do with his brother socially,
because he was *in trade*, whereas George moved in a very cul-
tured circle'. She was 'shattered to find from one of Evelyn's
writings that Dr Alexander Waugh, DD, had no right to the
coat of arms . . . he was a most unworldly man. . . .' I well
remember the mahogany hall chairs which he had had carved
with them.

In exchange for various useful clues, after some detective work
I was able to tell her that because he never qualified as a doctor
in fact George Waugh had no right to put M.D. after his name.
I was amused that his brother, who claimed to be the founder of
the Corn Exchange, was unacceptable socially to the prosperous
chemist.

Also, somewhat to my regret, I had to tell Evelyn that my
grandmother and her sisters never lived over the shop, but were
all born in Kensington. I sent him all the hitherto unpublished
material I could, to enable him to discover what sort of man
Hunt really was.

We agreed that there was some splendid stuff in *Pre-Raphaelitism and the Pre-Raphaelite Brotherhood*. My copyright in these
ponderous volumes had run out. My grandmother had 'edited'
much of the material, deleting passages from letters and diaries
she considered *unsuitable* for posterity. Various passages were
dictated to her by Hunt. By the early 1900s he was growing more
blind and could not read what she wrote. But the account of
his youth and of his adventures in Syria were still in his own
words—a bizarre blend of bravado, humour and pomposity in
the Victorian style. Graham Robertson in his book, *Time Was*,[6]
wrote: 'Holman Hunt always appeared to me particularly gentle
and unassuming and the strangely acid and vindictive tone of
his Autobiography came as a great surprise to most people.'

[6] W. Graham Robertson, 'The Spell of Rossetti,' *Time Was: Reminiscences.*
Hamish Hamilton, London 1931.

Evelyn and I were to meet again only three times and talk on the telephone twice. He acknowledged the innumerable papers I sent him by postcards mostly beginning 'thanks awfully' and ending 'your affectionate Coz'. In one of his letters, following our meeting at the Royal Academy private view, he expressed his disapproval of my escort. In another he regretted not coming to see me, that he had:

> 'not had the enterprise . . . it did not seem likely that you would be there over Sunday. Otherwise I spent the whole time . . . between White's, St James', Trumper's and Hyde Park Hotel . . . Ed told me (but I did not believe him) that they were making a film of your book. It would be ghastly would it not? Margaret Rutherford as Grand, I suppose. . . . Abandon your novel and go and lecture to the Americans. They would love it and you might find it exhilarating.'

Regarding his book on Hunt, 'we will meet, I hope before I go abroad, and talk of it'.

Some months after his death I wrote to Laura saying that I could not bear to waste such research as I had already done for the book that I had hoped Evelyn would write. Although it would be a travesty of what might have been, I would like to make an attempt myself to use the material. I was more interested in people than pictures; those more interested in painting than people may refer to Mary Bennett's 'catalogue raisonné' of the Holman Hunt exhibition arranged by the Walker Art Gallery, Liverpool, and the Arts Council, 1969. I wanted to tell the story in a manner that would appeal to the ordinary reader, interested in extraordinary men. But I hoped that it would not be entirely beneath the notice of scholars, if only because much of the material would be published for the first time. Such experts would of course be familiar with many facts that had appeared in the numerous works on other Pre-Raphaelites, their followers and admirers.

Although Laura searched the house from top to bottom, to our consternation the file was lost. I began again, and the following chapters are the result.

I might not have embarked upon this if I had realised how much work was involved.

28

Notes on Sources

UNLESS OTHERWISE stated in footnotes, my chief sources are my grandfather's memoirs, *Pre-Raphaelitism and the Pre-Raphaelite Brotherhood*, W. Holman Hunt, O.M., D.C.L., published in London by Macmillan & Co. Ltd, 1905, edited by Edith Holman-Hunt, my grandmother: the Iggulden collection of Hunt-Stephens letters at the Bodleian Library, Oxford, MSS Don e 66-68: the Hunt Bradley letters, now in the possession of the Princeton University Library, New Jersey, U.S.A., and the vast collection of family papers in the possession of Mrs Elizabeth Burt and myself. For the most part this mass of material has never been published. I have acknowledged in footnotes any extracts from Gabriel Rossetti's letters which are not quoted from *Letters of Dante Gabriel Rossetti*, edited by Doughty and Wahl, also any Woolner letters not quoted from *Thomas Woolner, R.A., Sculptor and Poet: His Life in Letters*, by Amy Woolner.

In the course of my research into the backgrounds of the different people involved in the first fifty years of the life of Hunt, his friends and the women he loved, I have assembled a substantial file of documents. This consists of birth, marriage and death certificates, extracts from census records, baptismal certificates, extracts from parish registers and ratepayers' records and extracts from medical journals, military records, contemporary periodicals and newspapers.

These cover a wide range of classes and people from Lord Ranelagh to Chelsea landladies, shop-keepers and footmen. A large proportion of this file is in duplicate at the Society of Genealogists, where it may be consulted.

My collection and that of Mrs Elizabeth Burt include daily

exchanges of letters which supplement and fill apparent gaps in the Iggulden Collection. The material was many times greater in volume than I had anticipated. There were not hundreds but literally thousands of letters and I found that many of them were crossed: that is to say the second page was written at right angles over the first, the fourth over the third, and so on. Subsequently, my grandmother and others, seeking for ever to suppress some aspects of the truth, had used scissors and a brush with indian ink, on the very thin paper, to devastating effect. Every modern method available has been used to decipher them.

Almost without exception, I have left the original punctuation and always the spelling. I have sometimes clarified abbreviations by adding the missing letters in square brackets. Deletions of irrelevant passages are indicated by four dots if a full stop was included and by three dots if only one sentence is interrupted. I have changed the ampersand, which appears in all the letters, into the complete word.

Several of the extracts from the letters quoted in this book, go into minute detail of behaviour and mood. The prevalent Victorian tendency to pour on to paper one's innermost thoughts, however evanescent, was shared by Hunt. The contrasting moods are often bewildering.

I first arranged in chronological order all those documents that happened to be dated. Then, the considerable minority that were undated had to be interpolated. This I have done to the best of my ability, using as guides their content, and clues such as addresses, ink, paper, watermarks, etc.

The reader will realise that this method is not infallible. My ideas of the correct sequence have more than once been upset by the acquisition of a new item and may well be upset again by others yet undiscovered. Even when precisely dated the sequence of letters is sometimes incongruous.

It is these intimate letters, together with the vivid recollections my grandmother, my father and my half-uncle, Cyril Benone, shared with me in my youth, as well as my aunt Gladys Holman-Hunt's memories recounted to her adopted daughter, Mrs Elizabeth Burt, which have allowed me to describe the behaviour and feelings of the main characters in this story with a freedom and confidence that might otherwise seem to be pure guesswork.

CHAPTER I

Lo! as that youth's eyes burned at thine, so went
Thy spell through him. . . .

D. G. ROSSETTI

IT IS boring when people of apparently humble circumstances are at pains to explain how they have come down
in the world through misfortune. However, there is no
doubt that in the seventeenth and eighteenth centuries Hunt's
ancestors owned large estates round Hull and that in spite of
much tedious litigation these were lost by his grandfather.

Hunt's father, like his father before him, became manager of
a large mercers' and drapers' warehouse in Cheapside: the family
lived on the top floor. His mother was Sarah Hobman, who was,
according to Hunt's memoirs, 'of stalwart horse-loving yeoman
stock'. I was told at an early age that the name Holman was a
corruption of Hobmand and that the Hobmans were of Danish
extraction. These explanations seemed incompatible.

Hunt was born in 1827.[1] He was christened William after his
father, and Hobman in deference to his mother's brother, who
had no children and was 'well-to-do'. My grandmother claimed
that even as a boy of eleven Hunt objected strongly to 'this
distasteful toadying to material expectations'. He disliked the
foreign name and, finding it written as Holman on his birth
certificate, announced that he wished to be known as Holman,
which henceforth he was.

William Hunt seems to have been an exceptionally well-
educated man for a warehouse manager in those days. I suspect
that this was mainly due to his inheritance of a modest library,
including some classics, various history and travel books and
others related to the arts. He was an amateur artist himself and
collected prints. He encouraged his son to draw when he was

---

[1] Contrary to the Dictionary of National Biography he had two elder sisters,
Elizabeth Ann born in 1823 and Maria born in 1825, and two younger sisters,
Sarah born in 1829 and Emily born in 1836. He had one younger brother,
Edward Henry born in 1832.

four, which kept him quiet for hours, and when he was five lent him a small paint brush and some cakes of watercolour.

To the child's terror he lost the precious brush between the floorboards. After various abortive attempts, he succeeded in replacing it with one made of a whittled stick and glue and silk and a small tuft of his own hair, hoping that this improvisation would placate his father, whose anger he greatly feared. After this he was limited to lead pencils.

At the age of five, his favourite day of the week was Sunday, which began with the clamour of City bells. Like all their neighbours, the Hunts put on their best clothes and went to church. After the evening meal and family prayers, his father real aloud from the New Testament. The child was enthralled by Christ's adventures: his imagination glowed with colour and visions of life as it was then in this marvellous place, the Orient. His father explained that the Holy Land and its customs had scarcely changed at all in nearly two thousand years. The greatest treat of all was when his father brought out his scrapbooks, excusing this personal foible with the dictum, 'a man without a hobby is a poor creature'. He kept up a running commentary as he turned over the pages of well-chosen illustrations—the natural and architectural wonders of the world, battle scenes, portraits of historical figures and reproductions of old masters. The children received a broader education than they would later on at school, but in spite of encouraging them to appreciate the arts, their father frequently uttered stern warnings that 'all flighty and unprofitable eccentricities should be suppressed', and that 'the only road to prosperity was the course of sober business'. Alas for sober business, the seed was sown.

About this time, Hunt's father moved to a much larger warehouse in Dyer's Court, backing on to Guildhall. The premises were built after the Great Fire over a honeycomb of ancient cellars. All day the place buzzed like a monstrous hive with the drone of the velvet-binding rollers, the rattle and whirring of machines winding thread into balls or on to reels. Mingled with the general noise was the shouting of the porters, the chatter of women in the packing room and the shrill laughter of the girl winders, whose teasing and petting was a source of embarrassment to the small boy. Until he was eight he spent his days there darting about from floor to floor or drawing quietly in a corner.

Often, he accompanied his favourite porter as he delivered bales to the wholesalers, bowed under heavy loads set on a 'knot' on his head. He became familiar with every inch of the City, its churches, civic halls, courts, yards, alleys and passages.

There were occasional visits to his comparatively rich uncle and aunt, the Hobmans, who lived at Rectory Farm, Ewell, in Surrey. Here he learned to ride and swim. He swam in the Thames whenever he could, and loved sailing and rowing; he started to box when he was ten. But although he enjoyed the English countryside, at heart he was a true Cockney, always preferring London and being glad to return there.

At twelve, after four years at a Spartan boarding school, he announced to his father that he was determined to be a painter. His father was appalled and declared that he would countenance no such nonsense: he would be placed in a strict house of business at once.

In silence, the boy decided to forestall his father. He knew the grim ways of a city warehouse only too well and could visualise exactly the pattern of his future. For two years, ten hours a day, he would deliver invoices as a messenger boy. Then, at fourteen, he would be promoted as a copying clerk and sit on a high stool in front of a desk carved with past victims' initials. For ten hours a day and ten shillings a week, he would copy invoices for the new juniors to deliver. The old head clerk would see that there was never a minute to read or draw.

Recently an aunt had sent him an illustrated book of travel. He yearned for adventure and above all else to paint.

There was no time to lose. He sought out a fifteen-year-old clerk with whom he had been at school and who was just leaving a job with an estate agent called Mr James, a man whose office was far superior to a clerk's den in a warehouse. With his satchel of exercise books under his arm he set off early next day.

Mr James was astonished to find a small, erect, neat figure waiting for his arrival. He listened good-naturedly as the lad declared himself proficient, after four years at school, in copying, mental arithmetic, vulgar fractions, decimals, algebra, and ciphering—I have his geometry book full of beautifully executed diagrams, with little sketches of the maths master in the margin.

At first Mr James's reaction was jocular. He suggested that the

33

smart young fellow should enrol himself forthwith in Her Majesty's service as a grenadier. Outwardly unperturbed, young Hunt proceeded to read aloud in a clear voice from a book he picked up from the table and then, taking a quill pen and paper, produced some lines of perfect copper-plate writing. Mr James was won over and gave him the job.

Hunt hurried home and told the news to his father, who was on the point of arranging for his acceptance into a particularly strict and awful warehouse. Incredulous at such precocity and independence his father was completely taken aback, but after a reassuring interview with Mr James, it was agreed that all was well.

Luckily, Mr James was an enthusiastic amateur artist. After office hours, he not only encouraged his young clerk to paint, but taught him how to grind and mix his own colours. Also, he pleaded with Hunt's stern father to allow him to attend an evening drawing class, and to spend his salary on weekly painting lessons from Henry Rogers.[2]

Mr Rogers was horrified by his small pupil's use of brilliant colour and declared that only an ignoramus like Constable attempted to paint trees and grass green 'like a cabbage'; sensitive artists like himself painted them brown and yellow.

At home Hunt had no privacy, being obliged to share a bedroom with his younger brother Edward, who complained to their mother about the smell of turpentine from clandestine still lifes and self-portraits kept hidden under the bed.

There were no Bank Holidays. Clerks worked on Saturdays, as on weekdays, until 8 p.m. Throughout his four years in the City, Hunt had only one free afternoon. It was in June and he spent it at the Royal Academy Exhibition, where he saw the Duke of Wellington, wearing a blue coat and white trousers, admiring a Landseer.

When Mr James retired Hunt enjoyed his freedom for two or three glorious weeks while his father sought to place him in a suitably grim house of business run by a strict disciplinarian who would stand no nonsense and would be as unlike Mr James as possible. Once more his son exasperatingly forestalled him and found his own job in the London agency of Richard Cobden's

[2] A City portrait painter whose style derived ultimately from Reynolds.

business. It was the time of the Corn Law agitation: Cobden had just entered Parliament.

Fortunately, the manager favoured his new young clerk, who was allowed time to read many books on art. Between routine tasks he was asked to design ornamental cloths for the commercial travellers to show as samples of what could be printed to order.

His father feared 'dire consequences of such hazardous deviations from sober business. Office discipline should not be relaxed for an instant'.

Hunt continued to pay for weekly portrait-painting lessons with Mr Rogers. There was less and less sympathy between them. The eccentric pupil had no respect for the orthodox rules and enjoyed nothing more than painting garish landscapes out of doors instead of in his master's studio: 'Drooping branches of brown trees over a night-like sky, or a column with a curtain unnaturally arranged, as a background to a day-lit portrait'.

Mr Rogers insisted that the figures in a picture should be placed along an S-shaped line. The parts of a composition should each culminate in an apex and the brightest light should always fall on the principal figure. One corner of the picture, even the sky, 'should be in shadow'.

To his parents' consternation and the disapproval of their neighbours, instead of donning his best suit and accompanying them to church on Sundays, Hunt escaped from the house before dawn with his paint-box and sketch-book.

'The year before I had gone every Sunday to church, but the combination of three services, the reiteration of prayers, palled upon me. I was brought to the conviction that I had reached the bottom of the preacher's mine of wisdom: I was listening to a learned parrot . . . I revelled in the blossoming trees showing their loveliness to the rising sun, and turned into secret lanes, and leas . . . beside a rushy river . . . I spied out the shy fish, and rejoiced with the happy birds, and summoned courage for my novice hand to interpret the rapturous charms.'

He was at that time in a lyrical mood. Later he bought Keats' poems off a barrow for fourpence,[3] and was inspired by them.

[3] *Life, Letters and Literary Remains of John Keats*, edited by Richard Monckton Milnes, Edward Moxon, London, 1848.

35

After about two years Hunt's amiable employer spoiled him even more. He was now required to work for only eight hours a day instead of twelve! Unwisely, Hunt confided to his brother, always a sneak, that he spent his freedom copying at the British Museum, or painting portraits in the City. Some days he spent 'journeying' for more established artists whom he met on these doubtful excursions.

On learning of this 'perfidy' on the part of the manager Hunt's father was outraged: he had warned him of such 'dangerous leanings'. The next day, he visited the office and declared himself appalled at such irresponsible indulgence which could only lead to the disgrace and ruination of his dissolute son.

Much concerned, the manager protested that the boy had an obstinate determination: were he treated as his father suggested he would just walk out! The father insisted that by law an employer could reject a minor's notice until a suitable replacement was found. After this noisy interview the manager reluctantly told his favourite clerk that he must work nose to grindstone for much longer hours.

Drudgery at the office was followed by frightful scenes at home or puritanical lectures. The younger children trembled: his mother pleaded. His brother was silent and smug as they undressed in their cramped bedroom. Only his sister, Sarah, who was two years younger than Hunt, gave him moral support.

She confided in whispers that some friends of their uncle's at Ewell had a nephew, a child of only twelve, who had been a student at the Royal Academy for over two years. She had seen his drawings: they were marvellous! He had won a gold medal four years ago. His name was Johnny Millais. He had never been to school. He spoke French—the family came from the Channel Isles—and his father played the flute. More amazing still, Sarah continued, quite unlike the Hunts the Millais family were thrilled, and actually encouraged the boy to be an artist. They even sat as models for his pictures! He had a studio in the house.

Sarah was urged to find out more about this extraordinary child.

Six grim months passed between boredom at the office and frustration at home. Hunt used to arrive home exhausted by nine o'clock, usually just in time for supper. The atmosphere was 'black and thunderous'. What a contrast, he thought, from young Millais' lot. Sarah fed him snippets of news.

Finally, one night, as he climbed into bed beside his now hated brother, his mind was made up: 'resolve growing daily in my soul the stronger'. He could endure it no longer. The next morning he requested an interview with his employer. He wished to leave as soon as a replacement could be found.

The manager, no doubt fearing another visit from his father, tried to bribe him with a rise and pointed out the advantage of a steady job although his prospects might not seem glowing now.

Hunt was polite but adamant. His employer gave him leave to go home early to face his father, and wished him luck.

My grandmother told me that when Hunt's mind was made up, he would stand very erect and speak out. His voice would sound confident and his bearing would be resolute and calm. The two or three—she included herself of course—who were privileged to know him well would appreciate the effort of control. His hands trembled unless he steadied them on some inanimate object.

So it was, no doubt, that day when he faced his father.

He knew that his parents were saving every penny to add to a small legacy towards retirement. He did not ask for material assistance. However, he begged to remind his father respectfully, he had earned his own living working in the City since he was twelve. He was now fit and aged sixteen-and-a-half. Rather than continue he would enlist in the army.

Unprepared for this attack, his father stalked out. Failure and hunger would tell: eventually his obstinate son would come to heel.

Three months later, an introduction to Sir Richard Westmacott resulted in his being given a card of admission to lectures at the Royal Academy, which was then housed in the eighteenth-century National Gallery.

As a result, he was privileged to attend the Academy prizegiving in 1843. All the students would be assembled, so perhaps he would get a glimpse of young Millais at last.

To Hunt, whose background was drab, the ceremony was grand and impressive. Powdered flunkies dressed in scarlet threw open the great doors: the distinguished Academicians solemnly

37

filed in. The President, Sir Martin Archer Shee, was absent. Turner, aged sixty-eight, had refused to deputise for him at the last minute. He brought up the rear of the procession and shuffled furtively into an inconspicuous place. At that time his best paintings were mostly in private collections and almost unknown to the students; by 1863 their value was to be multiplied fifteen times! Young Hunt knew his work and greatly admired it as true to nature. He was aware that Turner painted what he saw from his window and from the bridges on the river.

Hunt craned forward to get a good 'quiz'. He wrote in his journal of 'a stunted gentleman, unimposing in form, inelegantly dressed, and shambling in gait'. Perhaps his clumsiness was due to having 'a big head, with somewhat large features, which, although not handsome, bespoke the right to be at home in any presence'.

The solemn ceremony continued. At last, to Hunt's excitement, a voice boomed the magic name: 'John Everett Millais!' He had won the gold medal for drawing from the antique. Hunt noted everything: later he must report to Sarah in detail.

An angelic-looking blue-eyed boy was passed hand to hand over the heads of the laughing, applauding audience. Although fourteen he looked much younger, a little Lord Fauntleroy. His doting parents cultivated this image. Long fair curls tumbled round his pink face and over his lace collar. He wore a tunic, velvet shorts, white socks and buckled pumps of patent leather.

For Hunt it was love at first sight. He had wanted for so long to see his idol. As he cheered with the others tears streamed down his face. They were to love one another all their lives. Neither of them felt in the least self-conscious about the emotion they showed.

Years later, Woolner was to accuse them of being homosexuals in their youth. When Hunt wrote indignantly to Millais of this, Millais replied, 'I *can't* think how Woolner can have circulated any story about you and me. . . .'

Nowadays, no one would have thought anything else.

CHAPTER II

My friends and brother souls,
With all the peoples, great and small. . . .
TENNYSON

A WHOLE YEAR after the prize-giving at the Royal
Academy, Hunt was still struggling 'to pass the cursed
test' as a probationer. He worked incessantly, but failed
three times. As well as studying, he had to earn money to pay
for his keep at home and to buy painting materials needed for
his humble commissions.

One day he was drawing in the Elgin Room at the British
Museum when Millais looked in. He was fifteen, his hair now
short and curly. He stopped to admire Hunt's drawing and was
encouraging and friendly.

At the next attempt Hunt was accepted as an Academy
student.

Millais was still the youngest in the Schools, although senior
in achievement. For the first year or two he had been unmerci-
fully bullied (the senior students had even used him as a human
broom, grabbing him by the ankles and sweeping the floor with
his curls); but by now his charm allied to self-confidence had
established his personality. He was sought after—everyone's
darling—always surrounded by jokes and fun. School etiquette
forbade Hunt, a new boy, to approach the favourite.

Millais was in the Life School, but still looked in on the
Antique. He spotted Hunt one day and congratulated him: 'I
told you so: I knew you'd pass.' Pointing like a child he added:
'You've had your hair cut!' His own curls were gone: 'Look,
I've got a cockatoo crop.'

Millais was at once attracted to Hunt: 'You must call me
Johnny.' He invited him to tea at the Millais' Chelsea house.

It was impossible for Hunt not to envy the relaxed atmosphere
of gaiety and laughter. He was almost embarrassed by this ador-
ing family circle and its pride in everything that Johnny did.
Fascinated, he watched Johnny's affectionate teasing of his pretty

39

young mama as he wheedled her into making costumes or crimping false hair with hot tongs for indulgent relations to wear when they posed for his pictures. She was his willing slave. Mr Millais was forty-seven. He often obliged as a model wearing various wigs, whiskers or beards. Johnny patted 'good old Daddy' on the back. His parents were 'dear creatures'. For Hunt such liberties were unthinkable.

Not to be outdone, he told his hosts that his little sister Emily was posing for him with a watch to her ear. She was only seven. He would call the picture *Hark* . . .

They discovered their mutual acquaintances at Ewell.

'Do you play cricket?' Johnny asked. 'They give nice dances, why don't you go?'

Hunt confessed that he and his favourite sister, Sarah, had never learned to dance: he wished they had, or could.

Pirouetting, Johnny insisted that they must and should.

After this, 'our increasing intimacy induced confidential talk whenever we met'. They exchanged their views on art, their secret excitements and doubts. Hunt recited from his fourpenny Keats, and enthused about a book he had recently read where he had found his very own creed in print, expounded three years before by an Oxford graduate, John Ruskin. He knew the particular passage by heart: 'Go to nature in all singleness of heart, selecting nothing, rejecting nothing . . .' He had written in his journal that none could have felt more strongly than himself and that it was meant expressly for him.

Johnny agreed that they should rebel against the established artistic conventions laid down by the former President of the Royal Academy, Sir Joshua Reynolds: 'Silly old Sloshua Reynolds!' It had been his corrupting influence that was responsible for the brown sludge on the bogus old masters churned out by the students now.

Hunt was happy: he had found a friend. It was 1846 and he was nineteen. He and Johnny would stand together, two against the world. They would turn art upside down, 'spifflicate the sloshers and reach fame and riches'.

The Millais family treated Hunt as one of themselves, confiding dismay when their darling locked them out of his studio.

After this show of independence the boys were able to work uninterrupted far into the night on their pictures for the next

40

Royal Academy exhibition, drinking endless cups of coffee. To relieve the monotony, they exchanged canvases now and then.

'My dear old fellow,' Johnny would say, 'be a sport and do a bit of this drapery: so tedious, I'm bored stiff. I'll paint one of your heads.'

Hunt learned the commerce of art the hard way. He still ground his own colours, and bought seasoned panels of wood from a coach-breaker's yard for a few pence. Once, on thirteen days' work he made a profit of only two shillings. A shrewd fellow student commissioned him to make a painstaking copy of all the figures and the immediate background of Rembrandt's *A Woman Taken in Adultery*. The price was to be agreed on completion.

Hunt was aghast when he was offered fifteen shillings, and protested that a full palette alone cost a shilling a day. He was then accused of being very wasteful for using unnecessary madders and expensive pigments when he could have made do with cheap ones.

Unknown to their parents, the boys joined in a protest march of Chartists and narrowly escaped arrest for being involved in a breach of the peace. Hunt became an agnostic. They joined an arty and short-lived club called the Cyclographic.

Johnny taught Hunt to dance while Papa Millais strummed on the guitar. Hunt bought a second-hand velvet suit and Mama Millais made Sarah a dress to wear at parties.

When his son's pictures were actually hung in exhibitions Hunt's father was impressed against his will. Shortly after the boys met, the Millais left cards at the Hunts. Wearing his cylinder hat, Mr Hunt returned the call. He saw how differently they treated their son and may have wondered if he had been a trifle severe. At any rate his attitude changed. He took his son to call on the famous painter Varley. Soon after this he announced that at last he had prudently invested enough money to retire. The family would move from the top floors of the city warehouse to premises over a young upholsterer's shop which belonged to a Mr Wilson, at 108-109 High Holborn, Bloomsbury.

Better still, Hunt need no longer contribute a weekly sum for his laundry and food—in fact 'might consider in what respect his father could now be helpful'. Hunt was incredulous and rightly so: within a week the offer was withdrawn. After a

41

lifetime of 'sober business' old Hunt had been cheated out of quite a large sum. For the rest of his life it would require 'stringent and frugal economies for the family to keep their heads above water'. For the first time in his life Hunt went out and got drunk.

However, in spite of a hangover, he realised that his circumstances had improved on the whole. He was near his beloved British Museum and had his first studio—a room of his own.

Having struggled so long against such odds for his admission to the Academy Schools he worked hard and attended regularly. Out of the corner of his eye he watched the apparently carefree students who attended spasmodically: they were a wild and high-spirited lot. Secretly he envied them. Their ringleader was a strange but attractive young Italian called Rossetti. He had a haunting face. Hunt and he were on nodding terms.

Johnny now dressed very conventionally. He and Hunt agreed that they should not look like artists: both disapproved of conscious Bohemianism. Rossetti's flamboyant manner, eccentric clothes and shoulder-length hair were 'rather muffish'. Johnny's attitude to foreigners was prejudiced and very English. All the same, both he and Hunt were bound to admit that the designs this odd man sent to the Cyclographic were better than the others—and original.

Hunt was well aware that his family background was more limited socially than the Millais'. He knew he was unsophisticated. Just as he had been reluctant to make the first move towards Johnny, so now he waited for Rossetti to approach him.

It was surprising, as well as disappointing, that Johnny's picture was rejected by the Hanging Committee. His indignant parents took him to the country, so he did not attend the opening of the Royal Academy Exhibition. Hunt's picture (*The Eve of St Agnes*)—described in the Catalogue as *The Flight of Madeline and Porphyro during the drunkenness attending the revelry*—was well hung. Sure enough, at the private view, Rossetti sauntered up and declared himself lost in admiration. It was the best thing in the exhibition, superb, marvellous, miraculous. Such extravagant praise and torrents of superlatives accompanied by theatrical gestures embarrassed Hunt. He was flattered but tongue-tied for a while.

Unabashed, Rossetti continued to rave about Keats and finally

42

confessed that poetry was his passion. In a beautiful resonant voice, oblivious of the crowd, he recited from Shelley, Browning and Blake, and then from Dante in Italian. The effect was hypnotic: once more Hunt was bewitched. There were no girls in his life as yet and he was missing Johnny.

During the next few days his reserve was swept away as if in a whirlwind. He took Rossetti into his confidence over his and Johnny's ideas for artistic reform. He explained that recently other students had overheard them condemning Raphael's *Transfiguration* for its affectation—its disregard for simplicity—'it's pompous posturing'. Someone had said casually, 'So you are Pre-Raphaelites!' It was a joke really, but he and Millais had a bond. They were in league against Mr Sloshy-Slosh and the present taste. Giotto had painted from nature, used Tuscan models and real landscapes and live sheep. Once more a Renaissance was needed . . . That Oxford man, Ruskin, would understand.

Hunt and Millais—the two of them! At once Rossetti was wildly enthusiastic. They could count on him—now they were three! Surely Hunt could persuade Millais to let him join? Intrigue against authority appealed strongly to the son of a political refugee from Italy.

Hunt was delighted to see how much his theories excited Rossetti, but cautiously replied that Millais was away and until his return nothing definite about a secret society could be decided.

Rossetti hated delay. He insisted that Hunt should write and explain that he had found a fellow-crusader. He must convince Millais of Rossetti's dedication to the cause, that he was a devoted disciple, a loyal ally, a comrade in arms. Rossetti went off at a tangent, good and bad ideas tumbling out in English and Italian, prose, poetry and slang. He ended by insisting that Hunt should call him Gabriel and meet his family and friends.

Hunt was pleased. He promised to write Millais a line, and invited Gabriel to drink coffee at his studio.

Gabriel arrived wearing his black evening suit, as he usually did in the daytime, and a filthy, shabby overcoat which he had stolen from Madox Brown (later this was to cause an absurd controversy). His pockets were bulging with books, and crumpled scraps of drawings and manuscripts. The old Hunts were aghast at this weird figure with shoulder-length hair as they peered

43

through the lace curtains from the parlour window.

On opening the door, Hunt first drew his new friend's attention to the hideous furniture and fabrics displayed in Mr Wilson, the upholsterer's shop-window, 'wanting in artistic taste to a degree greater than could be found in any previous age or country whatever. With my youthful experience in designing patterns, I regarded decorative design as part of an artist's ambition and I declared that furniture and costume would remain as bad for fifty years . . . if we continued to leave the designing of them to tradesmen'.

He did not add that the twenty-seven-year-old Mr Wilson was making sheep's eyes at Sarah, and that Bill Peagrim, his shop-assistant, was intolerably familiar and flirting with one of Hunt's elder sisters, Maria.

Once safely ensconced in Hunt's room, Gabriel was full of compliments on his designs and experiments and roared with laughter at his accounts of adventures in search of authentic props—truth to nature!—such as his visit to Kew in search of a real palm tree for the background of *Christ and the Two Marys*. A huge, withered branch still stood in the corner of the studio. Hunt had carried it home in triumph all the way to Holborn. A dead bat had dropped out and lodged in his collar.

At night, in his so-called free time, he had sat for hours making line drawings of armour for his picture, *Rienzi*. He had worked by candlelight at the Tower of London where his father knew one of the officials. It was a spooky place.

There were many studies of dogs. Hunt had borrowed a couple of bloodhounds for *The Eve of St Agnes* from a friend, John Blount Price, who owned an estate in the country. How his mother had complained! They ate so much before they would settle down and scared his small sister Emily out of her wits.

Gabriel found these stories hilarious. He slapped his thighs so hard that tattered papers fell out of his pockets.

'My dear Mad,' he gasped, 'so serious and yet so comical!'

He had nicknames for everybody. After this Hunt was known as 'the Mad' or 'the Maniac'.

Gabriel took his leave, and begged Hunt to come and see him.

When he called, Papa Rossetti, wearing a skull cap, opened the door, and greeted him vaguely with 'Good evening, Mr Madox

Brown'. He knew that one of his sons was the latter's pupil and Gabriel had said that 'perhaps the Mad would come round'. In spite of his daughters' protests, he continued to address Hunt thus the whole afternoon. So many family friends were in and out: the Rossettis kept open house for Italian refugees, from politicians to organ-grinders. Gabriel emerged and introduced Hunt to his brother William and his sisters, Maria and Christina. 'Would they like Sarah, or she them?' Hunt wondered.

Hunt had never imagined such social confusion. At first sight the room seemed full of gesticulating people shouting in French or Italian—his school French was no help now. When he looked closer he could see that here and there were small groups, oblivious of the noise, immersed in games of chess or dominoes.

Instead of all the guests assembling round the dining table and saying grace, as they would at home, only a few drew up their chairs and settled down to the meal. Some wandered about plate in hand waving their forks in the air. Others jumped up and drifted back to the fire to join in animated political discussions.

Dazed with chianti and ill at ease in such a mob, Hunt eyed the tangled mound of spaghetti—an utterly unfamiliar dish— with horror.

To his relief, although he was hungry, Gabriel rescued him.

'Come on, Mad!' He was hustled upstairs to see Gabriel's 'crib' and his 'daubs', props and treasures.

In comparison with Hunt's orderly room the studio was an Aladdin's Cave, a jumble of bric-à-brac, rusty swords, scraps of rich brocades and tapestry, old dresses, moth-eaten wigs and feather fans, birds' eggs and shells, oriental pots, mostly chipped but still marvellous, picked up for a few pence. Junk of all kinds lay about between portfolios, canvases, paints, palettes and easels.

There were stacks of books. Gabriel picked up one at random, a German volume on witchcraft. Next, he proudly showed a collection of Blake's prose, poems and designs, bought from an attendant at the British Museum for ten shillings.

He was delighted by Hunt's reactions and read aloud from his latest discoveries—poems by William Bell Scott, 'a professorial fellow who lives in the north', and rhymes by Edward Lear, a dear old boy of at least thirty-five.

Relaxed at last, his eyes dreamy, in a magical voice Gabriel recited his own *Blessed Damozel*. Hunt was spell-bound. He

45

recognised a true poet and swore that he would never again attempt to write verse himself.

There was a bang on the door. William Rossetti walked in. Hunt immediately took to him, and made note of this in his journal. Gabriel had already told his brother of Hunt's and Millais' resolve. William and several others were anxious to join.

But Millais was still away and things were getting out of hand. Until recently Hunt had had so few friends: Gabriel had an enormous number and a vast acquaintanceship. If he admired an artist's work, he would write him such effusive letters that more often than not the recipient would suspect a hoax. Some months before, Madox Brown, always touchy, had been enraged on receiving extravagant eulogies of his generally unappreciated work from an upstart—a foreigner to boot. In a fury, he had seized his walking stick and stormed round to beat the daylights out of the insolent pup.

When Gabriel opened the door, Madox Brown had been quite disarmed and left his 'stout cudgel' with the inoffensive umbrellas in the hall. Before leaving he had agreed to take him on as a pupil.

Gabriel now explained to Hunt that the scheme just hadn't worked: he was fed up. Old Bruno had sat him down in front of a stupid pile of bottles—*still* life! What use was that? He longed to paint 'stirring romantic incidents . . . lovers rescuing ladies in mediaeval dress. . . .'

He pleaded with Hunt to take him on as a pupil.

Hunt said that at present this was impracticable. He was already teaching his sister and another pupil called Stephens; the crippled son of that official at the Tower of London, who came to draw twice a week and paid a shilling an hour. Mrs Hunt had grumbled that this did not cover the cost of his meals. Hunt quailed at the thought of Gabriel and his circus drifting in and out.

Seeing Gabriel's crestfallen expression he added vaguely that some day it might be possible when he could afford to leave home and have a place of his own. Gabriel was most persistent. Hunt must promise to call each day to supervise his work. He had decided to leave Madox Brown anyway and take a studio near a sculptor friend—'Good God, if ever there was a potential Pre-

46

Raphaelite it was Tommy Woolner!' Hunt must meet him at once, before Millais returned.

Within a few days Gabriel and William Rossetti took Hunt to call on the man who, in the remote future, was to become his brother-in-law. 'A handsome youth . . . somewhat beyond me in years . . . with dark eyes and thick blond hair.'

That night 'he guided us through the labyrinth of modelling-stools, pails of clay, plaster moulds and casts, on our way to the stove . . . a colossal clay figure stood mid space lit by candles just above the knees'. He applied wet cloths to this 'with the tenderness of a surgeon dressing a wound'.

Woolner was having a fearful struggle to survive. His father was a sorter in a country post office and unable to help him at all. To make ends meet he worked as a marble carver for others. A couple of years later Charles Collins, Wilkie Collins' brother, wrote to Hunt that Woolner's hated rival, the sculptor Maro-chetti, had far more hope of a coveted commission because he had 'gigantic studios, able assistants and furnaces where he heats his bronze . . . Woolner is his own assistant and [his] furnace is contained in a grate two feet square incapable of heating anything but a few chestnuts and the back of Rossetti's legs when his feet are on the chimney piece. What chance has poor T.W.?'

That first night when they gathered round the fire Gabriel held forth about the secret society which was to be formed. His description of its aims and ideals was somewhat confused. Every-one talked at once. Woolner was much impressed with the idea of a rebels' club or whatever it was: they could look on him as one of its keenest members. Hunt found 'his energy and burning ambition' appealing.

William also was anxious to belong. He had already joined Gabriel at the Life School, and 'applied himself at night in a steady manner to the pursuit of drawing, and regularly executed conscientious, although *rigid* transcripts of the nude'. He might not be exactly entitled to call himself an artist yet, but would soon learn to paint and surely become one. He was determined to give up that boring job with the Inland Revenue. This latest proposal was a challenge: Hunt felt that he should keep his end up. If William was eligible, why not his pupil? Fred Stephens, although lame since he was nine, was an excellent fellow.

47

When Gabriel objected that Stephens had never painted anything at all, 'Hunt retorted that as he had done nothing, nothing could be held against him'.

The Rossettis gave in and, not to be outdone, recommended yet another friend of theirs, James Collinson. 'A meek little chap', according to Hunt, but to them 'a stunner', who was courting their younger sister, Christina.

Woolner was such an entertainer that 'until four or five in the morning they rolled about on the floor with laughter'. His stories of Paris were capital and he smoked black tobacco in a clay pipe. (Hunt was soon to follow his example and become addicted. Millais, after resisting, at last succumbed and was to die of cancer of the throat years later. In his old age, Hunt could scarcely breathe for asthma.) .

The next morning, Hunt felt that this Pre-Raphaelite affair had got out of hand. Johnny should know what was going on: he had been away in Oxford too long. He sat down and wrote him another letter.

When Johnny went away they had been two against the world, then Gabriel had made up an obvious third. How to explain that three had now become *seven*?

On receiving the news, disturbing even to those 'dear old creatures Papa and Mama', Johnny hurried home. 'The Mad' was obviously dazzled by these crazy Italians. Perhaps Johnny felt a little out of touch and jealous. In another week there might be at least twenty more 'members'. Of what? He might well ask.

Hunt rushed to Gower Street as soon as he heard of the Millais' return. Johnny leant out of the window and shouted, 'Where are your flock? I expected to see them behind you!'

Hunt realised that Johnny was angry even before they were closeted in the studio. Although the latter admitted that Gabriel Rossetti was perhaps qualified to join in a combined effort of reform, Woolner wasn't even a painter, and . . . Hunt broke in and hotly defended his new friend's claims as a serious sculptor: he earnestly recommended him as an ally and something of a poet.

Johnny brushed this aside. Anyway Collinson was hopeless, half asleep most of the time, and as for the others, William Rossetti and Fred Stephens, they were mere outsiders—just a pair of amateurs. How could Hunt, of all people, imagine that a few drawing lessons from him, or a dozen visits to the Life School, could possibly make up for years of hard work and professional training? They were both over twenty, much too old to start. What was the point of it all? What on earth was Hunt after? 'Are you getting up a regiment to take the Academy by storm?' Of course he recognised the need to reform, but he was not a nihilist: he owed the Academy some loyalty. After all he had been their pride and joy for so long. The fact that his latest picture had been turned down by the Hanging Committee had upset Papa and Mama very much. Perhaps word had got round of his rebellious attitude and the powers-that-be thought he had become too big for his boots and needed a lesson.

His parents approved of his friendship with Hunt but, for heaven's sake, what would they make of the others?

Hunt sang his candidates' praises but to no avail. Then he patiently explained his hopes of the help they would prove in furthering his and Johnny's ideals. Johnny was unimpressed. All he said was: 'Yes, but all this is a heavy undertaking.' He was still annoyed.

Hunt became conciliatory. Nothing was *decided*. Johnny, as his best friend, should have the last word and he would stand by him. Johnny was not reassured.

Hunt tried again: 'If they fail, I don't see how they can interfere with us . . . Remember I have said I can agree to nothing finally till your return to town.'

Although the youngest of his friends, Hunt acknowledged Millais to be an infinitely superior and more professional artist. He was 'the best trained of all of us, he had a precocious capacity . . . a quick instinct which enabled him to pounce as an eagle on the prize he searched for. Favoured and young . . . firmer in will than many men ever become.'

By the time Hunt took his leave Johnny had somewhat relented. One day he would like to meet these odd new friends.

Hunt marshalled the Rossetti boys, Woolner, Collinson and Stephens and took them round to Gower Street. At the last minute Gabriel suggested they include Madox Brown, but Hunt refused. As it was, Brown scoffed at the whole idea as being extremely childish.

So many people have described this chaotic meeting and tried to assess its value that to make a synthesis of their accounts is

49

impossible. Stephens formed the simplest conclusion when he said that no one *founded* Pre-Raphaelitism: this meeting was 'a point of crystallisation at which seven very young men came together'. Gabriel Rossetti was to refer to 'the visionary vanities . . . of a group of boys who couldn't draw'. Some art historians still regard it as 'a boyish lark'. Others, such as William Gaunt,[1] as a 'strangely pregnant myth' or 'a fairy-tale'.

Hunt seems to have been more consistent in his aims than the rest, harping on a return to nature. Somehow an essence was distilled from the confusion of dreams and tastes, mediaeval and modern.

As usual, Gabriel was carried away, even suggesting they should all take an oath of chastity and abstinence from alcohol and nicotine. Fortunately for all, this proposal was turned down.

The meeting was a triumph for Hunt. As host, Johnny glowed with pleasure. Gabriel's charm was irresistible. Gabriel found that Johnny had 'the face of an angel'. Even Collinson kept awake. William Rossetti was appointed secretary—but again of what? Various suggestions were made, but in the end they all agreed that Gabriel's was the best proposal. It should be the Pre-Raphaelite *Brotherhood*! At once he set to work designing the lettering to be inscribed after their names on manuscripts, pictures, sculpture and personal correspondence.

Someone feared that if found on studio doors the initials would be misconstrued as Please Ring Bell. Never mind. They made a haphazard 'List of Immortals', placing stars by their names according to their estimation of immortal value. Shakespeare and the author of Job were awarded three. Surprisingly, Raphael scored one, so did Elizabeth Barrett, but many others, including Joan of Arc, Newton and Michelangelo, were starless. As an afterthought, Jesus Christ was put top of the list with four.

Some years later Millais was to write of his first encounter with the Rossetti brothers, 'I liked him [Gabriel] very much when we first met, believing him to be sincere in his desire to further our aims—Hunt's and mine—but I always liked his brother William much better. D. G. Rossetti, you must understand was a queer fellow, and impossible as a boon companion— so dogmatic and so irritable when opposed.'

During the autumn of 1848, after the Brotherhood was

[1] William Gaunt, *The Pre-Raphaelite Tragedy*, Jonathan Cape, London, 1942.

formed, Hunt sold *The Eve of St Agnes* for £70. On the strength of this he arranged to share 'a crib' with Gabriel at 7 Cleveland Street, Fitzroy Square, 'a cramped ill-lit studio' where they were disturbed by the whippings and scamperings of a school of small boys kept by their landlord Mr Simrad on the floor below. The landlady was drunk every afternoon and the Irish maid was a slut.

Hunt began his picture, *Rienzi*. William and Johnny obliged as models, and Gabriel posed for the principal figure. John Blount Price obliged with the horses.

Gabriel loved to keep open house in the Rossetti family tradition. Night after night hungry and rowdy friends knocked on the door. There was a permanent shortage of 'tin'. Hunt was obliged to neglect his next year's Academy picture and paint a lot of boring portraits to pay for the food and drink. By the end of the day he was exhausted: his pipe, newly acquired, would drop from his mouth and he would pass out full length on the floor.

Gabriel was painting his *Girlhood of the Virgin*. The lily held by the angel was made of wool, as fresh flowers were too expensive. The following year, Millais had to pay 5s. 6d. a pound for the strawberries in *The Woodman's Daughter*.

When Gabriel was working callers were ignored. He would meditate for hours in front of the canvas. Hunt wrote, 'he would refuse the attraction of home, meals, out-of-doors engagements, or bed, and sit through the night, sleeping where he sat for an hour at a time, recommencing his work when he woke. He ate whatever was at hand . . . when time came for bed the second night, he would ask me to leave him.'

The next morning 'he remained fixed and inattentive to all that went on about him, he rocked himself to and fro, and at times moaned lowly, or hummed . . . he peered intently before him, looking hungry and eager, passing by in his regard any who came before him, as if not seen at all. Then he would often get up and walk out of the room without saying a word'.

There was a succession of models for the small angel. Their fidgeting tried his patience so much that 'he revealed his irritation beyond bounds, storming wildly . . . and stamping about, until the poor child sobbed and screamed with fright. . . . After this scene, which raised clouds of dust . . . further work that day was out of the question'. Madox Brown wrote that the Virgin's drapery drove Gabriel into 'an almost maudlin condition of profanity . . . lying howling on his belly'.

Many people, besides Hunt and Madox Brown, have described the trials of living with Gabriel. We hear less from Gabriel about what he suffered living with the Mad. At times Hunt was almost a manic depressive. When in despair about his future or his work he would shut himself up in a poky bedroom above the studio and shiver with fear. He felt as if icy water were trickling down his spine. Alone in the dark, he raved, holding long noisy conversations with the Devil. He identified the forces of evil with a definite physical presence. He frequently lost faith in humanity and in his confused idea of God, but for him the Devil was always real. Perhaps some image was stamped on his childish mind from an illustration in his father's scrapbook. Like a man in a trance, he would wrestle with this terrifying beast—huge, snarling and covered with hair.

When the monster moved in, Gabriel, much concerned, would drag Hunt down the attic stairs, scolding but affectionate. He would light the lamp and the stove, and comfort him with cups of coffee. He chafed his hands and coaxed the Mad back to sanity with serious discussions of 'spiritual mysteries' or 'rollicking jokes'.

Like any couple of talented individuals who set up house together, they had to accept the best and worst. Their early mutual infatuation was based mainly on imaginary qualities with which they had credited one another. The love that followed was strange and tempered in a rare fire—also remarkable because it survived so long despite frequent disillusion.

The following spring they had almost completed their pictures for the 1849 Royal Academy Exhibition. Johnny Millais had finished his *Lorenzo and Isabella* in which he appropriately painted a student called Harris, who had bullied him at the Academy Schools, kicking the dog. All three proudly signed their pictures with PRB. There had been a definite understanding for at least nine months that they should all exhibit together at the Academy.

Gabriel panicked. He feared that the Hanging Committee would reject his picture; the Brothers were so unpopular. He decided to dissociate himself from Millais and Hunt and secretly to forestall them by sending *The Girlhood of the Virgin* to the so-called Free Exhibition near Hyde Park Corner.

This gallery was patronised by his previous master, Madox Brown. Artists were sure of their works being hung because they paid for the space required and because the exhibition opened a week before the other.

Hunt and Millais were astounded when he admitted what he had done—'He sneaked off without a word!' cried Millais.

William Rossetti was torn between loyalty to his brother and the Brothers. Old Mr Hunt, Papa and Mama Millais, and Johnny of course, were furious. But still Hunt loved 'the scoundrel' and felt sick at heart. Naturally, the others scoffed at anything he said in defence of such ungentlemanly conduct.

On Opening Day, because of the bad criticisms, Millais was obliged to reduce the price of his picture—already sold to some Bond Street tailors—by half. The tailors haggled and finally threw in a suit of clothes. He left London in disgust to paint backgrounds near Oxford, swearing never again to trust foreigners or read the papers.

Poor Hunt's *Rienzi* was not sold. Wherever he turned former admirers let him down. He was starving, and hawked his sketches round London from door to door. Various patrons, who had once been only too keen to commission him, now denied their interest and refused to accept the work. His paintings were no longer considered an investment by the many speculators who were anxious not to miss the boat as they had in Turner's heyday.

When Hunt was at his lowest ebb, the painter, Augustus Egg, came to call unexpectedly. He said how much he had admired *Rienzi* and offered to try to interest a collector. Hunt carried the canvas round to Egg's house in the Bayswater Road—miles away —the next day.

In the meantime, Gabriel had disappeared. His share of the rent was long overdue. He felt too ashamed to face Hunt and sent somebody round to collect his 'traps'. Then, the landlord refused to wait any longer. He seized all Hunt's possessions and all his work and threw him into the street. The schoolboys jeered from the windows and the Irish maid, who had long since failed to serve him at all, spat on the steps before slamming the door.

With as much dignity as he could muster, he set out on the long painful walk back to his father.

Only two days later a note arrived from Augustus Egg delivered by hand. The picture was sold. A cheque was enclosed for a hundred and sixty guineas. Later, Hunt discovered the curious fact that the buyer, a Mr Gibbon, was a philanthropist. He disliked the picture so much that he kept it shut up in a cupboard in case anyone should see it.

Hunt wrote in his journal, 'When I presented the cheque at the bank, I requested to leave the money on account and have a cheque book [his first—he was twenty-two]. I went with a reserved air and paid off the landlord . . . I had no studio and was fagged with long, hard and anxious work. . . . With a replenished purse I went off to Lea Marshes for a month; the river and the meadows were pure and beautiful . . . it was not difficult to find a rich landscape for my *Christian and Druid* picture.'

Gabriel had now sold his *Girlhood of the Virgin*. It had good notices. The *Athenaeum* critic said that 'its spiritual attributes, and the great sensibility with which it is wrought, inspire the expectation that Mr Rossetti will continue to pursue the lofty career which he has so successfully begun'.

According to Hunt, 'it appeared pure and bright, and was the more attractive by reason of its quaint sweetness. The Marchioness of Bath bought it for eighty guineas'.

Here was an excuse to break the ice. Gabriel was his pupil after all. As soon as Hunt returned from the Lea, he called to offer congratulations. Gabriel wept. Without one word of reproach Hunt took him in his arms like a naughty child.

Hunt wrote later in his journal: '[This] seemed a good opportunity to go, together with Rossetti, to see ancient and modern Art in Paris and Belgium, as we had long planned to do.'

I have no record of what Johnny Millais thought.

CHAPTER III

Eat thou and drink; Tomorrow thou shalt die.
                    D. G. ROSSETTI

DURING THE quarrel, not only William Rossetti, but Woolner and Collinson too, had been in an awkward position. It had, after all, been Gabriel who introduced them to the other Brothers; he was their sponsor. Everyone except Millais, who took longer to come round, was thankful to hear that the misunderstanding was over. They had all missed the parties in Fitzroy Square.

As keeper of the PRB *Journal* William wrote with relief of the two Brothers' imminent departure for the continent. Gabriel, chastened since the reconciliation, was anxious not to run the slightest risk of upsetting Hunt, and wrote, 'I find that by delaying our departure I should be inconveniencing Hunt. I therefore start with him for France and Belgium on Thursday at half-past one, without going at all into the country with Woolner.'

Throughout the journey, Gabriel wrote continually to William what he called 'Proems', mixtures of poetry and prose. From one of these, headed *Between London and Paris, 27th Sept. 1849 . . . 3rd Class*, it would seem from the disparaging refrain that they had invaded a compartment reserved for ladies whose demeanour and dress did not appeal to him.

Once safely installed in Montmartre lodgings recommended by Woolner, Gabriel was 'obliged to write this on English note-paper, as Hunt has ruined the last sheet of French we possessed [Surely he meant the other way round?] by endeavouring to concoct an indecipherable monogram of the PRB to be signed to passports etc'.

Each morning, they breakfasted at a *laiterie* kept by a certain Madame Charles and patronised by 'impecunious and reckless painters'. They were students, bearded fellows under police surveillance, as they had taken part in recent political demonstrations. One morning, their places were vacant. They had been arrested by order of Monsieur le Président.

Hunt noted to his journal that Gabriel was 'the perfect travelling companion'. Limited to schoolboy French himself, he was lucky that Gabriel was a born *boulevardier*, though for an Italian refugee he was surprisingly insular. They both reacted to everything abroad like typical narrow-minded Cockneys. Foreigners were ridiculed for their 'utter muffishness' and they condemned anything unfamiliar as absurd.

Gabriel made it clear in his letters to William that neither he nor Hunt fancied French girls: 'My dear sir, we have not seen six pretty faces since we have been at Paris, and those such as would not be in the least remarkable in London. As for the ball last night, it was a matter for spueing [sic]; there is a slang idiocy about the *habitués* . . . and the females, the whores, the bitches—my God ! !'

However, a few days later they revised their opinion, if only for a few hours. 'Hunt and I begin to like Paris immensely. . . . Last night we went to Valentino's to see the cancan. As the groups whirled past us, one after another, in an ecstasy of sound and motion, I became possessed with a tender rapture. . . .'

Not forgetting that their tour was originally intended as part of their artistic education Gabriel wrote, 'Meanwhile Hunt and myself race at full speed along the Louvre, and yawn from school to school, wishing worn-out those masters known as old.'

Millais shared their prejudice for some years to come. After an Exhibition of old masters, he declared himself 'truly disgusted . . . this Art is in truth as Egg says perfect rot . . . I don't care a rush *light* about it'.

After eighteen days in Paris Hunt and Gabriel had spent most of their money, so they took a late train to Brussels and sat up all night in a third-class carriage. Gabriel passed the time as usual composing sonnets or writing to William. It does not sound as if Hunt was an ideal travelling companion. 'Poor Hunt, who has toothache and can't smoke, has asked me twice for brandy. . . .' At other times Hunt 'would jerk himself, and then fall forward in his sleep', with his head on Gabriel's shoulder. They both deplored 'the beastly victimisation of English travellers'.

In Belgium, they scoffed at everything it was conventional to admire apart from Van Eyck's and Memling's pictures—and the local wine. Hunt busily wrote his journal; they both wrote letters. There is no doubt that when they got home they seriously considered publishing their impressions of the tour. Years later, however, Hunt was embarrassed when Madox Brown's son-in-law, Hueffer, 'the clever genial critic of *The Times*', published some 'old papers . . . in the handwriting of Rossetti and myself, entitling the find as a journal of our tour in France and Belgium'. In this account, they 'were able to dismiss the whole Louvre with one word "slosh" . . . from Rembrandt to Rubens'.

Prompted by my grandmother, Hunt pompously excused this later as 'reckless talk. . . . Although I was prone to enjoy any surprising nonsense, I should certainly have put my veto upon any such publication as expression of our *sober* conviction'.

Fifty years after this little jaunt, when she assisted Hunt in editing his memoirs, she persuaded him to revise many of his youthful opinions which she considered damaging to his public image. In any case, he was by then too blind to read what she wrote.

I will quote only three examples of 'respectable' views of which she approved. *La Source*, by Ingres, was 'a truly excellent picture . . . notwithstanding its timid restraint as to colour. . . .' while Delacroix's fashionable and contemporary work 'was to me not admirable either in plan or form, and in colour, stainy and nauseating. . . .' In fact French modern art was 'stilted, stagey . . . coarse and ugly. . . .'

Gabriel thought that Delacroix was a 'beast'. Delacroix, however, recorded in his journal 'profound admiration' for *The Order of Release*, which Millais sent to the Paris Exhibition of 1855. He could not remember if it was painted by Millais or Hunt, but found it 'singular in its observation and, above all, in its sentiment'.

Gabriel and Hunt returned to London and an enthusiastic welcome from the Brothers, who were agog to learn about 'the abominations of the continent'. They brought back two souvenirs: 'an extraordinary self-concocting coffee-pot for state occasions of the PRB' and 'a book containing a receipt for raising the Devil'. It is to be hoped that this work included the 'banishing rites' of particular interest to Hunt.

Among their friends, only Madox Brown, who much admired

the work of German painters, was shocked by their opinions. Perhaps it was he who persuaded them not to publish, and so prevented them making fools of themselves.

During the next two years Hunt gained an ever increasing circle of friends. In 1850 it was through Millais that he met the Combes at Oxford. Thomas Combe was Superintendent of the Clarendon Press and Printer to the University. Millais recommended 'the old boy' as 'a brick . . . a true Stunner!'

Hunt too found the Combes the 'salt of the earth' and for many years Thomas Combe played a fatherly role in his life. He was a steadfast friend and patron, acted as Hunt's banker and business adviser, and was responsible for investing profitably the proceeds from the sale of pictures.

Mrs Combe, or 'Mistress Pat' as she was called, was Hunt's idea of 'a perfect lady'. During his search for a suitable wife she behaved like a match-making mother.

Hunt's and Millais' high opinion of the Combes was not shared by Gabriel Rossetti. A few years later he found them and their parties terribly dull. But Mr Combe was useful. Being churchwarden of his parish, he knew everyone.[1]

Mrs Combe's rich uncle, Mr Bennett, was a gay old spark; he too found them very dull when he stayed with them. Indirectly, it was he who was responsible for Hunt's ultimate success with the Combes at Oxford. He advised young men 'to put good port wine under their waistcoats' if they wished to survive as long as he.

Hunt and Millais were not particular about what they drank in their early twenties and suffered from 'severe attacks of claret'. It was only later that Tennyson was to teach them discrimination. Millais soon became a *bon vivant*, and would 'down [his] cares with champagne'. For many years he sent Hunt many 'royal presents of wine' and, when he was living in Scotland, 'succulent salmon for breakfast, dear boy'.

From the Brothers' letters it is obvious that Charles Collins and Jack Tupper were frequently intoxicated. Tupper was an Academy student friend of Hunt's. At one time Stephens was

[1] In 1857 Gabriel, William Morris and Edward Burne-Jones attended church with the sole purpose of spotting potential models among the congregation. After the service, those old bores, the Combes, could be relied on for introductions to pretty girls.

surprised if he ever found him sober; on another occasion he looked 'as if he'd been drunk every night for over ten days'.

Charlie Collins, too, was an ex-student with whom Hunt had lost touch. Millais reintroduced them in 1850: 'as good a little chap as ever lived'.

He was the son of William Collins, R.A., and brother of the writer Wilkie. As a child he had been 'dandled on the knees' of Constable, Turner and other celebrities. Now he was Dickens' favourite and was eventually to marry one of his daughters. For forty-six years he and Hunt were very close friends and Hunt drew him on his death-bed (April, 1873).

The Rossettis brought Hunt a pupil called Robert Martineau, who painted *The Last Night in the Old Home*. He, in his turn, introduced Hunt to Edward Lear. At first Hunt found Lear too old: he was fifteen years his senior, and gave drawing lessons to Queen Victoria. But gradually they too became tremendous friends.

Lear kept a Book of *Hunte* (sic) and declared that he had learned more about art from him than from anyone else. He saw the comical side of being taught by such a young master and called him 'Pa' or 'Daddy', while Hunt addressed Lear in letters as 'Dear Infant', or as 'Child'.

In return for Hunt's somewhat stern instruction Lear gave him lessons in Italian and French. He also encouraged his passion for travel and advised him on matters of etiquette—how to address royalty and titled people, not to write *Esquire* after his signature: 'Such a proceeding should be wholly [sic] limited to business letters, or between stiffly polite correspondents.' I am sure that none of the Brothers realised that Lear suffered from epilepsy and syphilis.

Another life-long friend was Arthur Hughes, 'a brother-brush' if not actually a Brother. Perhaps his best-known painting is *April Love*. Years later he painted a beautiful portrait of my great-aunt Alice as a wedding present to his friend Woolner.

His nephew, Edward,[2] also an artist, fell in love with my mother when he was fifty and she was eighteen. I have a fine drawing of her dedicated *To Gwendolyn, from her painter man*.

My grandmother carefully preserved the original of a notice

[2] Edward Hughes completed *The Lady of Shalott* and the later version of *The Light of the World* now in St Paul's, and various other of Hunt's pictures.

which Watts Phillips[3] stuck on Hunt's studio door sometime in 1850:

MISSING

'A young man who answers to the name of Holman Hunt, he is about the middle height—of a fair complexion, *very good looking*, with a countenance denoting great intellectual activity, shows however, at times, much absence of mind which his friends might pardon had it not extended to "absence of body". He is also somewhat eccentric in his habits, talks well and wisely upon Art and may be known by the letters PRB being stamped on his forehead.

'Any persons or person who can give information as to his wellbeing or whereabouts are requested to communicate immediately with Mr Watts Phillips of Oak Villas, Forest Hill, and will be well rewarded for their trouble.'

'N.B. When last heard of the unfortunate young man was talking wildly about Jerusalem and is suspected to be on the road to Jericho.'

Millais once told Boyce,[4] who recorded the fact in his diary[5], that 'Hunt had a morbid conviction of his own ugliness'. Contemporary sketches scarely justify such modesty. The self-portrait I have of him in his teens is of an attractive boy with thick copper-coloured hair, a sensual mouth with a dimpled chin, and large round eyes set wide apart. Burne-Jones described him some years later as 'a tallish slim man with a beautiful red beard, something of a turn-up nose and deep-set dark eyes: a beautiful man'.

Certainly he was always self-conscious about his nose, which was short and retroussé. In 1860, when he had become famous and there was a craze for autograph collecting, he sent a batch of specimens to Mrs Harriet Collins[6] to distribute at Oxford, with the instructions:

[3] Watts Phillips (1825-1874) was a dramatist, novelist and designer of Irish extraction. He had been a pupil of George Cruikshank, but was known principally for his plays and novels.
[4] George Price Boyce, water-colourist 1826-1896, friend of D. G. Rossetti.
[5] Diaries from The Old Water Colour Society's Nineteenth Annual Volume 1941.
[6] Mrs Harriet Collins, mother of Wilkie and Charles.

'Look over very carefully and decide which is the best, and then give it to the most aquiline nosed lady of all those who have done me the honour to apply for my signature; but don't talk to me about snub-nosed four-foot-tenners, for fear that in the course of two or three years, I should have an eldest son like the preceding portrait with no nose at all, for I can't afford him any of this important feature if my wife does not come to me well dowered with the Duke of Wellington's nose.'

The word 'proboscis' is crossed out and the letter is illustrated with a caricature of the child to be expected from such a union. He added:

'To all ladies who have written for autographs lately, I have replied that I am making a collection of photographs and in return I shall be glad if they would send me theirs—*but they have not done so*. If you find an example of my particular ideal, mind you get the photograph and send it to me instantly.'

The Brothers' letters frequently refer to the 'graceful pretty girls' they meet and 'pipes and wine without stint'. Obviously, Hunt was as susceptible as any normal young man and even positively inclined towards marriage at an early age if he could afford it.

CHAPTER IV

Free love—free field—we love but while we may.
TENNYSON

EIGHTEEN HUNDRED and fifty was a significant year in the personal lives of all the Brothers. In January, Hunt moved into new lodgings at 5 Prospect Place, Cheyne Walk. His new landlady was a widow in her early forties called Mrs Bradshaw. She was not a stranger. She kept the Chelsea stationer's shop where he often bought pencils and paper. Her unmarried daughter, Sarah, was a governess.

In spite of the great affection remaining between them Hunt decided not to share a studio with Gabriel again. But Gabriel was a frequent caller and found 'Hunt very comfortably settled'.

Mrs Bradshaw proved a landlady less prejudiced against artists than Gabriel's who, the following year, pinned a notice in the hall: 'Models to be kept under some restraint, as some gentlemen and artists sacrifice the dignity of art to the baseness of passion'. Gabriel remarked, however, that 'at half past ten o'clock, Hunt was requested to allow his gas to be turned off, as the family went to bed!!, which did not exactly meet his views or intentions'.

Gabriel spent hours in the Chelsea studio. Although he could neither row nor swim he loved the river. Hunt wrote that they enjoyed nocturnal excursions in a little rowing boat in 'the star-checked gloom, passing the floating barges, and the ghostly houses on the banks and haunted by echoes. . . .'

Day and night, model-hunting was a sport much enjoyed by the Brothers and their friends. They roamed the streets with arms linked pursuing their prey. Indignant pedestrians were jostled off the pavements. Pretty girls were surrounded and captured like birds in a net.

Some were game and fell victim to the laughing boys' flattery and persuasion. The band agreed that Millais and a friend called Walter Deverell,[1] who now shared a studio with Gabriel, were the best looking and that they should do the talking. Millais' curls were now darker and shorter; he was nineteen. Woolner was quite handsome until he grew a beard which obliterated most of his face. Hunt was strongly aware of sexual attraction. But perhaps Rossetti, being dark and Italian, appealed most to the English girls.

When they hunted further afield their brashness was tempered with courtesy. One of them described how they accosted an elegant courtesan in the fashionable West End as she descended from her carriage. Bowing low and doffing their hats, they implored her respectfully to pose for them—just head and shoulders. Not being asked for more intimate favours by such an attractive group of boys she flounced off, offended.

The 'suitable girls' they met were heavily chaperoned and would be thought inhibited prigs nowadays. However idealistic and romantic, these youths were as sexually inquisitive as their King's Road counterparts today—their curiosity even less frustrated perhaps than in our permissive society. At the time William Acton[2] wrote:

'Many thousand young women in the metropolis are unable by drudgery that lasts from early morning till late into the night to earn more than from three shillings to five shillings weekly. Many have to eke out their living as best they may on a miserable pittance for less than the least of the sums above-mentioned.'

Is it any wonder, he asks, that 'urged on by want and toil, encouraged by evil advisers, and exposed to selfish tempters, a large proportion of these poor girls fall from the path of virtue? Is it not a great wonder than any of them are found abiding in it?'

Some people might think that in the days before antibiotics young men tried to resist the temptation of sexual adventure for

[1] Walter Deverell 1827-1854. He was an ex-Royal Academy student and the son of the secretary of the School of Design. When James Collinson resigned from the Brotherhood, Deverell was recommended by Gabriel Rossetti as the seventh Brother.

[2] William Acton, *Prostitution considered in its moral, social and sanitary aspects in London and other large cities*, Churchill, London, 1969.

fear of venereal disease. Surprisingly, Acton reports the contemporary and general medical opinion:

'It is a fact that no other class of females is so free from general disease and that as a rule prostitutes are endowed with "iron bodies", with extremely resilient and resistant constitutions. If we compare the prostitute at thirty-five with her sister, who perhaps is the married mother of a family, or has been a toiling slave for years in the over-heated laboratories of fashion, we shall seldom find that the constitutional ravages often thought to be necessary consequences of prostitution exceed those attributable to the cares of a family and the heart-wearing struggles of virtuous labour.'

'The author of *My Secret Life*,' says Steven Marcus in *The Other Victorians*,[3] 'provides us with a good deal of information about how part of sexual life in Victorian England was organised or institutionalised.' He goes on:

'As we read his accounts of the London streets and parks at night, we are reminded in one respect at least the London of 1850 still bore considerable resemblance to the city of Boswell's *London Journal*. If one wanted to take a prostitute—or any woman—to some place indoors, "accommodation houses" of various degrees of costliness were to be found in every part of London. In the sixties and seventies "any coffee house with the word *beds* on the windows was also available for sexual use".'

Most nights there were innocent meetings of the PRB round a glowing stove in Woolner's crib. Drinking coffee from the famous continental pot and smoking their pipes, they were joined by new and enthusiastic friends to discuss the publication of a magazine.

Woolner produced the sculptors Hancock and Bernard Smith. Hunt sponsored his friend John Tupper and John's brother George, a printer. Millais brought along Arthur Hughes and Charles Collins. Madox Brown brought Thomas Seddon, the landscape painter. More and more interesting men came each

[3] Steven Marcus, *The Other Victorians*, Weidenfeld and Nicolson, London, 1967.

64

time: as keeper of the PRB *Journal* William Rossetti noted their names. The poet Coventry Patmore was somewhat older than the rest. He 'preferred Hunt to them all because of his integrity', but 'Woolner was the brilliant talker'.

The Brothers called Patmore 'the Vampire'. It was he who introduced them to Tennyson and a wider literary circle.

They were all determined on artistic reform. They sat up until dawn arranging their contributions and discussing methods of promoting *The Germ* as it was at last decided to call their magazine. Although Gabriel Rossetti professed to detest music, he would lead the singing as they marched home through Chelsea, or went down to the river at sunrise for a swim. Night-capped neighbours threw open their windows, growling disapproval at the noise they made.

Hunt's poverty was such that at one of these literary gatherings he offered forty drawings for sale at a sovereign each. Having tasted success by selling *Rienzi* the previous year, what he dreaded most was returning once more to his father. 'Sober business' in a strict warehouse loomed horribly near. It became increasingly difficult to persuade his sisters and their friends to sit to him for nothing. And in any case, they were not the feminine types he admired.

To begin with all the boys' relations had been delighted, even flattered, to pose, but the novelty wore off and these unpunctual amateurs, often preoccupied with domestic responsibilities, proved poor substitutes for professionals. There was an endless choice of beautiful women and girls only too anxious to sit for a shilling an hour or seven and sixpence a day—twice as much as they could earn in a week in a more respectable career. This modest sum was scarcely prohibitive when shared by three or four artists gathered round with their easels. The rate of pay was confirmed by Mrs Frith, first wife of the successful painter, to Gabriel Rossetti's mother, who enquired on behalf of her son regarding his employment of a ravishing shop girl, Lizzie Siddal, whom Allingham,[4] the Irish poet, and Deverell had recently discovered.

[4] William Allingham 1824-1889. He spotted Lizzie Siddal first 'through the glass among the bonnets and gowns. He was an excise officer in Donegal, loved London. Eagerly . . . read his Irish poems about fairies to his Pre-Raphaelite friends . . .' William Gaunt, *The Pre-Raphaelite Tragedy*, Jonathan Cape, London, 1942.

In the spring of 1850, Hunt searched for a suitable model for a picture he wanted to paint. Envious of the others' success at finding their ideal in Lizzie Siddal, he now prowled alone. At the end of March, Gabriel Rossetti wrote to his brother William:

'Hunt . . . has been to Battersea Fields after gypsies, as he wants to get some women with good hands of a proper savage brownness. . . . He found a very beautiful woman for what he wants, fit for Cleopatra; she consented to sit for five pounds an hour, but finally came down to a shilling, and fixed the day to come. His Cleopatra asked for a pot of beer, over which she and a most hideous old hag, her mother, made their bargain.'

On another lone-wolf expedition he picked up a very young stunner with red gold hair. When he followed her home, he thought she was Italian. She was in fact English and lived in Chelsea. Her name was Annie Miller.

She 'lodged with her sister in Justice Walk, behind my studio'. Although she was only fifteen, she was already a part-time model. Thus began a relationship that was to haunt him for years.

Annie's beginnings were humble. Her father, Henry Miller, was a soldier who had fought with the 14th Dragoons in the Napoleonic Wars. Having been wounded (though not seriously), he applied successfully in 1832 to the Royal Hospital, Chelsea, for a pension. The same year he married a charwoman and moved into an over-crowded cottage in Royal Hospital Row next to a public house called the Duke of York.

Shortly after the Millers' marriage their first child was born, a son baptised Henry at Holy Trinity, Sloane Street. A daughter, Harriet, followed within ten months. Two years later, in 1835, little Henry died and Annie was born. It seems that the Millers did not bother to baptise the girls.

Their mother died soon after, aged thirty-seven. By then Henry Miller was forty-six and unable to cope with the two surviving babies.

He left Royal Hospital Row and took them to his brother and sister-in-law, George and Bess Miller, who struggled for survival in a Chelsea slum, conveniently near another public house, the Cross Keys.

66

George Miller was only thirty—a cordwainer or cobbler. Bess was a laundress, aged twenty-eight. Their first child was born in the workhouse.

Henry and his two little girls, Harriet and Annie, were welcomed by George and Bess. At least Henry could contribute a few shillings a week from his meagre pension for their keep.

They all huddled together in squalor in the cellars behind the Cross Keys with the Moseleys, father and sons, all three chimney sweeps. There were various other 'lodgers' including an impoverished clerk John Hughes. He was the only one amongst them who was literate and in the future was to prove most useful to Annie's aunt as a scribe.

The girl's father, Henry Miller, 'drove a horse and cart with bricks, mortar and rubbish, till he could not walk fast enough to keep up with the horse. . . .' Then he was engaged as an odd-job man by the same builder, 'polishing harnesses and cleaning boots and shoes, for which he was paid twelve or fourteen shillings a week' to add to his pension.

When Annie was ten she was put to work and joined her sister looking after the children of the man who had taken her father's place with the horse and cart—a Chelsea neighbour named Hill, whose wife had more profitable things to do in the afternoon.

In order to provide food, or small luxuries denied them, many working-class mothers or artisans' wives at that time indulged in casual prostitution. For fear of fire, their small children were left locked up in the house during the day in the charge of a girl of nine or ten. If at all pretty she would have something to sell herself in a year or two through the agency of the local procuress, who was usually a family friend. The girl would lose her virginity soon anyway, so she might just as well sell it at a price to a gentleman with a taste for rape. Were she 'unlucky', abortions were comparatively cheap: her parents would still make a net profit.

Hill told Hunt that in those days the Miller girls were 'both dirty and infested with vermin'. His wife 'had killed some of the lice . . . Annie's hair was remarkable for its wild and rank abandon'. She grew up 'totally without education . . . could not read or write a single word . . . or [knew] her letters . . . was without even the habits of cleanliness . . . living in the

67

foulest of yards' [Cross Keys Court]. She was 'allowed to prowl about the streets using the coarsest and filthiest of language . . . in short was in a state of absolute neglect and degradation'.

When the girls were in their early teens, their father was seventy, past work and a nuisance to them all. He was admitted as a Chelsea Pensioner to the Royal Hospital, and pottered about the neighbourhood wearing his medals and red coat.

Aunt Bess then put Harriet and Annie to work as servants at the public house. Harriet's looks were not remarkable, but all the artists noticed Annie, swobbing spilt beer and filth off the floor, dodging the drunks and horses in the yard as she clattered about in rags and wooden clogs.

She was a natural flirt and, according to Hill, well aware from a very early age of her physical attractions, and 'being bent upon getting fine clothes and indulging her love of flattery, she became a professional model' from time to time.

Doubtless her aunt was relieved. Had Annie worked in a shop she would have earned only three shillings a week and contributed nothing for her keep.

It was risky for an attractive girl to become a domestic in private service because maids were either fair game for the master and sons of the house or a prey to the menservants. If such lapses came to light, the maids were instantly dismissed without a reference.

Even then, Annie can have had few illusions. She must have known that as a prostitute in Chelsea she could have earned three or four shillings per client, and that gradually, as her wardrobe improved, she would be able to work her way towards the West End: the rate in the Haymarket was five times as high.

She could have dreamt of becoming a prosperous courtesan, with an establishment, her own brougham, several servants and an income of £4000 a year. With her looks, this dazzling future was more than possible. Such a career would far from jeopardise her chance of making a good marriage. William Acton drew attention to the frequency with which 'the better inclined class of prostitutes became the wedded wives of men in every grade of society, from the peerage to the stable'.

CHAPTER V

The lost days of my life until today. . . .
D. G. ROSSETTI

AT FIRST Hunt was proud of Annie Miller. His fellow artists raved about her. She was not only beautiful, but 'such a jolly girl'. He had been somewhat shocked by Gabriel Rossetti's cynical attitude to women: 'They are so much nicer when they have lost their virtue'. Until he met Lizzie Siddal, Gabriel attributed to models the morals of whores—after all, the words were synonymous.

When called to account for speaking in a scornful way of Madox Brown's protégée, Emma, the uneducated daughter of a poor farmer, he explained, 'I regard *all* women as being absolutely loose-tongued and unreliable, so that to suggest such qualities in one of them does not seem to me particularly disrespectful.'

Although young Emma obliged them all by coming round with her broom and sweeping out their studios, Gabriel Rossetti mistrusted her. She gossiped to the sensitive and jealous Lizzie Siddal about his flirtations, which upset her and made her disagreeable.

Hunt knew that it was out of the question to introduce Annie Miller to his family circle.

Miss Siddal was refined and considered herself superior to the other models; she resented being totally ignored when Gabriel's and Deverell's friends and relations drifted in and out of the studio. In polite society models were a joke.

Woolner, the lively raconteur, entertained the company with his investigations of their susceptibility which he had made for Charles Darwin: '. . . how far they would blush the first time they stripped for the "altogether".' Gustave Moreau had known one who had actually blushed all over.

When at last Madox Brown married his Emma he wrote her a good example of the prejudice:

'I will tell you an amusing anecdote. Mrs Warton, the Model, came to sit to Mr Lucy the other morning; she came while I was gone to breakfast. She is rather a pretty girl. When I was there, Mrs Lucy was jealous of her husband. I said I did not think so—but why?—"Why," says the woman, "while waiting for Mr Lucy here this morning, Mrs Lucy came into the room and pretended to look for a book. And she says. "Are you come here to sit for Mr Lucy?" Says I, "I don't know, I'm sure, which of the gentlemen I'm wanted [for]— I believe it is for Mr Lucy," says I. So she says, "Are you going to sit undressed for him?" And I answered her. "I'm sure I don't know if he wants me to." "Well," says she, "I'm sure I can't think however a woman can be so nasty indelicant [sic] as to take off all her things before a man; it is a filthy disgusting thing to do, and I can't think how they can get any woman to do [it]. I wouldn't," says she, "no, that I wouldn't."

'Mrs Warton answered not a word to increase her choler; so with that she flounced out of the room, with her face as red as a turkey-cock's.

'Mrs Warton would have it that she was on the tiles peeping down through the skylight; because it rattled with the wind, and Mr Lucy looked up once now and then, and told her it was the wind. But nevertheless the story is sure to go unimpaired all over London, as Mrs Warton, being pretty, seemed to derive satisfaction from the idea of Mrs Lucy's being jealous.'[1]

The months following the discovery of Annie Miller were financially disastrous for the Brothers. She was much in demand by other painters, but Hunt could not afford to employ her. Lizzie Siddal had graciously consented to pose for the Early Christian girl in his Druid picture.

That spring, *The Germ* 'went bankrupt with a debt of £33' after only four issues. The unfortunate printer, George Tupper, bore the brunt of the loss, and besought Fred Stephens to be present to overhaul the accounts at the last meeting to prevent it 'degenerating into a Poetico-spouting-railing-trolloping-mistifying-smoke-scandal. . . .'

[1] 'Ford Madox Brown (1821-1893)', *English Diaries of the XIX Century* edited by James Aitken, Penguin Books, London, 1944.

Some good came of *The Germ*, however: William Rossetti was at last able to leave his post as an Inland Revenue clerk; he was offered a job on the *Critic*, a weekly paper. Also, it introduced Lizzie Siddal to Tennyson's work. She first read his poems on an old copy wrapped round a pound of butter.

When May came Gabriel Rossetti decided once more to forsake the Brothers and sent his *Annunciation* to a gallery in Portland Place where it was sure to be hung. (He referred to it later as 'the *White Eyesore*'.) Woolner had sometimes posed as the angel. Millais had finished *Christ in the House of His Parents* or, as it came to be called contemptuously, *The Carpenter's Shop*. Although Hunt had been working on his picture for months it was still not to his satisfaction, but there was no time left to improve it. He gave it a long-winded title: *A Converted British Family Sheltering a Christian Missionary from the Persecution of the Druids*. He and Millais submitted their pictures to the Royal Academy Exhibition of 1850 signed with PRB after their names as usual. Until then, in their innocence, they had thought that the meaning of the secret insignia was a mystery to everyone except the Brothers.

But, on Opening Day, to their horror, a hostile press ridiculed the Brotherhood. Dickens led the attack with his famous article in *Household Words*. *Pre*-Raphaelite indeed! What arrogance those whipper-snappers showed in condemning Raphael, the great master! These upstarts had grown too big for their boots; their heads had been turned by their undeserved success the previous year. They had actually sold their pictures! Their theories were absurd, even *wicked*, perverted and blasphemous . . . no words were bad enough.

Who had betrayed the secret society? An urgent meeting was called to investigate this serious matter.

To William Rossetti's shame and the others' dismay Gabriel confessed. Under great pressure, he had confided in an inquisitive sculptor, who in his turn had passed the information on to some opportunist who had sold it to a newspaper.

Millais was disgusted. He had always thought that Rossetti was 'a queer fish', and never liked him much. Hunt made customary excuses for his beloved Gabriel: he was a foreigner after all, 'not like us', he always behaved like a spoilt child. Sooner or later the secret was bound to leak out: so many of his

71

friends knew it already. But to the once-proud parents of Hunt and Millais, the treachery of that 'sly Italian' was beyond the pale.

No one suffered from the bad publicity more than Hunt. In the city, his father was a laughing stock. What did you have to do, he wondered, to succeed in the world? Was it possible without influential friends? Perhaps he should have sent his son to a public school—Westminster or St Paul's? Night after night, Sarah went to bed in tears; she was so teased by other girls.

Once more Millais was obliged to reduce the price of his picture—already committed to Farrer, the dealer—from 300 guineas to 150. Hunt's painting remained unsold. In desperation he was obliged to accept any job that was offered and copied William Dyce's Academy picture for £15.

More bad luck was to come. A so-called friend who had borrowed quite a large sum disappeared to the continent and never returned. And Thomas Creswick, R.A., who had commissioned the picture, *Claudio and Isabella*, the year before, declared that the designs submitted were hideous and called off the deal.

Hunt went to see Augustus Egg and poured out his tale of woe. Egg thought the sketches were admirable. Touched by Hunt's hungry look—he was so earnest and talented, so thin and drawn—he agreed to take over the commission for £25. He paid half in advance.

Once Hunt's debts were paid this money did not last long. He was without the price of a penny stamp to post a letter when he found half-a-crown down the side of a chair. For a few days this kept him in food.

It was a godsend when he was offered the chore of cleaning and restoring the paintings of Rigaud at Trinity House. This was the only public work ever offered to Hunt. He was paid two guineas a day and took on Stephens as his assistant to fill in 'the flat shading'. Hunt wrote in his memoirs: 'I stood on a springy plank, dashing away with large brushes . . . almost asphyxiated by the fumes of wet white lead on the walls.'

By mid-July 1850 the work was done. It was time to go every day to the Lollard Prison at Lambeth Palace to paint the background for Augustus Egg's promised picture. His everyday clothes were in rags, his decent suits at the pawnbroker's. He was hounded by creditors and behind with the rent, as usual.

This time it was Millais who came to the rescue. He and Charles Collins were painting backgrounds at Oxford. Hearing of Hunt's plight, he wrote frequently to cheer him up, addressing the letters grandiloquently to *The President of the PRB*, beginning one, for the first and last time, 'My dear Bill'.[2] Hunt hated the abbreviation and Millais understood, having lately begged everyone to stop calling him Johnny. The letters mostly end with 'With Brotherly love', and such postscripts as 'Hurrah hurrah [repeated 6 times] for the PRB!' and 'Write, write!!' and 'Work away Old Sugars!' Charles Collins joined him in sending 'Brotherly affections'.

During this Oxford visit, when Millais was twenty-one and Collins twenty-three, they became very fond of each other; and Millais was anxious for him to be accepted as a member of the PRB. After all, Hunt and Gabriel between them had sponsored William Rossetti, Woolner, Collinson and Stephens: now it was only fair that they should accept his one and only candidate. He and Charles Collins were so certain that the Brothers would agree that, in anticipation, Collins signed his sketch of Millais and a letter to Hunt with the initials PRB. However, for some reason Woolner fought savagely and successfully against his election. Millais was of course upset and Collins was deeply offended. He was already suffering from unrequited love for a girl at Oxford and this added insult to injury.

Fortunately, Mr and Mrs Thomas Combe took the two young men under their wing that summer and invited them to stay at the Clarendon Press. Mistress Pat made delicious pies. They discovered a 'large acquaintance of college men, many of them really stunners . . .' who esteemed artists greatly and were mad about Hunt's Druid picture. They attended college gaudies, 'moist fishing excursions', and masked balls, and even 'tried to mesmerise some ladies'.

In fact there were good days and bad. As usual on these painting expeditions, it rained a great deal and Collins was 'dreadfully annoyed by flies and children'. Millais confessed in

[2] Even in intimate letters, as a rule, Hunt and his friends used no Christian names and ended 'Yrs', or 'Yours Truly'. For the sake of brevity I have only quoted exceptions from the norm.

his letters to Hunt that in searching for subjects to set against their inevitable backgrounds his 'invention was exceedingly costive'. And in another:

'I regret to say there is a dreadful inclination coming on both of us to *drink*; it may be the excess of misery brought on by breathing *pure* country air. We acknowledge to be real London Cockneys and long to imbibe city atmosphere, see smoky faces, square vegetation, dead leaves and green railings, and behold the great men in Art walking in dignified calmness on London pavement, *hoary headed* tutors. I cannot help thinking we have been asses to have followed the principal of nature and common sense, it is so disgustingly laborious and unremunerative. . . . We have recently made a great many converts and shall make many more if we do not die of Delirium Tremens. Collins cannot go half an hour without a swig at pure brandy—the bottle is before me now. . . . At night I read *Kenilworth* which is entirely made up of slothy mine hosts and gloomy cavaliers, it certainly is damned rubbish. We find pleasure in reading Pickwick *it is so funny*.

'Every aged collegian is an amateur and paints in *bold watercolours* . . . I might say without joking that every Don has a *Madonna* by Carlo Dolci, the favourite artist down here. . . .'

They were not entirely dependent on the weather and on painting backgrounds for so-far-subjectless pictures; Mr Combe commissioned Millais to paint his portrait and Mrs Combe's rich old uncle, Mr Bennett, commissioned Collins to paint his.

Hearing that his beloved Hunt was in such straits, Millais did everything he could to interest these new patrons in his welfare. Like true Brothers he and Collins raved about the unsold *Christians escaping from the Druids* wherever they went. Mr Combe had already seen and admired it at the Royal Academy.

At last Mr Bennett confided in Millais that he would like to give his niece and her husband a handsome present in return for their prolonged hospitality. Young Millais knew the answer! But of course, Hunt's Academy picture was the very thing! The Combes would be thrilled; and what an *investment* —only 160 guineas! A mere bagatelle for Mr Bennett. In a few years, it would be worth ten or twenty times that amount.

Mr Bennett agreed to consider it. Millais wrote urgently to Hunt who had recently improved the picture: 'Have [it] sent down to Oxford . . . *as I am sure* you will sell it. . . . Have it packed up in a wooden case . . . *you will not regret it; recollect I shall be the showman'*.

Who better, indeed? Mr Bennett agreed to buy it.

Hunt borrowed the money to dispatch the crate.

Within two days, a cheque on Coutts' Bank arrived; but it was not signed by Mr Bennett. Perhaps Mr Combe paid for his own present in the end.

Mr Bennett looks a lively ninety in Collins's portrait. He grumbled without shame to fellow guests about his 'over-temperate host'.

Many 'black-frocked' clergymen were invited to dine, and meekly followed Mrs Combe when she shepherded the ladies out of the dining room for *tisanes* and *conversaziones*. Small wonder, since a silver chamber-pot (which eventually descended to my father) was handed round for the comfort of those gentlemen remaining. Mr Bennett detested what he called the 'High Priests and Levites'; he was glad to see the back of them. But he always complained loudly that his niece's husband was most *un*civil not to remain behind with his civilised guests to pass round the wine.

Night after night, in his cups, Mr Bennett persisted in his carping to Mr Combe, until the latter was goaded to suggest politely that if his hospitality was found so lacking, perhaps Mr Bennett would care to find another host.

Mr Bennett left in a huff, shaking his last will and testament, and his fist, warning the Combes that they would have cause to regret their rudeness. They were both disinherited.

Thanks to Mr Combe's integrity, Hunt was not made a victim of this ill-timed family feud. He was able to pay his debts and redeem his suits. Solvent at last, he could now afford to see more of the delicious Annie Miller.

Despite Gabriel's petty betrayals over the last two years Hunt was still devoted and forgiving. In October, he, Gabriel and Stephens booked rooms at Sevenoaks for a weekend of 'picnics and painting real girls under real trees' at Knole Park. Hunt wanted a background for his next year's Academy picture, *Valentine and Sylvia.*

At the last minute Lizzie Siddal refused to go: Annie Miller would be there. It seemed Hunt had now become her protector. Lizzie had detested the girl from the moment she saw her. She considered her insensitive and vulgar, and hated her vitality and bursts of immoderate laughter. She scented danger. Gabriel was obviously attracted. As for Hunt, she had disliked him ever since he and Fred Stephens had played 'a disgraceful hoax on poor Jack Tupper, by passing her off as Hunt's wife'. Touchy and neurotic, with no sense of humour, she resented this pleasantry as 'disrespectful'. She had only agreed to sit to him as Sylvia because Gabriel had persuaded her.

On wet days, Hunt embroidered the dress she was to wear with silver thread and pearls. I was forced by my grandmother to wear it about seventy years later. It smelled musty. I suffered agonies of embarrassment.

Lizzie Siddal did not miss much that weekend at Knole. The Brothers struggled to paint backgrounds with their umbrellas up. As Millais and Collins had discovered at Oxford the previous year, such excursions seldom lived up to idyllic expectations: 'Rain, rain, rain, nothing but rain for the martyrs of art.' Gabriel Rossetti wrote to his mother:

'After an interval of extreme anguish, Hunt and myself were obliged to beat a retreat soaked to the bone. I find I shall never be able to get on without a change of nether garments, which article of dress proved this morning unable to withstand three hours' cataract. Will you therefore take the trouble to send me somehow my other breeches (the pair with straps), and to wrap in them any Italian grammar you can spare, as Hunt wishes to avail himself of my law [sic] in that language.'

Hunt soon bombarded William Rossetti with long Italian letters.

To Lizzie Siddal's satisfaction a dispirited and bedraggled party soon returned to London. But Hunt refused to give in to the English climate and went back to Sevenoaks and worked there on and off, sometimes with Stephens, until November.

In May of the following year (1851) Hunt sent *Valentine and Sylvia* to the Academy. It was badly hung. The critics were more

76

venomous than ever. 'If the attacks the year before had been a storm, this year they were a hurricane.' Kingsley and Macaulay joined in, and the latter wrote: 'Pre-Raphaelitism is spreading. I am glad . . . it is by spreading that such affectations perish.'

Carlyle, however, professed to see 'some sense and hearty sincerity in it' as did many of the older painters.

Madox Brown wrote Hunt a generous letter:

'Your picture make me feel shame that I have not done more in all the years I have worked. You will now have one long course of triumph, I believe—well you deserve it. Your picture seems to me without fault and beautiful to its minutest detail, and I do not think that there is a man in England that could do a finer work. . . .'

Although Millais and Hunt had agreed to keep secret their new technique of painting over a wet white ground, Millais, on impulse, told Madox Brown, who was becoming closer and closer to the Brothers. Madox Brown wrote to Lowes Dickinson: [3]

'As to the pure white ground, you had better adopt that at once, as I can assure you, you will be forced to do so ultimately, for Hunt and Millais, whose works already kill everything on the exhibition for brilliancy, will in a few years force everyone who will not drop behind them to use their methods.'

Once more, nobody seemed interested in buying Hunt's picture. He was in debt again and seriously considered emigrating to Australia to become a cattle breeder. Woolner and others had already decided to seek their fortunes in the gold mines there.

Millais begged Hunt not to leave. Success was just around the corner for 'dear Will Huntikins', he said. He and his parents insisted on his accepting a loan. Equally concerned, Coventry Patmore approached Ruskin, stressing Hunt's plight and pleading the Pre-Raphaelite cause.

[3] Lowes (Cato) Dickinson 1819-1908. He became increasingly attached to the Pre-Raphaelites after 1853 when he rented a studio in Langham Chambers next to Millais. He was one of the founders of Morley College and taught painting there with Ruskin and Dante Gabriel Rossetti.

Ruskin then wrote his two famous letters to *The Times*, 13 May 1851, declaring:

'there is not a single study of drapery, be it in large works or small, which for perfect truth, power, and finish could be compared for an instant with the black sleeve of the Julia, or with the velvet on the breast and chain mail of the Valentine of Mr Hunt's picture.'

He praised the 'marvellous truth in detail and colour', and said: 'there has been nothing in art so earnest or so complete as these pictures since the days of Albert Dürer'.

Doubtless to Annie Miller's delight, Ruskin's only criticism of the picture was 'the commonness of feature' and 'unfortunate type chosen for the face of Sylvia'.

Ruskin's letters did not have an immediate effect. The picture remained unsold during the Royal Academy Exhibition. However when Hunt submitted it to Liverpool 'it was awarded the £50 prize. It was sold in November to Francis McCracken, a Belfast shipping Agent, "who had never seen it, but who was interested from what he had read about it". In the following January, John Miller of Liverpool also offered to buy it, at a reduced rate'.[4]

[4] Mary Bennett, *William Holman Hunt*, catalogue raisonné, The Walker Art Gallery, Liverpool, in conjunction with the Arts Council of Great Britain, 1969.

CHAPTER VI

Was it a friend or foe who spread these lies?
D. G. ROSSETTI

A. C. GISSING, author of a biography of Hunt, headed his chapter about this period in Hunt's life with the accurate, if somewhat ambiguous summary: 'Work and Happy Intercourse, 1851'.

By August, Hunt and Millais had already decided that the subjects for their new pictures were to be *The Hireling Shepherd*[2] and *Ophelia*. They left London for Ewell in search of backgrounds. Both had had a large acquaintanceship in the neighbourhood since they were boys.

I have a small oil that Hunt painted in his teens, of the Hobmans' kitchen. It shows his mother standing by a stone sink looking out of the lattice windows. There are chickens pecking grain off the red tiled floor. My grandmother insisted that the figure was that of a servant, but 'Sarah Hunt' is written faintly on the back of the panel, with a sketch of a man wearing a cylinder hat.

The Brothers took rooms at Worcester Park Farm, which was originally built as a 'hunting-box' for one of Charles II's mistresses.

Even at Ewell their search for pretty girls continued relentlessly. They pursued across the fields 'two graceful damsels', who turned out to be housemaids working for some family friends—probably the Glyns.[3] Millais had hoped that one would pose as

---

[1] A. C. Gissing, *William Holman Hunt: A Biography*, Duckworth, London, 1936.

[2] Evelyn Waugh may not have been justified in accusing Hunt of cruelty to goats in Syria later, but the sheep that Hunt painted in *The Hireling Shepherd* certainly suffered. Various yokels were employed to hold them down and when the wretched animals struggled or rebelled, they were lifted up some height from the ground and dropped to render them insensible—a horrifying process which, according to Millais, resulted in their losing quite a lot of wool.

[3] The Rev. Sir George Lewen Glyn had been vicar of Ewell since 1838. He had inherited the baronetcy on the death of his brother in 1840.

Ophelia. Sitting on a fence, they discussed their ideals of feminine beauty, tracing examples in the mud with the points of their walking sticks. Then, glancing at these, they looked up and laughed with surprise; each had drawn the other's profile exactly! My grandmother often stressed that when they were young, they loved one another as *brothers*. Had her beloved not admired Millais' physical beauty, he would never have married her or her sister Fanny, whose profiles so resembled his, although of course they were dark and he was fair.

Waiting in the fields to pick up girls seems to have been a favourite if dubious form of recreation for young men of the time. Certainly Stephens found it relaxing when staying with stuffy, conventional people. He wrote in a letter (undated) to Hunt:

'A country house is really a Terrible place in the way of shackling a fellow's movements. I was so reduced once that I actually bribed my friends stable man to let me out o' nights for quiet prowls, but my reputation was gone through sitting on stiles and smoking in peace, and the rustics believed I waylaid the milk girls; of this I was perfectly innocent.'

The fun enjoyed was often spoilt by a guilty conscience. Millais wrote to Hunt from Winchelsea, Sussex, the following year:

'Now I am going with Halliday to smoke a sigaret [sic] upon a stile—what a difficult thing it is to behave properly. At this place there are lots of pretty girls who insist upon coming out bonnetless in the moonlight and invitingly passing and repassing us, dallying in hopes, and I have an almost insurmountable desire to stop them and speak, as most youths would, and when I get back to my bedroom I think what a fool I have been, and make up my mind to begin again. If I remember right it was the same with you at Fairlight!'[4]

Among some family papers, I found my grandmother's somewhat naïve explanation of one of these escapades, which was to cause much trouble for Hunt later.

[4] Near Hastings in Sussex.

80

She wrote:

'Hunt and Millais were staying at Ewell, where Hunt was painting the background for *The Hireling Shepherd* and Millais was painting the background for *Ophelia*. They were in their early twenties.

'Two girls, who proved to be sisters, crossed the field where Hunt was painting and he thought one of them would be a most suitable model for the Shepherdess picture. After casual conversation he suggested that she should ask her mother (her home was near) if she would allow her to sit as a model to him. At the same time Hunt properly gave a reference as to his respectability in the name of Sir L. Glinn [Sir George Lewen Powell Glyn]. Hearing nothing, eventually Hunt went to Kingston and saw the mother and brother (who was a seller of groundsel). The girl's name proved to be Emma Watkins.

'When the mother had made enquiries, she sent her daughter up to his studio in Chelsea to sit for the Shepherdess.

'The first time she came with her friend, a sailor, the second time also, but the third time she came alone. When Hunt asked her why she had come without her friend, she said that her mother thought it unnecessary. After this she came several times alone. Rossetti, Stephens and others were in and out of the studio, as she sat, or rather reclined, for the pose. For some reason the group of artists who became acquainted with this model nicknamed her "The Coptic". She was engaged to marry the sailor.

'At last the Coptic announced that she would like to lodge near the studio in a place found by her friend as it would be easier than coming up to London daily from Kingston. Hunt's Chelsea landlady was a Mrs Bradshaw. She said that the lodgings suggested by the friend were not suitable and suggested that the Coptic also should lodge with her, as Hunt also lived in the house it would be more convenient for all concerned.'

Emma Watkins must have been greatly impressed by the young gentlemen's courteous behaviour. The author of *My Secret Life* wrote at the time, 'Anyone can have a field girl, nobody cares'.

Charles Collins joined them for a while at Worcester Park Farm. His mother, Harriet, was a very different type from Mrs Combe. Far from leaving the dining-room at the conventional time, she enjoyed nothing more than to sit talking and flirting with the boys far into the night, while they smoked and drank their wine. Hunt and Millais pretended to compete for her favours, and all three shared 'rollicking jokes'. Her letters to Hunt began, 'Son of my Heart', and ended, 'Ever your loving Harriet'.

Charles Collins was not as popular with Millais now as he had been the year before at Oxford. He was 'hipped in love' and consoled himself by becoming High Church and indulging in what Millais called 'monkish nonsense'.

Charles had flaming red hair, and blamed this for his romantic failure. Assisted by Hunt he made several attempts to dye it a less offensive colour.

As well as working on the background for *The Hireling Shepherd* during the day, Hunt was painting on moonlit nights an ivy-smothered door in an owl-haunted orchard. He was not afraid of ghosts, and four years earlier had been restrained by a quaking companion from chasing one across the fields. To shelter himself from the cold he sat in 'a sentry-box made of hurdles' with his feet in a sack of straw.

This background presented the usual challenge: a subject was required. Whom should he paint standing by the door? For what purpose could the figure, man or woman, be standing there?

It was on the night of the blackberry pudding row that he found the answer.

Charles Collins refused a helping of blackberry pudding. Millais was furious with him. How could he resist such a tempting dish? It must be some ridiculous self-imposed penance . . .

Reluctant to become involved, and having wolfed his own share of the pudding, Hunt got up and left the table to sit by the fire, sketch-book on his knee, pencil in hand as ever. He brooded on backgrounds and moonlit doors overgrown with weeds . . . He racked his brains for suitable subjects: Tennyson's poems, Shakespeare's plays, the Bible . . . Christ! . . . What was that text—in *Revelation*? 'Behold, I stand at the door and knock'. While the blackberry pudding argument raged his pencil flew over the paper.

Poor Charles went up to bed in tears to say his prayers. (He had recently changed the pretty girl in his flower garden picture into a nun having *Convent Thoughts* while contemplating a passion flower.)

Millais came over to see what on earth Hunt was so busily drawing. He explained. Millais clapped him on the back. They sat up drinking far into the night.

Besides Papa Millais, various neighbours called at the farm, including Hunt's uncle Hobman. He suggested that the gigantic water-rat in Millais' picture should be scraped out: it would look as if it was going to spring at Ophelia's throat. Millais had painted it indoors on a wet day from a dead one which had been caught in a trap.

Other friends came down from London. Coventry Patmore encouraged Millais to keep a diary. For a while he did, but later his son censored it. The Combes paid them a visit. They much admired Hunt's moonlit background, and, being devout Christians, thoroughly approved of the subject. Wilkie Collins also came and was horrified to see how thin Charles had become through fasting.

By November, bad weather had driven them back to London. Millais had not been as lucky as Hunt in picking up a model in the country. Gabriel lent him Lizzie Siddal for Ophelia. A martyr to art, she lay resigned to her fate in a cold bath.

Hunt was shortly joined at his lodgings in Cheyne Walk by his shepherdess.

To a field girl, the comparatively luxurious existence of an artist's model must have been bliss. To recline in a warm studio instead of grubbing about among mangold-wurzels and kale, frozen and soaked to the skin—that was the life for Emma Watkins!

Although there was no boating on the Thames until the spring, she revelled in the Chelsea parties, and was a great success with the boys. Hunt was obviously teased about his new acquisition. It was Gabriel who nicknamed her 'the Coptic'.

Laughingly, Hunt protested that she was already engaged to be married; they all enjoyed pulling his leg. One of these fine days, her jealous fiancé would arrive! They stormed up the stairs and banged on the door with a stick, imitating the gruff voice shouting for 'Emma!' They took it in turns to act the part of the sailor home from the sea. Such a situation was bound to create hilarious studio gossip; Robert Brough, the satirical writer, certainly heard the story, and wrote it, although he did not succeed for some years in getting it published. So did Annie Miller, living just around the corner. She must have been piqued when Hunt imported a rival stunner, and furious at her success: the girl was nothing more than a red-faced country bumpkin.

Hunt was preoccupied and determined to finish *The Hireling Shepherd* for the Royal Academy Exhibition the following May. Not content with painting Emma Watkins and the shepherd during the day, he was painting *Christ at the Door* at night.

The lantern, which he designed, cost £7 to make. The door was a board pinned with trails of ivy. The lay figure, draped in his grandmother's tablecloth (cut up and ruined by a tailor), stood with a lump of clay on its head, holding the lighted lantern in one wooden hand. Hunt wrote to Combe in February 1853:

'. . . the oil lamp belonging to the lantern does not give light enough so I have gas fittings made,[5] which go admirably, *only* the lantern becomes red hot . . . then I take to camphor . . . but this after much trouble, in adjusting the lamp to the lantern, either smokes too much as to make the room unbearable . . . or goes out entirely. . . .'

However, he rigged up 'an elaborate arrangement'—a makeshift tent—of screens and Venetian blinds to get the right sombre effect. He often worked until four o'clock in the morning, squinting through a gap in the hangings at this weird *maquette*. When there was no moon, various friends called hoping the Mad would be free for 'grub' or to go dancing (Gabriel's new studio was over a 'hop-shop'). Madox Brown 'found Hunt terribly fagged painting his moonlight picture'.

He was cooped up indoors most days, and working and smoking far into the night. He missed taking regular exercise, having always been keen on keeping physically fit. When the clock struck four he laid down his brush, turned out the gas

[5] By Henry Childs, Annie's sister Harriet's young admirer who was the son of the Chelsea barber.

and sprinted down Cheyne Walk to the river and back before falling into bed.

Sometimes he and William Rossetti hired horses and galloped full pelt along Oxford Street into the fields nearby. Game was still shot in that area as late as the 1850s.

Hunt was not only an enthusiast for sculling, swimming,[6] shooting, riding and dancing, but also, since the age of ten, he had been mad about boxing. In fact, he held forth to the Brothers and their friends on 'the Noble Art', saying that 'it was due to our ancestors' pugnacity that England was great' and that 'we were *degenerating* into a generation of milksops'. It was due to him that William Rossetti, Boyce, Tupper and Stephens all took boxing lessons from a man called Read. Ruskin was coached by the great Tom Sayers.

It is interesting that at the same time, Armstrong, Lamont, Du Maurier and Poynter, who shared a studio in Paris, 'divided their time between painting and swinging Indian clubs, boxing with one another and indulging in strenuous horse-play'.[7] Even Whistler, having first despised such physical jerks, at last took boxing lessons from a pro.

Hunt's Indian clubs[8] descended to me, as I described in *My Grandmothers and I*.

In the spring of 1852, William Bell Scott paid his first call at the Chelsea studio. From Hunt's pictures he had expected him to be rather sedate and grim. He was 'astonished . . . and greatly entertained by the irrepressibility of his mirth and the uproariousness of his humour', and wrote in his autobiography:

'The lay figure held a lighted lantern, and Hunt, painting by good daylight . . . peered into the mysterious gloom. . . . The arrangement had a bogey effect. . . . He was at that time, however, a Hercules, though not a giant, and after an

---

[6] Hunt taught William Rossetti to swim.
[7] James Laver, *Whistler*, Faber and Faber, London, Second Edition 1950.
[8] They were terribly heavy. I, as an overgrown child, was made to use them by my Hunt grandmother. Swinging the clubs like a human windmill, I sometimes lost grip with one hand. The club would fly across the garden or the attic and crash against the wall. I expected to see my arm attached, dragged out of its socket. 'How barbarous! Most unsuitable for *girls* . . .' my other grandmother would exclaim.

economical dish of savoury fish and ginger beer, which my long walk made excellent, evening coming on, we crossed the street and jumped into a wherry, the management of which he was quite accustomed to, and he pulled me up to Hammersmith and back again.'

I can only guess at what kind of relationship Hunt enjoyed with Annie Miller and Emma Watkins during this period. The latter does not appear in any other of his paintings. Certainly, the sailor returned to claim her, as all Hunt's friends had predicted.

Hunt was by no means confident in the success of these two pictures. His debt to the Millais family worried him and he applied for the job of official draughtsman to Layard's Mesopotamian expedition, but his application arrived one day too late.

CHAPTER VII

Hope sows what Love shall never reap.
D. G. ROSSETTI

THE HIRELING SHEPHERD was hung on the line in May 1852, and eventually sold for 300 guineas, although a review written by the *Athenaeum* critic was scarcely complimentary:

'Like Swift [Hunt] revels in the repulsive. These rustics [the models] are of the coarsest breed, ill-favoured, ill-fed, ill-wanted. . . . Their faces . . . too flushed and rubicund suggest their over-attention to the beer or cider keg . . . and touched as if both had fed on madder, or been busy with raspberries . . . and would be none the worse for a course of brimstone.'

All the same this led to another commission, which was to bring him in a further hundred guineas and to win him a prize of £50. It was painted at Fairlight and finally called *The Strayed Sheep*. At last Hunt's debt to the Millais's was paid.

He needed a change. The Combes invited him to Oxford for Eights' week and 'Commem'. Mr Combe took charge of his money and invested it wisely. Mrs Combe, having grown increasingly fond of their protégé, who was now twenty-five, tried to produce suitable girls for him to escort to parties, but her choice was not at all to his taste. Not taking much care over punctuation and illustrating the letter with a sketch of a plain, spotty girl, he wrote to Stephens an undated letter complaining:

'Imagine the above face on a young lady of 4 3/2 [sic] feet high, and tell me if ever in all your life (and you *have had* your trials I know) had to walk out with such an odious creature. The beauty referred to is here, and it is my unfortunate lot to have to take her about all day over the town, and at night to parties in the colleges to which I am invited alone with Mr and Mrs Combe (who assure me that my hosts, the doctor and fellows, will be delighted to receive any lady with me) so it is generally supposed that I am engaged to the grinning, costive looking Virtue, and I have no help but those arising from stratagems calculated to risk my reputation in the eyes of the good, angelic Mrs Combe. for instance last night at Exeter Coll. I managed to fall in love with a stunner in the company, which fact I communicated to Mrs Combe as an apology for my want of attention to Miss Costive and it answered capitally.

'But today having taken Miss Costive to breakfast at Baliol [sic] I found another stunner [Miss Georgina Andrews] in the room with whom I fell in love again and walked off leaving Miss C—to Mr Jenkins[1] a MA who has more claim to the honor of martyrdom than myself: and then it did not answer at all, for I was caught in St Mary's at the Bishop's sermon, and was compelled on leaving to give up my sweetheart to her Ma and Pa. and to take the indigestable to the Theatre to a grand concert. thence to dinner—thence to see a balloon ascent and back home where I had a headache which nothing but a pipe and the fresh air would dissipate. which being granted. procured me one hours relief.

'Tomorrow is Commemoration Day, consequently the first thing I shall see on going down to breakfast will be this creature in her bonnet ready to pounce on me immediately I have reluctantly admitted that I am unable to eat any more. when I shall have to take her to the Theatre, and remain with her until two. and in the evening to another College Party.

'This misery has been growing on me for the last week and today has arrived at such a pitch that I find it quite impossible to think of any other circumstances so I will close my note, begging you to commiserate me. and to reminder me to Jack Tupper etc.. I shall return as soon as possible. perhaps a week.'

His moods change rapidly. Within perhaps a few hours of

[1] The Rev. John Jenkins was then a fellow of Jesus College and became the Dean of Jesus and Bursar about ten years later. Hunt painted his portrait that year (1852) and said of him, 'I never knew a man more pure in mind and deed. . . . It was a boon to have known him.'

88

writing this he was replying to 'a long affectionate letter' from Walter Deverell which delighted him 'not so much from any unusual brilliancy in it but from the spirit of brotherly love which I have every desire that you possess for me, being manifold in pages'.

Deverell was anxious to know if Hunt was thinking of seeking his fortune in Australia with Tommy Woolner and other artists. Hunt did not give any family reasons nor his pursuit of sweethearts and stunners for remaining in England, but stated:

'I have only a few men of our circle to keep my thoughts homeward. I do not know what I should do away from Rossetti. It is true, that I have not seen him or heard from him a long time, but I know him to be in the same land somewhere, and that at any time he can be found out and spoken with when necessary and this is enough, but to have the dark world seperating [sic] me from Gabriel, Brown, Stephens and yourself William R. for this life, is not what I will bring to myself rashly, for fear of the cold desolateness of the shadow of death's valley being anticipated by my soul's meanderings. . . .' [The rest of this sentence is indecipherable having been deliberately and successfully censored in indian ink.]

It is very strange that he did not even mention his devotion to Millais as a reason for staying. He went on to describe his visit to the Combes at Oxford:

'With a good friend or two I could be happy, in this town. . . . Alone it would be rather dull, if not disgusting were it not that my good host is such a glorious fellow. . . .'[2]

He returned to London to paint Christ's face. At the end of June, he asked Christina Rossetti to pose for this because he admired 'her gravity and sweetness of expression'. Christina never sat professionally, she was a poet, and her mother brought her to the studio. No wonder she looked grave, posing in the dusky tent while Mrs Rossetti knitted away by the window. Perhaps it was then that she was inspired to write that well-known sonnet beginning 'The PRB is in its decadence'. She stared

[2] Letter No. HM. 12917 in possession of Henry E. Huntington, Library and Art Gallery, San Marino, California, U.S.A.

with foreboding into the future and saw the Brotherhood disintegrate.

Last year, she had refused to marry James Collinson—one of the seven Brothers. Disillusioned, he had resigned from the PRB and gone to Stonyhurst with the intention of becoming a priest, hoping to enjoy the tranquillity of 'monastic' life. The authorities, however, had set him to work like everyone else at menial tasks not at all to his taste—cleaning boots, digging and scrubbing. He decided that after all his true vocation was artistic, left the Jesuits in disgust, and started to paint again. He was infirm of purpose: she would never marry him.

Woolner too had become bitter, having failed to land any important commission. Next month he was emigrating to Australia with other disgruntled artists. Even Tennyson—'the Great Alfred'—had said that if it were not for his delicate wife he would accompany them. He believed there were huge fortunes—tens of thousands a year—to be made there for the asking.

It was already obvious to her that William Rossetti and Fred Stephens would soon give up painting altogether—like Charles Collins, they would take to writing, or become critics . . .

Everyone knew that the Mad longed to fulfil his childhood dreams and visit the Holy Land. If, as it was rumoured, this extraordinary picture of his for which she was sitting was indeed sold to the Combes for hundreds of pounds, then these dreams would become reality. Unlike Gabriel, he was prepared to work like a maniac.

But Gabriel, like Millais, Tom Seddon and other friends, had sworn that he would accompany Hunt to Syria. Christina knew, however, that her brother would never escape: he was too firmly caught in Miss Siddal's web.

'The Sid', as they called her now, was coming to sit to Hunt again, in spite of her dislike of him. She was flattered perhaps that her hair should serve to frame Christ's face. Christina must have tried to imagine the side-whiskers and beard which the Mad would paint on her own cheeks and chin.

He talked endlessly of his forthcoming trip to the East. What would become of Millais then?

Millais had been too young last year to become a Royal Academy Associate—both he and Hunt had applied. Millais would certainly apply again and succeed. But he loved the Mad so emotionally, so dependently: how could he live without him? According to studio gossip, young Mrs Ruskin was sitting to him for a picture called *The Ransom*, which subsequently became his *Order of Release*.

During the autumn of 1852, Hunt went down to Ewell now and then to perfect details of the background of his moonlit picture. Millais could scarcely endure his absence even for a few days and wrote:

'I do long for you to be back and to see each other in the evenings . . . I am tremendously dull here and have positively no person except Charles Collins (who is frightfully chilling) to associate with. I really don't know what to do sometimes. I run off to Hanover Terrace merely because it is an object, jest with the old lady, Harriet Collins say about a dozen words to her lay figure son, and tumble out into the freezing night, miserable . . . I met Gabriel there the other day. He appeared to me to be just the same as ever, flinging his legs up upon any object within reach and humming in a moody way. He attends Wells Street Church I think pretty regularly . . . (Charles does not quite understand him).'

Whatever their motives, people found regular church attendances was in fact the equivalent of a weekly cocktail party; it was the way to make new acquaintances.

During this winter Hunt 'had the happiness to be chosen as one of the original members of the Cosmopolitan Club'. When G. F. Watts left his Charles Street studio 'his artistic and other friends' continued to use the premises and forgather with 'an ever increasing circle of remarkable men of differing intellectual activities'. It was here that Hunt first met Thackeray and Layard.

Millais was missing Hunt more than Hunt was missing him. When Hunt disappeared again to Ewell for a few days, Millais wrote on 4 November 1852, pathetically and ostensibly to ask him to bring back some ivy, adding:

'I hope you will finish by this week as I truly *long* for your return having no friend in London except Charlie and he does not in the least sympathise with me, he is more like a walking lay figure than ever. . . .'

And yet again a few days later:

'Charley Collins has just gone home from here, after dining with me, he wants a three weeks old baby to paint in his picture, and we both went round into our mews to see a coachman's wife's infant, but it was too old.

'I pity him painting such a frightful thing as a child of that age, they look strangled, and purple, and otherwise horrible to behold. He also wants a girl for the principal head, and wrote to Siddal mentioning his acquaintance with Gabriel, but was answered in the most freezing manner, stating that she had other occupation, so that the poor little chap is quite at a loss for work.

'Whilst I was in the city on my way to the Tower [of London], Mr Combe called, it was unfortunate, not a soul was at home, he left saying he could not possibly call again, they are not coming to Town as I expected to see the Duke's [The Duke of Wellington's] funeral. . . .'

On 1 January 1853, Gabriel Rossetti wrote to Tommy Woolner in Australia:

'Hunt has just returned from a Christmas [with the Combes] at Oxford, jollier than ever, with a laugh which answers one's own like a grotto full of echoes. . . . We have been amusing ourselves since dinner with trying to sketch heads from memory. . . . Here is Hunt. It is one of William's queer portraits, but it has something of him. It looks like a fellow who would have a try at anything, even to making the sun stand still—and indeed he has done that, on his canvases which are more vivid than ever. You have heard from him, and will know that he is at last coming into his rights . . . as Tennyson says . . .

"has found the stubborn thistle bursting
Into glossy purples that outredden
All voluptuous garden roses." '

Hunt saw little of his family now: the Combes had taken their place. His sister Sarah had married Wilson, the upholsterer, and Maria was engaged to the shop assistant, William Peagrim.

Three weeks later, William Rossetti wrote, less expansively than his brother, in the *PRB Journal*: 'Our position is greatly altered. We have emerged from reckless abuse to a position of general and high recognition. . . .'

It was a spring for jubilation. In May, Hunt's *Claudio and Isabella*, commissioned for £25 as long ago as 1850, was well-placed at the Royal Academy Exhibition. Lord Grosvenor wanted to buy it for three hundred guineas. Augustus Egg urged to accept this offer, but Hunt insisted on keeping to the bargain that they had made when he was desperate.

Effie Ruskin wrote delightedly to her Mama that Millais' painting of her was attracting such a fashionable crowd that one could scarcely see it for bonnets.

Hunt was now established not only as an artist, but as a social success. His new tailcoat was beautifully cut and the envy of Charles Collins, who wrote asking for his tailor's address. The tailor's name was Poole—he was the man who lent £10,000 to Louis Napoleon and thus helped to create the Second Empire. Earlier in the year another, less distinguished, tailor had misunderstood Hunt's instructions and made part of the famous tablecloth into a tailcoat for Christ to wear in the moonlit picture.

It dawned only gradually, even on Hunt's closest friends, that he seriously contemplated going to Syria as soon as circumstances permitted. Surely, they said, it was rank folly to leave London just as he was on the crest of a wave?

If the Combes bought *Christ at the Door*, he would soon have about £1,000 to invest—the equivalent of £5,000 today.

He and Millais were asked everywhere to parties. Being delicate, Millais disliked late nights, and longed to escape to the North with the Ruskins, his exciting new friends, for a few weeks of painting and fresh air. John Ruskin had vaguely commissioned a portrait.

Millais went with Hunt to a crush at the Monckton Milnes' in Upper Brook Street. Effie Ruskin was there and begged Hunt prettily to come with them. On the way, they were all invited to stay with the Trevelyans at Wallington near the Scottish border. Although Millais' own brother, Bill, had agreed to join the party, Effie knew how lost he would be without beloved 'Will Huntikins'. Both she and her husband had taken Hunt's acceptance for granted. She confirmed the invitation by letter and was surprised when he politely refused, pleading pressure of work; *Christ at the Door* was not finished yet and a new commission had cropped up through Augustus Egg. Millais brushed Hunt's refusal aside. The old boy would join them later, until then they would write to each other every day.

In fact, the reason was Annie Miller, the fruit of success—he felt that he had experienced True Love at last. She was now eighteen.

Mr Combe invested more and more money as it rolled in. Being religiously inclined, he was sympathetic to Hunt's resolve to concentrate on popular biblical subjects. Perhaps he could convert agnostics? And where else but Bethlehem and Nazareth would he find the strictly authentic backgrounds and props and models he needed for these?

In those days all right-minded people were agreed that art must carry a message. Kingsley, Thackeray and Dickens used their talents to improve the lot of mankind. Hunt felt that he should join the crusade—and not just because this point of view was the fashion. Mr Combe was impressed by young Hunt's sincerity. He intended to use his gift to bring the man in the street nearer to Christ as He actually lived.

Hunt confided his more intimate aspirations and problems to the 'angelic Mrs Combe'. Only she would understand that he *must* take a wife with him to the Holy Land. After all he might need a nurse, after falling foul of some dread disease—plague, cholera, or smallpox: according to Layard there were *lepers* everywhere! In such an emergency, the sheltered stunners he met at London or Oxford dinner parties might prove broken reeds. He had already ordered potassium permanganate, but what did she think?

Certainly the newspapers were full of alarming reports: it seemed that there was political unrest in the East. War was threatened, revolutions . . . the parents of some frail, upper-class girl might well object to her risking her life in an outlandish place like the Holy Land.

Hunt comforted himself with the thought that any fool with half an eye, even a woman, could learn to shoot: a tall, thorough-bred English girl was more than a match for some miserable, stunted Arab.

All the same, how could he tell if the refined, aquiline-nosed young ladies whom he met at *conversaziones* speaking melodious Italian in Tuscan accents would pick up Arabic as quickly? According to Layard French was not enough. To begin with, too, it might prove difficult to find a suitable house. Would a *lady* (Mrs Combe should know) be happy for a while camping in a sandswept tent or a gutted tomb? Would it appeal as a domestic challenge, sleeping in a flea-bag in the desert, maybe stewing camel steaks over smouldering dung?

Mrs Combe thought not.

The more he talked, the less could she visualise the daughters of the intellectual people she knew or those of the well-endowed county neighbours, accustomed to riding to hounds, jogging along on donkeys through germ-ridden dust under a tropical sun, pestered by flies, pursued by howling jackals, while vultures hovered.

At one point, in desperation, she offered herself to accompany him. It would make a change after all. She had no boy of her own: her youth and looks were withering away as a printer's wife at Oxford.

Hunt returned to London no wiser and, having suffered from agonising toothache, wrote Mrs Combe a bread-and-butter letter: 'On Saturday I took a violent remedy (pray don't read this aloud . . . such a fact being made public would fatally stand in the way of your humble servant's matrimonial intentions), I went to the Dentist and had four teeth extracted (with no anaesthetic)'. Later Millais wrote: 'Dear Boy, how do you eat now?' He recommended 'chliriform [sic] as somewhat deadening sensation.'

Hunt was tough, but his heart still ached: he was torn between two ideals and ideas of marriage. Perhaps at no other period have young men found the rival attractions of the virtuous and the fallen so equivocal.

To be sure, Miss Georgina Andrews, whom he had lately met at Oxford, was a lovely girl, gracious and full of charm, but the formal courting of virtuous girls involved wearisome, time-wasting interviews with prospective in-laws—the discussion of settlements with solicitors, and all sorts of tedious, incomprehensible horrors. Respectability was as stifling and restricting to an artist as conventional clothes, regular meals, or being forbidden to smoke indoors. Outrageous, as Woolner said. Having complied with such unreasonable demands, as often as not, the groom found he had opted for a pig in a poke—the melting sweetheart might change overnight into a cold, domineering wife, a *malade imaginaire*, or something worse.

As an alternative, there were the women, condemned by the righteous as 'tainted' or 'lost', with whom one felt perfectly at ease, wearing any old clothes in the relaxed atmosphere of one's own or one's friends' studios—frying sausages, falling in love, sharing jokes, attending private views without the bother of introductions.

One really got to know where one was with a girl, dancing and drinking at hop-shops or pleasure gardens like the Cremorne or boating by moonlight on the river, unhampered by chaperones.

Nor were such larks any longer counted as sinful. The rescue of fallen women, or those in danger of corruption, was noble and fashionable now. Society had a guilty conscience at last for poverty-stricken lost innocence. Well-meaning ladies in prim bonnets, armed with tracts, and brandishing stout umbrellas to ward off pimps, pursued prostitutes through the streets, pleading with the unfortunates to repent and enter Homes of Hope founded by Lord Shaftesbury. More often than not their efforts were scorned and the crumpled tracts tossed into the gutters.

Even Gladstone was an enthusiast for rescue work. 'At some cost to his reputation, for there was an unworthy suspicion (shared unfortunately by the Queen herself) that his . . . care for prostitutes was not wholly [sic] disinterested . . . he even took them back to his own house where they were cared for with all kindness by Mrs Gladstone.'[3]

Many a distinguished man was inspired to save and improve a seedy soul. Pygmalion's example was popular. Madox Brown had hidden young Emma for years while he educated her: she was almost presentable now. Soon he would marry her. There were more successes than failures—though to be sure, according to gossip, Augustus Egg's choice had been most unfortunate.

Every day that Hunt saw Annie Miller, the scales tipped

[3] James Laver, *Age of Optimism*, Weidenfeld and Nicolson, London, 1966.

further in her favour against one of Mrs Combe's hypothetical stunners. Better the 'Queen of Devils' one knew![4]

Supposing he were to pay for Annie's education—elocution and dancing lessons? Of course she had a Cockney accent . . . her laugh was rather loud . . . but no one would suspect in a year or so that she had been born in a slum and had worked as an artist's model. Admittedly, some of her personal habits were objectionable; summed up in a word—*uncouth*. He would have to take a well-bred, sympathetic and *charitable* woman into his confidence. Who?

Stephens was always talking about some grand and respectable lady, a Mrs Bramah, the aunt of his new well-to-do friend, Tom Diplock, a medical student.

It was rumoured that Gabriel was toying with the idea of marrying that moody Lizzie Siddal and she was only a shop girl, but after all he was a foreigner. Annie's education would cost about £200—a tidy sum: this would have to be withheld from Mr Combe who would certainly disapprove. Fred Stephens would have to be put in charge of this affair: he was a *reliable* friend; he could keep accounts and send reports of Annie's progress to Syria. To earn enough for those little feminine extras, the bonnets she loved so much, she could continue sitting to artists they knew, who could be trusted not to ask her to pose in the nude. He drew up a list of them—Millais, Halliday, Egg, Boyce, Stephens.

Before revealing these plans to Annie, he talked the whole matter over with Stephens, who was at present much in debt and reduced to copying pictures at £10 each for Augustus Egg.

Stephens agreed with this scheme in principle and said he would ask Tom Diplock to introduce him to Mrs Bramah, but in return for these services he begged to borrow in advance some of the money that Hunt would leave with him—of course he would keep strict accounts and repay the loans, as they were needed, into the fund for Annie Miller.

From this moment, not only was Stephens beholden, but condemned to the thankless rôle of go-between.

To Hunt's astonishment, when he returned to Annie and earnestly explained these constructive ideas, far from appearing

[4] Christina Rossetti is rumoured to have called her this.

97

grateful, she seemed incredulous, almost stunned by his proposal. She went home early in a strange mood. For days she did not come near his studio.

Perhaps her intimate favours had made him feel guilty and responsible for her future. Surely, now it was not for her to reject him? He wrote distractedly to Millais in the North.

After much thought and discussion with her Aunt Bess and sister Harriet, Annie reached her only possible conclusion. Henry Miller, her father, refused to call on Hunt to discuss the matter. Although Hunt's intentions were matrimonial, no question of marriage would arise until he returned from Syria—in the meantime, the Mad, as he was so rightly called, would pay for her education. Mrs Bradshaw's daughter was already teaching her the three R's and if she learned to dance and talk properly, and 'etiquette' from Tom Diplock's aunt, why, she might even land a West End nob and end up at a swell address in Maida Vale.

She knew that Hunt was terrified of her succumbing to just such a 'degrading temptation'. With this fear in his mind, and hoping to impress upon her the horrors she might expect from such a life, he was starting a new picture. He had asked her to pose for him now, in an expensive, fashionable nightgown—fine linen trimmed with hand-embroidered lace—as a kept woman alone with her lover! But at least such a risqué picture would be the talk of the town—she might be 'the belle on the line' at next year's Royal Academy Exhibition.

Since Hunt's intentions had become matrimonial, every day he lectured her, or dreamed up some boring idea, to warn, or illustrate, how shocking and *dreadful* were the wages of sin.

Within a few days, Tom Diplock agreed to introduce Stephens to his aunt, Mrs Bramah, and to Hunt's relief Annie called and condescended to sit for this controversial picture.

Stephens, instead of confiding in Mrs Bramah that Hunt's interest in his model was matrimonial, or at least emotional, spoke of his feeling protective, and his fear of her 'sinking to the lowest' once he was abroad and unable to employ her.

All their friends were agreed that she had 'the *makings* of an excellent woman' and felt she should be saved at all costs.

Mrs Bramah was an ardent member of various fashionable and recently formed societies for the rescue of the fallen. She had heard from her nephew, Tommy, that his friend Hunt had a true vocation as a religious painter. Stephens impressed her as serious and earnest.

It seemed that Hunt had known this poor motherless girl since she was a child of fifteen. She lived in that slum in Cross Keys Yard, down the road, behind the rowdy public house. She had doubtless heard that when the Enumerator compiled the Census three years ago, he had not dared enter that filthy cluster of hovels round the court house—it was teeming with criminals and prostitutes—and most enumerators were retired constables and therefore used to disagreeable work in sordid surroundings.

Mrs Bramah agreed to see his protégée to make enquiries about a dancing class. While Annie was sitting to Hunt in Cheyne Walk her deportment and etiquette lessons began.

CHAPTER VIII

Rain, rain, and sun! a rainbow in the sky!
A young man will be wiser by and by. . . .
TENNYSON

A L L T H E I R lives the Brothers suffered from rheumatism as a result of their devotion to outdoor backgrounds. The weather in Scotland during the summer of 1853 was worse than any that Millais had endured in England.

He wrote to Hunt complaining of 'the horror of this climate (!) Rain all yesterday, rain again today . . . it is truly disgusting . . . almost the whole day we play battledore and shuttlecock . . . four days incessant rain, swelling the streams into torrents. . . . The dreariness of mountainous country in wet weather is beyond everything . . . poor William [his brother, sometimes referred to as Bill] has given way to whisky and execration . . .'

By the autumn he was 'still working out of doors in spite of my resolutions to the contrary. I believe I shall kill myself for the cold and damp is intense. I have had a kind of tent made to protect me against showers, but it only serves as a tube for the wind to drive through, chafing the back of my head in a most disagreeable manner.' Not long after, 'my tent has been washed away and a heavy iron fireplace has been thrown over by the strength of the current . . . hail, rain, thunder and lightning.'

He was always delicate, and having a fine, fair skin, he was tormented by mosquitoes and midges. When they went away together Hunt was never without witch hazel and Pomade Divine, hating, as much as he, the disfiguring bites and stings.

Cossetted as a beautiful child by a doting mother, Millais was narcissistic and terrified of any threat to his looks. He knew that his physical beauty appealed to Hunt, who had felt protective towards him since they first met. Hunt would not condemn such fears as effeminate and vain. On a Sunday in August he felt able to write unself-consciously to him:

'Will and myself had a bathe under a shower of water which was almost as severe as a soldiers whipping. I of course kept my delicate person from such treatment and meekly sat in a pool looking on at the swimmer's evolutions, which were of a marvellous kind, his desire being to teach me how easy swimming and floating is, which (with due respect to ye Whales) appears quite the reverse—I have had letters from Collins who strange to say is actually bathing also, his dislike to water was always much greater than mine for I could take a shower bath, and one could not induce him to commit his body (for fear of drowning) within a coffin bath of hot water. . . . Goodnight, write when you can for it is almost my only pleasure.'

Millais had an accident and knowing Hunt's admiration for his profile, could count on concern and sympathy: '. . . when bathing, in ducking my head I struck my forehead and nose against a rock at the bottom. The blow was so violent that I thought the outline was gone for ever, it bled awfully, streaming all down my nakedness. The first kind remark Will . . . made was you have broken your nose. I felt so weak from lack of blood that Ruskin hurried home for whisky . . .'

Happily for all concerned, the famous profile survived. Every sketch Millais made in Scotland included a self-portrait. Hunt never recommended boxing for Millais, whose personal vanity and snobbery were a bit of a joke among the Brothers. When describing him to Edward Lear, Hunt said Millais was someone for whom everyone offered to carry parcels because he always expected to be spoiled. When William Bell Scott pointed out a little red mark on his eyelid, Millais said with a smile: 'There are spots on the sun, you know!'

No wonder he missed his indulgent friend. For months they kept up an unbroken chain of letters. Millais was always imploring Hunt to join him in Scotland: 'I wish old boy you were here . . . Although this place is so beautiful and Bill is with me I feel very lonely and miserable . . . I wish you were with us here.'

Hunt wrote screeds to Millais in return, mostly about Annie. Millais, who shared all the news he received from his parents, Charles and Harriet Collins, and the Combes, with the Ruskins and his brother William, replied: 'I destroy your letters, at least most of them I have received here that I think you would not wish to be seen. . . .'

It is unlikely that to begin with Millais took Hunt's passion for Annie very seriously. She was only a model, a passing infatuation. The old Maniac was always susceptible and falling 'madly' in love with stunners he picked up in the streets or in the fields or at parties in London and Oxford. It meant nothing. He had never been jealous of Hunt's girls. But Hunt was well aware how much Millais resented his friendship with Gabriel and tactfully brushed enquiries aside saying that he rarely saw the Rossettis although in fact they were very close. Reassured, Millais wrote back, 'I am sorry you see nothing of Gabriel Rossetti as I think it is a pity that an old friend should gradually get shy of *us*. Does *Seddon* still intend going to the Holy Land?'

From his frequent letters Hunt soon noticed a change in Millais' relationship with the Ruskins. At first they were 'the most perfect people—he is so gentle and forbearing . . . benign and kind, a good fellow and a pleasant companion'. But gradually Ruskin sank in his estimation: he was 'not of our kind' and he 'had never heard a man contradict himself like he does', and 'he is not a man who respects a person more for living with them'.

Effie Ruskin, however, gained every day in favour. She was 'the most delightful unselfish kind-hearted creature' he ever knew, 'the sweetest creature that ever lived . . . the most pleasant companion one could wish. . . .' In fact having the acquaintance of Mrs Ruskin was 'a blessing'.

Even Harriet Collins was told, 'You really have cause to be jealous of Mrs Ruskin for a more delightful creature never breathed.' He was teaching her to draw and paint. 'If it were not for her being such a captivating person I should feel disgusted with such aptitude.'

By the end of August he was writing to Hunt, 'It would be quite impossible to stay here if it were not for Mrs Ruskin who is more delightful every day . . . I have given up reminding him of his own remarks [Ruskin] for he always forgets, his great hobby now, is illuminated twelfth century drawings; dragons passionately biting their own persons, and bodiless fiddle-players, and hooded jesters terminating into supple macaroni, you know the kind of thing. . . .'

Still more alarming and indicative was the letter he wrote to Charles Collins: 'I confess, I should feel considerably better for a wife in Scotland. There is such want of humanity. These chilling mountains make one love little soft, warm, breathing bodies.'

There was no need for Hunt to read between the lines. What a hopeless situation! It was worse than his own with Annie Miller yet he shared in the dilemma. Ruskin had been, and was still, the Brothers' idol and champion: he had rescued them in their hour of need. As for Mrs Ruskin, there was no future for Millais with her—she was Ruskin's wife and that was the end of it as far as Hunt could see. But if Millais were to get himself 'into a scrape', whatever the risk to Hunt's career, there was no question as to where his loyalty would lie.

What a coincidence that he and Millais, so familiar with their love for each other, should become simultaneously involved in the unfamiliar love of women! The emotional tie between them was overwhelming: at any other period, it would be difficult to imagine their relationship remaining platonic.

If Millais' familiarity with Ruskin bred contempt, Ruskin's was tempered by fascinated bewilderment. His opinions of Millais' character, in letters to his parents, are more revealing than anything Hunt ever wrote of him: 'Millais is a very interesting study. I don't know how to manage him, his mind is so *terribly* active—so full of invention that he can hardly stay quiet for a moment without sketching, either ideas or reminiscences—and keeps himself awake all night planning pictures. He cannot go on this way.'[1]

And a few days later: 'Millais is chattering at such a rate—designing costumes—helmets with crests of animals, and necklaces of flowers, that I hardly know what I am writing. . . .'

By the end of the summer, Ruskin was no wiser about his guest, and repeated:

'I don't know how to manage him and he does not know how to manage himself. He paints until his limbs are numb, and his back has as many aches as joints in it. He won't take exercise in the regular way, but sometimes starts and takes races

[1] *The Works of John Ruskin*, edited by E. T. Cook and Alexander Wedderburn, George Allen, London, 1903-1912.

103

of seven or eight miles if he is in the humour: sometimes won't, or can't eat any breakfast or dinner, sometimes eats enormously without seeming to enjoy anything. Sometimes he is all excitement, sometimes depressed, sick and faint as a woman, always restless and unhappy. I think I never saw such a miserable person on the whole. He is really very ill to-night, has gone to bed and complains of a feeling of complete faintness and lethargy, with a headache. I don't know what to do with him. The faintness seems so excessive, sometimes appearing almost hysterical.'[2]

My grandmother often said that Millais would never have married Euphemia had it not been for 'inclement weather'. At the time I was not sure what this meant. All that concerned me then was that the battledore and moth-eaten shuttlecock, with which we played sixty years later with Thackeray's grandchildren, had been presented to Hunt by Millais at the end of that wet summer, by which time he had become an enthusiastic player. Perhaps Hunt had tossed that shuttlecock back and forth in his Chelsea studio with Annie Miller. My grandmother threw away nothing except papers.

Although Millais had escaped the rigours of the London season, Hunt's social life in London was increasingly demanding.

Christ at the Door had become *The Light of the World.*

A friend of Augustus Egg's, Thomas Fairbairn, was delighted with the idea of another picture, to be called *The Awakening* or *Awakened Conscience.* What a laudible message! Naturally, he was unaware of the artist's personal interest—that the *model* who posed so well as the whore was to be saved. As he watched the picture progress, at least she appeared by her expression to be extremely receptive.

Hunt was more fortunate than Gabriel Rossetti in finding an *avant garde* patron actually to commission a picture of such a controversial subject; Ruskin warned Gabriel that it was 'a dread-fully difficult one'. He was very uneasy about it, having 'natur-ally a dread of subjects altogether painful', although he did not mean that 'an entirely right-minded person never keeps a mis-tress'. In Victorian England the subject was taboo. Gabriel

[2] J. H. Whitehouse, *Vindication of Ruskin*, Allen and Unwin, London, 1950.

shrugged his shoulders: let the Mad get on with it for now.

Carriages drew up in Cheyne Walk, bringing callers anxious to meet the successful young painter and see his new paintings. He was only twenty-six, original and attractive.

His studio, full of packing cases, already bore signs of his imminent departure for Syria. 'My room, with windows free, overlooking the river, was as cheerful as any to be found in London; but I had not made any effort to remove traces of the pinching [and scraping] I had suffered until lately.'

When the lovely Marchioness of Waterford (who was herself a good amateur artist) and her sister Lady Canning called with an introduction from 'that clever young critic, Mr Ruskin', he was relieved to find that his shabby furniture did not deter them in the least, indeed:

'the beautiful sisters were supremely superior to any surprise. It might have seemed that they had always lived with broken furniture by preference; and when Lady Waterford, taking a chair by the back, placed her knee in the perforated seat, and so balanced her queenly person as she stood looking and talking, it might have been thought that the chair had been prepared for that especial purpose.'

The Light of the World strongly appealed to Lady Canning, who, a few days later, wrote asking the price. Hunt therefore wrote to Mr Combe, offering him first refusal at four hundred guineas, 'which he immediately remitted to me, so the picture became his'. It had not yet been exhibited, and was not quite finished.

Carlyle, who lived nearby in Cheyne Row, did not share Lady Canning's opinion of the picture. When he and his wife had visited Hunt the year before, he had been full of praise for The Hireling Shepherd and Strayed Sheep, but now he regarded The Light of the World with horror. It represented a complete contradiction of all the Pre-Raphaelite principles which, previously, Hunt had so earnestly explained when condemning Raphael's Transfiguration for 'its pompous posturing'. Carlyle had approved the young rebels' realistic approach and their sincerity.

'"You call that thing a picture of Christ!" Carlyle trembled with indignation before the "mere papistical fantasy".

' "Do you suppose that Jesus walked about bedizened in priestly robes and a crown, and with yon jewels on his breast, and a guilt [sic] aureole round his head? . . . Don't you see that you're helping to make people believe what you know to be false, what you don't believe yourself?"

'He raised his voice well-nigh to a scream, and Mrs Carlyle standing behind, put up her emphatic finger and shook her head, signing to me.'

Carlyle went on to denounce all artists, except perhaps Dürer, for their portrayal of Christ. ' "And when I look, I say, 'Thank you, Mr da Vinci, thank you Mr Michael Angelo, thank you Mr Raffaelle [sic]; that may be your idea of Jesus Christ, but I've another of my own which I very much prefer'." '

Da Vinci was particularly criticised for his *Christ Disputing with the Doctors*, which made ' "Him out to a puir, weak, girl-faced nonentity, bedecked in a fine silken sort of gown, with gems and precious stones bordering the whole, just as though He had been the darling of a Court, with hands and fingers that have never done any work . . . [whereas] I see the Man toiling along in the hot sun, at times in the cold wind, going long stages, tired, hungry often and footsore, drinking at the spring, eating by the way. His rough and patched clothes bedraggled and covered with dust . . . surrounded by His little band of almost unteachable poor friends, I see a Man worth seeing the likeness of, if such could be found . . . lean and prematurely sad . . . until, with face worn and distorted, He ends His life of misery upon the Cross. . . ." '

Much disgruntled, the Chelsea Sage took his leave. He paused in the hall in front of a portrait of Hunt's father: ' "And who may that shrewd-looking man be with the domed and ample cranium?" '

In his memoirs Hunt tries to justify his inconsistency of purpose in betraying the original Pre-Raphaelite ideal in *The Light of the World*, but at the time there is no doubt that he was deeply impressed by Carlyle's condemnation of the picture. It brought him down to earth. He was more anxious than ever to seek the authentic backgrounds in the Holy Land, and to discover for himself what clothes Christ had worn, what tools he had used and how he had lived. It was now that Hunt decided that one of the first important works he would paint in

Syria should be *The Finding of Christ in the Temple*, which no doubt, he hoped would be favourably compared one day, by Carlyle at least, with da Vinci's *Christ Disputing with the Doctors*.

Eventually Christ's dress for this painting found its way into the prop-box, or Hobman chest. I used to wear it as an overall for spring-cleaning. I hated it, and spilt Bluebell polish all over it. The fringe round the hem tickled my legs.

Many people and circumstances, apart from Annie Miller and *The Awakening Conscience*, combined to delay Hunt's departure for the East. He was well aware from Millais' unhappy letters that the less he wrote to him about Syria the better. Millais was comforted by reports in the newspapers of threatened war: 'You can't go abroad before the Turkish question is settled and that won't be yet a while.' He was struggling to finish Ruskin's portrait. It was not until August that he realised through letters from Charles Collins and the Combes how advanced were the plans.

'Mr Combe speaks of your paying a farewell visit at Oxford previous to your Syrian voyage, as though you were going off in a fortnight's time. Is this true? If so you are only fit to be potted like ship's provisions for such a determination. I should like to get back before you start so let me know something about your intention.'

Three days later, he wrote:

'I am very anxious to know if you are really going to Syria immediately . . . I should not like you to go without my asking you a favour [to join him later] . . . I am writing this in my bedroom resting this scrap of paper on my thigh, which limb as you know is none of the broadest—Tell me what you are painting and have you finished the Moonlight [picture]? Now I am going to bed to act another part in a dreamland with which I soothe myself to sleep.'

If ever a man was truly lovesick, it was Millais. His confused feelings for Euphemia, a married woman, made him long to escape from a situation which, as yet, he did not understand. He was only twenty-four. Having scoffed at Charles Collins for consoling himself with religion when he was 'hipped in love' two years before, now he wished:

'there was a kind of Monastery that I could go to—I am beginning to be perfectly sick of life, and only find comfort in prayer. Charles Collins is completely right in his manner of living . . . I don't sleep very well at night and am sure if my face in the slightest degree told of my restlessness, and suffering, it would be lined like a Bradshaw railway map, instead of remaining smooth and youthful as a schoolboy. Write soon again please for it is a real mercy.'

He grew ill with panic. He must leave the scene, forget Euphemia, disappear with Hunt to the East or, as a last resort, join him for a while in Florence or Paris. 'I am sure we would get on so delightfully together as we have heretofore.' Never again would he stray far from his beloved and protective friend: their relationship was wonderfully uncomplicated and happy— their flirtations with pretty girls such fun, so innocent . . .
He wrote to Hunt:

'Now there is almost a certainty of war will you still persist in going to the East? If so I am sure you will be cut up and eaten by the Russians. I had a letter from Mrs Combe yesterday—she speaks of your departure as inevitable and seems to think that she may accompany you, which would be splendid for you as she is a wonderful person in sickness. I hear that they bought the *Light of the World*. . . . My dear fellow, I can't tell you the depth of dull melancholy I have fallen to since I have been away. I quite hate the thought of your leaving me positively friendless (with the exception of Charley). I do believe you will never see me again if you stay away long. I have at night dreadful wakefulness and the most miserable forebodings. I wish you would not forget your original promise that you would write for me to meet you . . . I don't think I could live in London somehow when you are gone. I have not any place to go to. You will think all this very weak but I don't profess to be otherwise. I shall go with you to Oxford when you spend the promised week with them [the Combes]. . . . Here I am at 24 years of age sick of everything . . . I don't believe there is a more wretched being alive. . . . Goodnight you runaway'.

During this emotional crisis, when sublimating his sexual frustration into religion, Millais was drawn much closer to Charles Collins. He also wrote screeds to him and confided the fear that 'Hunt rarely prays'.

As far as Euphemia was concerned, the sooner Hunt left the better, as long as he left alone. By now she returned Millais' love—and well understood her own feelings. She was only a little older than Millais, but having been married four years and having led a sophisticated social life in Venice she was far more mature.

Whether or not it had already occurred to her, or had been suggested, that she should have her unconsummated marriage with Ruskin annulled, it was clear that Hunt's attraction and influence on Millais were greatly to be feared. There was no time to lose. In his present mood, he would follow Hunt to the ends of the earth as soon as the portrait was finished. She would be doomed to remain Mrs Ruskin, in name only, for ever.

Millais was by no means alone in dreading Hunt's departure for the East. As the time drew nearer, almost all of his friends seemed desperate either to accompany him or to join him at a later date.

Thomas Seddon, a landscape painter, called by my grandmother 'that impractical joker', left for Cairo where Hunt promised to meet him as soon as he could get away.

Gabriel Rossetti was frantic. How could the Mad abandon him? How could he live, let alone write or paint, without him? Lizzie Siddal was constantly ill, sulking or making scenes; he too longed to escape from a wearisome relationship. Hunt was a rock, one of his few reliable friends. Gabriel wrote one Tuesday night that autumn of 1854 from Newman Street:

'. . . I hope to God—and I use the words most solemnly concerning one of the dearest hopes I have—that you are not going to start before the next exhibition, in order that I may at least have a chance, by the sale of a picture I shall then have ready, of accompanying you on your journey. . . . For

109

indeed, should this not happen at all, of which I have thought so much, I feel that it would seem as if the fellowship between us were taken from me, and my life rejected.

'I can trust you my dear Hunt, for knowing, much better than these words express, the reality which they have for me while I write them; being indeed, I suppose, the most serious words I ever wrote in my life. . . . Affectionately your PRB. D. G. Rossetti.'[3]

Even Madox Brown resented being obliged to stay behind tied to young Emma, his new wife. About eighteen months before, on a bleak day at Gravesend, he and Hunt and the Rossetti brothers had seen Woolner off to Australia on an emigrants' ship. This event had made a deep impression on him and inspired him to paint *The Last of England*. He was dogged by bad luck and poverty and even this, one of his best pictures, was attributed to Hunt by the *Athenaeum* critic. Ruskin loathed his work and always abused him.

To add to Hunt's many emotional and practical problems, Walter Deverell, one of his and Millais' dearest friends, became seriously ill with dropsy. His parents had recently died leaving him no money to support innumerable younger brothers and sisters. The handsome Deverell was penniless. Hunt was always dashing round to his sordid crib with grub or coals for his empty grate. He wrote to Millais describing poor Deverell's plight, and between them they scraped up ninety guineas to buy one of his pictures anonymously. However, the illness persisted.

Ruskin was so moved by Hunt's letter (which, for once, Millais shared with him) that he wrote to his parents suggesting they might show a little kindness to Deverell 'in the way of a shape of rice . . . or a little sweet sherry . . . Everett [Millais] is very fond of him and was crying about him all the morning.'

Millais was still intolerably depressed and continued to bombard Hunt with letters, thinking him just about to leave:

'My dear old friend, God knows I will miss you . . . I am almost glad that I do not see you start as I believe I should groan myself into a fever—you must write continually. . . .

[3] Collection of Mrs Janet Camp Troxell.

The desire which I expressed . . . was that you would permit me to join you at Cairo when we would return together. I would make the journey entirely for recreation and pleasure and therefore unencumbered of canvasses and gallipots—I could easily return to see you off; but will rather escape such a melancholy business. In truth I don't think I should have the strength to say good-bye—scarcely a night passes but what I cry like an infant over the thought that I may never see you again—I wish I had something to remember you by, and I desire that you should go to Hunt and Roskell and get yourself a signet ring which you must always wear . . . get a *good one* and have your initials engraven thereon. . . . It is wonderful how with all the suffering I endure in thinking of your leaving, Deverell's illness, and the other calamities, how I still go on with my work, sitting numbed in the biting cold, twirling little brushes upon a broken china palette, and doing about the size of a fiveshilling piece in a day . . . I should like to go to sleep for a year and awake and find everything as it was when you lived in Cleveland Street [Fitzroy Square] when you were straightened for food, and we all went nightly to disclaim against Rubens and the Antique—Those were happy times to these . . . it is nevertheless my wish, but not so great a wish as that I may meet you stepping lightly down the gangplank and returning to the old friend you know— Poor Jack—Write by return of post.'

Much touched, Hunt duly ordered a small gold ring, set with a round sardonyx, which he wore until he died. It is now in the possession of Mrs Elizabeth Burt, the adopted daughter of my aunt, Gladys Holman-Hunt. The stone is engraved with his initials combined with an M. Inverted, the monogram cunningly turns into the letters PB.

Augustus Egg consistently argued that Hunt was most ill-advised to go. For different reasons, Ruskin decided belatedly that it was his duty to write Hunt a letter on 20 October:

'I can't help writing to you tonight; for here is Everett lying crying on his bed like a child—or rather with that bitterness which is only in man's grief—and I don't know what will become of him when you are gone—I always intended . . . to try and dissuade you from this Syrian expedition—I suppose it is much too late now—but I think it quite wrong of you to go. I had no idea how much Everett depended on you, till lately—for your own sake I wanted you not to go, but had no hope of making you abandon the thought—if I had known sooner how much Everett wanted you I should have tried. I can be no use to him—he has no sympathy with me or my ways . . . he has nobody to take your place . . . if you wait to take care of Everett till he gets somebody else to take care of him, you may go [to the Holy Land] with fully ripened power, and save *him* besides. I never saw so strange a person, I could not answer for his reason if you leave him. Instead of going to Syria, I think you ought to come down here instantly: he is quite overworked—very ill—has yet a quarter of his picture to do in his distress—and we must go to Edinburgh—and leave him *quite alone*—Think over all this. Yours ever faithfully and in haste. J. Ruskin. Don't say anything about this letter to him.'[4]

It was Effie who told Millais that Ruskin had written this letter to Hunt. Then Millais himself wrote again; and yet again: on the last day of October, before returning to London, he declared:

'If you have no objection I will gladly join you in Florence next Spring as I am really dreadfully unwell, scarcely a day without a headache . . . I feel so horribly impatient to do something. Quiet is never rest to me as the whole time I remain doing nothing I feel under the lash of some demon. I can understand so well your desire to get away into new scenes, it is the only thing left for us . . . I have sent the picture of Ruskin home for the weather is terrible and would have killed me . . . I have a headache coming on from writing . . . I cannot go out I feel so tired and there is nothing to occupy me indoors, I so long to see your old familiar face again and hope you will not leave before I return . . . if you will wait for a week I will join you and go to Paris as I want some trip to amuse me. . . . How about the stinging flies in the East? The gnats here disfigure me horribly.'

4 Collection of Mary Lutyens.

By now the foggy London winter had set in. Hunt's picture of Annie and her conscience was incomplete because there was no adequate light by day. If it were to convey a forcible message, it must be shocking. He was a realist, but on his sister Sarah's advice, as a sop to the squeamish, he had added an almost imperceptible line on the sleeves, to indicate that under her nightgown the whore was not *naked*. This *camisole*, or *Spenser*, although only suggested, would however stop at the waist. He decided she should clutch a Paisley shawl round her hips—for warmth perhaps. She must not actually *sit* on her lover's knee so scantily clad. Now, surely nobody could find *The Awakening Conscience* offensive. Annie found the pose exhausting.

As her future guardian and mentor, Stephens sometimes seemed a broken reed. He needed new boots and was always in debt. Tupper had understandably sent him a strongly-worded letter only the other day. Fred 'would not like to have a repetition of its tones, therefore, if you can enable me to overcome the Beast I shall be most grateful and more so if you could find something which I could do to assist you and lighten the weighty pecuniary obligations I am under to yourself'.

Hunt replied:

'I am now in as serious monetary pass myself—have not yet finished the *Light of the World* so cannot claim anything from Combe and have not a single sketch finished by which I can get the means for persueing [sic] my present expensive task . . . All my packing cases are here . . . I am Tired— oh so Tired and wish I could rest—sleep or die from my weary labours.'

He had in fact already received Combe's cheque for four hundred guineas, but perhaps he had returned most of it for Combe to invest or maybe he felt that if he lent Stephens any more money it would diminish the fund set aside for Annie.

Already, her dancing lessons were arranged. Mrs Bradshaw's daughter had proved an excellent governess. Annie had made much progress lately with her pot-hooks and alphabet. Later, Miss Bradshaw's friend, a Miss Prout, would supervise her studies of geography, history and arithmetic. He hoped, however, that Mrs Bramah would succeed in correcting the petty faults, those 'objectionable habits', which made her unacceptable in polite society. As a successful artist's wife, she must be at ease in the company of the *great*, not only 'nobs', but the most distinguished intellectuals in the land.

Hunt was always fastidious, constantly brushing his copper-coloured hair and scenting it with sandalwood oil, so my grandmother said. As soon as his means permitted he had his clothes made in Savile Row. Could Mr Combe approve of such vain extravagance?

The more Hunt visualised Annie as his wife, the more he became aware that she was not yet refined. Her wild beautiful hair was still unkempt. It must be properly dressed. She must carry a cambric handkerchief instead of sniffing, or wiping her nose on her dress. Her laugh must be *restrained*, she should 'attend more to her person' and change her linen daily. Apart from petticoats she must wear *underclothing*. (The author of *My Secret Life* complained that in the early 1850s 'more and more this fashion of wearing drawers seems to be spreading, formerly no woman wore them'.)

Public lavatories being non-existent, it was a common sight to see women squatting in the side streets, and the Strand especially 'was a favourite place for doxies to relieve their bladders . . . mostly they went in twos . . . for a woman likes a screen, one usually standing up till the other had finished.' Coping with drawers and buttons would have been an additional problem to holding the hems of their skirts out of the already over-flowing, stinking gutters.

To Euphemia Ruskin's and Lizzie Siddal's relief, as well as fobbing off other friends, Hunt succeeded in dissuading both Millais and Gabriel Rossetti from accompanying him to the East. It was vital anyway that these two should not arrive simultaneously. He must go ahead like John the Baptist. It was always his belief, he said, that an artist should not live in any old sordid crib, even in the Holy Land, but in an elegant house surrounded by beautiful things. This excuse appealed to Gabriel Rossetti who was keener than ever on collecting bric-à-brac, such as the blue and white china that Tissot had encouraged him to buy. Gabriel's emotional problems changed from week to week; until Hunt left he would spend every available moment with him. He wrote to Madox Brown that the date of Hunt's departure was constantly changing: 'Till he is fairly off I will not fix an evening . . . as it might possibly interfere with some opportunity of meeting *him*.'

As a parting gift he sent Hunt a daguerreotype of the *Girlhood of the Virgin*, painted when they shared a studio in 1848, with the two sonnets describing it. As a dedication he quoted four lines from Taylor's *Philip van Artevelde*:

'There's that betwixt us been, which men remember
Till they forget themselves, till all's forgot,
Till the deep sleep falls on them in that bed
From which no morrow's mischief knocks them up.
                                    from D.G.R.'

Hunt framed these souvenirs of Gabriel and kept them on his table till he died, just as he always wore Millais' ring. He was never parted from these reminders of the intense love he felt in his youth for these two very different men.

Millais was not so depressed now he was back in London near Hunt and Charley Collins, but even if Hunt went away, just for a few days, he would write.

Millais still suffered from blinding headaches and lately protested that he did not care if he were elected or not as an Associate of the Royal Academy, but once he heard that he was accepted he was extremely pleased.

Hunt convinced him easily that in his present delicate state pioneering was not for him. It comforted Millais to imagine the beautiful Arab horses, soft-footed turbanned servants, exotic models, and he agreed to wait until Hunt was ready to send for him and had learnt a smattering of Arabic. In the meantime he would keep an eye on Annie, he could use her for a couple of heads maybe. The 'old boy' was certainly 'badly hipped', but then he had fancied Annie for a long time.

Presumably Hunt spent Christmas in London with his parents —although there is no record of their meeting. He left on 13 January, and wrote later in his memoirs: 'I was waiting for one bright day to finish *The Awakening Conscience* before leaving England. At last it came, and by four o'clock I had accomplished all.' It was Annie's last sitting to him. He left her with her aunt in Chelsea. He described the rest of the day.

'I took a cab and made a round of calls on my friends to say goodbye. . . . Millais came back with me and helped me to pack. Some bachelor friends rallied me, saying that they should go and dine leisurely and come on to my lodgings later. When they arrived I had gone, and Millais had accompanied me to the station. As I had not had time to dine, Millais rushed to the buffet and seized any likely refreshments he could, tossing it after me into the moving carriage. What a leave-taking it was with him in my heart when the train started! Did other men have such a sacred friendship as that we had formed?'

CHAPTER IX

A queen with swarthy cheeks and bold black eyes,
Brow bound with burning gold.

TENNYSON

FOUR DAYS after Hunt left London, Millais wrote to Euphemia's mother on January 17: 'The oldest and best friend I ever had left me on Friday on his way to Syria. . . . As soon as I finish Ruskin's portrait I shall join him at Cairo and begin a new life, or rather try to end this one.' He was as yet ignorant of Euphemia's plans.

When she confided in her parents and friends that her marriage to Ruskin was still unconsummated, they all advised her to have it annulled.

Hunt wrote to Millais at length throughout his journey. Before sharing the first letter with Charley and Wilkie Collins, and Gabriel and William Rossetti, Millais thoughtfully inked out a paragraph describing an amorous encounter which Hunt had enjoyed on the train. He thought it was:[1]

'not desirable that they should see it . . . owing to the little impropriety in the French railway carriage which would alarm them mightily particularly as it is generally understood you are principally induced to go to the East from religious notions and such an effort could be certainly misunderstood—would appear a contradiction'.

Hunt replied surprisingly and later my grandmother deleted the following passage from the letter to Millais quoted in his memoirs:

'. . . your account of my intention as understood by my friends generally, to employ myself in the illustration of scriptural subjects, which I learn is announced publicly in the

[1] Letter begun February 7 and finished February 13, 1854. (Millais papers M.A. 1946) Pierpoint Morgan Library of U.S.A.

Daily News as the object of my travels, is most amusing when considered with the fact that I have not a single intention formed about work of any kind.'

He spent three hectic days in Paris under the wing of a young painter called Brodie, who proved an experienced guide with catholic tastes. They had met at Madame Charles's *laiterie* five years ago on Hunt's trip with Gabriel Rossetti.

Hunt stayed at a very old hotel in the Rue Jean-Jacques Rousseau. He was convinced that the place was haunted and his room possessed by evil spirits. At night, as soon as he blew out the candles, he was tormented by his familiar but dreaded devil, disguised as Death. If he slept at all, he suffered from such nightmares that he, and the other inmates, were woken by his blood-curdling screams of, 'it's death, death, *death*!'

To general relief, after three nights he decided to pack his traps and proceed to Marseilles, travelling slowly down the rivers and canals or taking an occasional train. In the markets of Provence the fruit and flower stalls were 'gorgeous'. He was much attracted by the 'comely daughters of the Sun'. At last, he took a P. & O. steamer to Alexandria. When the boat called at Malta he posted a letter to Gabriel.

Gabriel wrote at once on February 7 to Woolner in Australia:

'I had a long letter yesterday dated Malta, from the glorious old boy . . . William's letter . . . will tell you how Hunt—the world's great man at last—is off "for the East indeed", and of what pictures he has painted, celebrated already before the town has ever seen them—and how during his last months here he had become such a swell. . . .'[2]

Hunt wrote in his memoirs, having referred to his journal:

'It was a delightful voyage, with porpoises racing the vessel and flying-fish shooting through the prismatic arcs of the waves even on to the deck. How sweet too, it was to look over the gunwale into the lapis-lazuli water, dense as a dyer's vat,

² Amy Woolner, *Thomas Woolner, R.A., Sculptor and Poet: His Life in Letters*, Chapman and Hall, London, 1917.

marbled all through with engulfing veins. Egypt showed itself very unimposing with its low sand dunes, and for landmarks only the lighthouses, Pompey's Pillar, and the many windmills which owed their origin to Napoleon.'

On reaching Alexandria, he changed to an untidy and dirty little boat 'captained by a native, and the crew were uncontrolled and unmannerly . . . before sunrise we were landed at Boulak'. A grisly old sheik supervised the unpacking of the cargo which was to be transported by camel to Cairo.

A wide, rough road wound through a jungle of palm trees and sugar cane to the capital of Cairo. The dilapidated bus, drawn by asses, creaked along amongst the horses, cows and goats, giving way to the Bedouins on their camels, passing snake charmers squatting in the mud, and jugglers with chained baboons. 'Now a clamour of screeches heralded a funeral procession with the women tossing dust over their heads, and the corpse borne, face uncovered, dressed as the man was living. . . .'

On entering the city,

'the Tom-Tom sounded and joy-cry rang out its peal of notes. This was a marriage company, with the child bride under a canopy of gold embroidery, walking with shuffling feet. Mother and female relations dressed in old, harmoniously coloured and traditionally decorated silks.

'Through all the confusion, water-carriers rang their brass tazzi [sic] and mingled their shouts in the name of the Prophet. Above all swept the searching hawks, circling and crossing, sometimes swooping down into the busy crowd to seize undefended prey.'

Looking back fifty years later, Hunt regretted the passing of so many characters from this vivid scene:

'. . . the Pasha in his gorgeous carriage with running footmen, the priests solemnizing the return of the Sheik from Mecca on his white horse; the devout who threw themselves down to be trampled upon. . . . The Greeks in smart jackets and short starched petticoats, and parties of closely-veiled wives in the charge of fat eunuchs. . . .'

Seddon was waiting for him, smoking a hookah with four other Englishmen in Williams' Indian Family Hotel. Hunt made a special effort to appear typically British when abroad. Even for those days he was patriotic to excess. In his opinion, since his arrival in Cairo, Seddon had 'gone native'! Admittedly, he had made progress with the language, but he was far too familiar with the locals, humouring them and praising their childish antics, instead of keeping his distance in a dignified manner. He had even gone so far as to adopt their dress. When mounting the high Arabian saddle on his donkey, too, he was most inept. These unfamiliar garments were easily disarranged. Hunt recalled the Bantu proverb: 'Even the slightest wind suffices to expose the anus of a hen.'

Much shocked, Hunt wrote a complaining letter to Gabriel Rossetti. As if this was not enough, Seddon had developed an unnatural passion for snakes. He had actually invited a serpent charmer to the hotel as his guest, sitting cross-legged on the floor chanting solemn incantations to immunise himself against venom while the noxious creatures crawled all over him.

This was not only dangerous, but a most distasteful spectacle for all their European acquaintances to witness: it looked as if the fellow was pandering to superstition. The Arabs were too big for their boots already—not that they had any—only the other day a Mr Shepheard, who owned a small hotel, had been attacked.

However, Hunt's main purpose in writing to Gabriel Rossetti was to answer his questions about the expense of the trip and the cost of living in the East. Williams' Indian Family Hotel charged seven shillings a day for full board and lodging. The journey out including first-class train fares cost £30 exactly. Another ten pounds had gone on victuals, tips and odd hotels, including three nights in Paris. He and Seddon had agreed to economise and share the expense of a tent. It was essential, of course, to engage a servant each. Their wages would be £1 10s. od. per month in the town, where they could find other perks and backsheesh, but £1 more in the desert.

After a few days spent exploring the citadel, bazaars, mosques, fountains and tombs of the Caliphs, they decided to camp near the Sphinx.

'[A] very moderate expedition daily provided us with birds for the pot; all other food we purchased from the Arabs . . . after experiencing the unparalleled hardness of a bed in the sand, violent gusts of wind battered the tent, until it was torn up, flapping about like a mad thing, and admitting a tornado . . . fastenings came undone and the canvas was beyond all control. Seddon on his side was also holding on to the loose folds like an octopus . . . the tent was literally turned inside out, and we were rolled over and over as though in a blanket pudding, while books, clothes, carpets and drawing materials were scattered about the desert, some of them irrecoverably lost in the sand. This experience induced us to have a vacated tomb swept out for our abode.'

Hunt's servant was a Greek whom he chose to call Gabriel.[3] Seddon's was an Egyptian 'treasure' named Hippo. Needless to say, '. . . the latter was a serpent-charmer and never went about without one or two reptiles as bulky as one's wrist, coiled up inside his Kamise. . . .' Four years previously, the Pasha had sent him to the London Zoo 'in attendance on a hippopotamus'.

Surprisingly, Hunt found these camping expeditions beneficial to his health. However, he and Seddon repaired intermittently to the hotel, where he wrote complaining to the Combes:

'The great want is a—(don't be horrified) a wife, for there is no female society—it is true there is a Mrs Major Britt in the hotel but then she is a Plymouth bother [sic] [the next few words have been obliterated by my grandmother] so of course it is impossible to talk much to her. . . .'

Every few days he wrote long, illustrated letters describing his adventures to Millais. A paragraph in one of these was also censored. It advised him, before leaving for the East, to grow a beard and to make himself look as old and unattractive as possible, for fear he should be captured by predatory tribesmen.

Millais, who wrote just as frequently, replied:[4]

[3] Gabrien in some letters.
[4] Begun February 7 and finished February 13. (Millais papers M.A. 1946) Pierpoint Morgan Library of U.S.A.

'For divers reasons I think that it is necessary that I should cultivate a beard before joining you amongst those peculiarly addicted people, so according to Christian custom, I think I shall look less like a boy and escape without attention.'

Beards were not yet fashionable for young Englishmen but Hunt was now:

'persuaded to overcome my Anglican prejudice in favour of a clean chin. I should not do so, however, if I found it disguised my nationality, for that is worth every other pretention [sic] one travels with; it finds one in cringeing obedience and fear from every native, every dog when told one is an Englishman runs away yelping. With this nationality indeed, and a fist, I would undertake to knock down any two Arabs and walk away unmolested.'

He admitted:

'the country is very rich and attractive, but I am inclined to dislike it on that account, for I have no patience with the fates when they tempt me to become a *paysagist*.

'The pyramids themselves are, as one always knew extremely ugly blocks and arranged with most unpicturesque taste. . . . The only association that I value is that Joseph, Moses and Jesus may have looked upon them to make reflections which are riddles for us. There are palm trees about which attract my passing admiration but for all else one might as well sketch in Hackney Marsh. The desert is beautiful but I could not settle down here. . . .

'[Seddon] when present shatters every serious devotion to thought with some intolerable and exasperating attempt at a practical joke and with his own unbounded joy at the same. I must not complain however for I was fully prepared for this disagreeable feature in his character and I must say Seddon's good nature and his ability for useful arrangements go much beyond my expectations.'

Apart from exploring the interior of the pyramids, Seddon insisted that they should climb up to the top of them, 'declaring his determination to write his name on the top . . . I contented myself that mine would not be found there, but he retorted, "Oh, isn't it though? I took care to write yours as large as mine."'

While he was writing this letter to Millais, the post arrived, bringing with it one from Millais himself, the letter for which he had 'for so long, ardently wished, but has left me depressed in spirits'. It was packed with news, good and bad, of their mutual friends:

'Poor Deverell is dead. Very curiously he died whilst I was in the house. . . . After you went away he got much worse but never to the last imagined he was dying . . . I saw him but once more since you left and then he was so impatient and drowsy that I did not stay above three minutes. . . . His death was very extraordinary as he was most perfectly sensible, indeed he seems not to have understood that his last convulsion was death, for he sat up in his bed and said I cannot stand this choking, and endeavoured to throw off the bedclothes, all the day he had been complaining of suffocation but not much of pain.'

Hunt was very distressed and replied:

'God help poor Deverell! I was prepared for the fatal news, but not the less affected by it. The longer I live the less certainty I feel as to the course to be taken and I almost determine to do nothing. I am ashamed at the little enthusiasm I feel even with the novelty of my present life.' [The following passage was deleted by my grandmother.] 'I am perfectly unaffected by the feeling for work of any kind. I wish I could conquer the increasing weakness for it leaves me in danger of losing every opportunity that passes before me. . . .

'I hope you will come out in the autumn. Seddon will have gone back by then, and I will have made some way with the language if possible . . . one has so many prejudices to overcome towards the annoyances which exist here, I wish we could meet abroad and travel and work together for a good while, with occasionally another or two companions (Halliday

for one). The country offers nothing to me but landscapes . . .
you know I want figures.'

Millais' feelings about his own work were equally negative:

'I am not painting anything except Ruskin's portrait which
I am heartily sick of as it will never give him satisfaction—I
hear flocks of people are going to see your modern picture [The
Awakening Conscience] at Egg's who are mystified by the
subject.'

In answer to Hunt's enquiries about his young sister, Emily,
Millais wrote that he intended inviting her to meet his cousin
as he thought they might make a good match. Hunt was
delighted: 'your proposition to entertain my little sister at tea
with your cousin gratifies me beyond anything that could be
made'.
Millais shared Hunt's letter with Emily:

'[She] spent an evening with us last week. She was delighted
with it, but jealous of its length in comparison with what she
had received therefore write her a long letter next time. I have
not seen any of her drawings as she did not bring them with
her, although I told her it was your wish that I should look
over them; however next time she comes to our house, she
will bring them. . . . What a great girl your little sister has
grown. I remember her on the back seat of a chaise with your
uncle Mr Hobman. We were all struck with the wonderful
resemblance between her and yourself. . . .'

Alas, nothing came of these match-making plans, but there
was plenty of news of other gossip—although Millais still
sounded depressed:

'I generally spend the evening with Halliday who improves
upon closer acquaintance. Sunday I took him to the Collins's
where we dined together. Charles is working gradually from
his old picture which is really very good indeed, the colour
especially. I shall certainly join you next Autumn. I shall
begin the Flood, [The Deluge] which I shall be able to paint

anywhere and take about with me, it will be necessary to paint all kinds of heads in that, therefore it will be an advantage.

'I have not seen Gabriel, he did not come and spend the evening when I asked him, and I don't much relish the idea of calling to see him . . . I don't see more of my brother William than you do in the country . . . Stephens has called once or twice when I have been out, I met him at William Rossetti's where he was as listless as ever, I cannot think how I can help him at present . . . Patmore is dreadfully in earnest in his solicitations for me to spend an evening with him I have double share since you are gone.'

A few days later, Millais continued this long letter on 13 February 1854 to describe a new friendship he had made since Hunt left:

'I have not written for two or three days as I have been in the Country with Leech the Punch draughtsman. I accompanied him last Friday afternoon to see him hunt, intending only to sit quietly on horseback and watch the persuits of the sportsmen, but when I got amongst the redcoats to the peril of my life I must join them in the scramble to the astonishment and horror of Leech who looked upon me as insane as I went most cleverly over the first ditch I ever leapt in my life, the excitement was so great that I wanted to jump everything but judiciously restrained. Since this exploit I have been very stiff, as in the days when I travelled on my grey nag upwards of fifty miles which was hard work to one who does not ride above twice in the year. I like it so much that I am going to purchase necessary boots and spurs. I rode so well that other huntsmen were quite surprised when they heard it was my first attempt. From sticking fast to the animal my legs are a frightful state of blister and it is most painful for me to sit down. . . .'

Leech introduced Millais to fishing, stalking and shooting, as well as fox-hunting. He took him to his own bootmaker in Oxford Street: 'Ah Sir,' said the shopman, 'what a fine leg for a boot . . . same size all the way up.' Leech was determined to make a man of him, or a country gentleman at least. No doubt Euphemia Ruskin was pleased.

However, Millais was not all that manly as yet, and in the same long letter characteristically referred to his personal appearance.

'The wart you will remember on my *left* underlid has been removed by Sir B. Brodie who burnt it away with some terrible acid. The pain was intense at the time nearly as great as toothache, and since the cauterising the only inconvenience I have suffered from has been the festering away of the part which now seems almost like the other ego. . . . God bless you old boy and keep you until I join you in the Autumn. Everybody sends their love to you, Ever affectionately yours, John Everett Millais.'

By the same post, Hunt received a letter from Gabriel and a note from Stephens enclosed with more letters from his parents and Emily—doubtless poor Fred could not afford the stamp. When writing to Hunt about his financial worries, Stephens' style was formal: 'My dear sir, it is totally out of my powers to meet this Bill on the 23rd instant.' There followed the usual excuses: '. . . commissions have fallen through etc.' But there was not a word about Annie. No wonder Hunt felt depressed; he must have read these letters over and over again, and aloud to Seddon perhaps.

Clearly there was no sympathy between Millais and Gabriel Rossetti. Millais was unaware that 'the queer fish' had ever considered joining his own beloved Hunt in the East.

For fear of provoking jealousy by writing to Gabriel without warning Millais (who might then find himself with a *fait accompli*), Hunt threw in a casual reference to the plan, completely out of context, between other items of news in his reply: 'I intend sending a letter to Gabriel . . . he wishes to learn about the expenses of living here, so I will leave that subject entirely for his perusal.'

The next censored letter from Millais took me a lot of trouble to decipher with assistance from the Victoria and Albert Museum. Once I had succeeded it became obvious that although Millais was aware of Hunt's jealous infatuation for Annie he did not take his matrimonial intentions towards her very

126

seriously. He regretted the loss of one of Mrs Combe's approved stunners and expected Hunt to feel the same:

'Combe and Mrs Pat came to town to see the pictures for the R.A. . . . don't be disgusted by the way this letter is put together. One thing I fear to relate because I know your tender heart was once moved by her charms. Miss Georgina Andrews is no more single. This morning I received wedding cards from Mr and Mrs Thomas Patmore—South American sugar planter brother [of Coventry Patmore]. So much for the wonderful management of Mr Combe and Mrs Pat. I feel you will utter one deep sigh in the desert and your life will be forever writched [sic] . . . Annie Miller has been sitting to me and I have painted a little head from her. She is a good little girl, and behaves herself very properly—she is not sitting to anyone else but Rossetti.'

This information must have made Hunt feel uneasy. Annie would always be 'a good little girl' with Millais. He had not wished to hurt Gabriel's feelings by actually forbidding her to sit to him, but his name was not on the list of approved artists.

This last letter from Millais included the first reference to the Spring Exhibition at the Royal Academy, also the news that Papa and Mama Millais were moving from Gower Street into the country.

'I must have a painting room in Town, and I suppose a bed, until I leave [to join Hunt in the East], before which I must go into Wales to finish the waterfall in Ruskin's portrait. . . . Deverell's picture [which he and Hunt had bought anonymously for ninety guineas] is in my room now and is *quite beautiful*. I never saw it before the other day. His family have left the house where the poor fellow died and are living Brompton Way. . . .

'All hunting is now over. I went to the last meet, but the ground was too hard for both horses and hounds. . . . I see a great deal of Leech . . . Yesterday we took a walk in the Park together and very nearly every woman we saw was lovely.

'I went with Halliday to see the pictures which have been sent in to the R.A. and a more dreadful lot of things I never saw. Maclise has a marriage on a battle-field, containing some hundreds of figures. . . . The impression is moustachios, frowns, chain-mail and pearls.

'Frith has something really much better than usual—a scene on Margate Sands. The only truly good work I saw is by Inchbold, who has painted a lovely landscape with the sea and cliffs (not in the least like yours) quite original and exquisitely truthful and refined. . . .

'I never see the Ruskins now, except Ruskin himself, who is to sit to me again next Thursday. I have been out very little, into society, it is Winter, deriving scarcely pleasure from anything. The desire to work gets less every day of my life.

'I shall die a pauper if I do not alter soon. I try sometimes to think of subjects but nothing ever seems worth painting. . . .

'I hope, old friend, I shall soon be with you. The summer will pass quickly enough and I shall be, please God, alongside of you. I assure you I feel very wretched here although I have some friends left. I long to hear again from you. . . .

'The Rossettis have had a letter from Woolner who is getting on very well as a sculptor in Australia.

'God bless you, old boy. Keep yourself alive and well until I join you. . . . I keep all your letters.'

Whereas Seddon was quite content to paint landscapes, and disappear into the desert with snake-charmer and tent for days, Hunt, like Millais, needed figures for his pictures.

Misconstruing his master's signs of frustration, Hunt's well-meaning Greek prowled about the warren-like bazaar, and seized unsuspecting women, bundling them squawking through their veils on to the rump of his ass, or dragging them back to Hunt's cave near the pyramids.

Obviously, Gabriel could not understand why this show of initiative met with such stern disapproval. His young master appeared a fine shot, a brave horseman, and virile. It seemed that he did not prefer boys, and then the answer dawned on him: one stupid woman at a time was not enough! Gabriel knew how and where to cater for such tastes. He led Hunt to a brothel,

'. . . so I went with him without question into a house where I was followed by scrutinising eyes through windows and door-cracks on each storey.

'Going up the outside staircase, I found myself at last at the top of the house entering the guest-room. This was a small chamber without much furniture, but surrounded by divan seats in front of a rich lattice-work *ushrebeeah*, where people sit for the cool air in the heat of the day.

'No one was present, so I had leisure to examine the objects in the room and speculate upon the beauty of the houris in the house, and to make some study of the manner in which I would [the next few words are undecipherable under the Indian ink] arrange the figures which I should have to do that same day; and here I heard women's voices outside, and shuffling of feet.

'Four or five entered veiled, with a duenna. They ranged themselves in a rank with their backs against the door. With but only twenty words of Arabic, and a great deal of impatience, I could not afford much ceremony; so after I had fired off the nineteenth, I thought it time to walk up to the most graceful figure and utter the still unexhausted twentieth, "Ya bint".

'The shy daughter of the full moon lifted her veil and squinted. "The evening star" had lost her front teeth, the "sister of the sun" had several gashes in her cheek, while the "mother of morning" had a face in shape like a pyramid. [Next sentence illegible.]

'I told my man to express my regret that heaven had not bestowed on me enough talent to do justice to that order of beauty, and I took my departure by giving a *backshish* to the old woman; Had a fight with a man or two in going downstairs, and an encounter with several dogs in the yard, and I found myself in the street with my man behind me in a state of utter bewilderment at the turn affairs had taken.'

Eventually Hunt succeeded in recruiting as a model 'a full-grown damsel' from the North. He found her among the *fellahin* who were clearing sand away from the base of the Sphinx. Unfortunately, her friends were anxious to see what went on in the white man's cave. They shook their sand-laden cloaks all over the wet oil-paint and when Hunt shouted at them she and they ran away.

According to Hunt's notes the *fellahin*, or peasantry, unlike the town or desert Arabs, varied very much. The women and girls of the north were lighter in colour—beautiful, slender creatures, scantily clad and unveiled. They carried pots on their heads and were therefore wonderfully graceful. They had oval faces, high cheek-bones, enormous eyes and straight black hair, and were 'at their best at twelve or thirteen'. In contrast, the *houris* from the Delta were dark-skinned and painted their lips deep blue. They tattooed a floral device on their foreheads and wore necklaces of coins and cheap pearls over their cotton smocks: 'no use to painter or man.'

When he finished this particular picture in England, he called it *The Afterglow*. Before leaving Cairo he succeeded in finishing one other painting.

'One day when I was mooning about the bazaars, I had my attention drawn to a young tradesman courting a girl; she had come duly veiled, and prepared for an idle visit to his shop-seat.

'In an unlit corner I could watch the growth of his natural curiosity, and his pleadings to be allowed to satisfy his eyes as to the features hidden under the black *burko*. To raise up the veil was an act for which there could be no toleration; to press it close so as to see the outline of the face, the mouth, and the chin, was the utmost propriety could allow . . . I seized upon this symbol of human interest in the unknown as a good theme with which to put to the test the possibility of undertaking my first subject picture in the East. . . .

'The young man I found to sit as the lover had questioned me during the day as to my object, but went away apparently quite at his ease, and evidently more than satisfied with his gains. Next morning, however, he failed to appear, and when I met him afterwards he accosted me in great indignation, saying that I had tried to deceive him, for no sum in the world would he come again, for he had met a *Moalin* who had told him that my real purpose was to obtain the portraits of true moslems, to return with them to England, to call up Satan, to bargain with him as to the price he would pay for the souls of my victims, and that thus I should become rich beyond conception. In time I found other models who came reluctantly and stayed sulkily.'

It seems extraordinary that despite his meetings with Layard and other orientalists and with extensive reading that until Hunt arrived in the East he seems to have been unaware that the likeness or image of a person was a positive Moslem prohibition. It was utterly forbidden for a human being to try to reproduce what only God could create in the original. In Hunt's letters he refers to a 'stupid *superstition*' that the possession of the representation of an individual 'gives the owner power over the model's life and will'. He even expected the locals to sit in the nude and complained of their refusal.

The wife of the English Missionary in Cairo warned him that a search for models was a matter of the greatest difficulty; she had once induced her servant girl to sit—'but never again. . . .'

The backgrounds for his previous pictures had been painted from nature, but the models had posed against them in his studio. He could have left the figures until he returned to London with 'authentic props and costumes'. But no problem could have a straightforward solution for him.

By now more and more letters full of gossip from England were arriving. Less than three weeks after Millais' last letter his spirits had improved: 'It was fun playing croquet with pretty ladies'. To Hunt's astonishment he had now apparently abandoned all thoughts of coming to the East but:

'I have plenty of news for you. First (which I know will interest you as you are aware of the circumstances) Mrs Ruskin, that was, has been taken away by her parents who have been in London arranging everything for her release, which she will most likely have in about four months time from now. The Exhibition [at the Royal Academy] is open and your picture [*The Light of the World*] the only picture considered by thinking men.'

He went on to say that the Russian war and the Ruskin divorce were '. . . the principle Topics of conversation in Town'.[5] Now that his plans were changed he took it for granted that Hunt would abandon the East forthwith:

[5] He mentioned that cholera was raging in parts of London.

131

'When you return you will know me as the party at the quay with the largest pair of moustaches . . . I am glad to hear that your beard does not promise expatriearchal [sic] appearance to your London friends. . . . When I meet you stepping lightly down the plank, my legs will not be entangled in its length when we embrace—Tell Seddon if he brings a snake near me when he comes I will shoot him on the spot. . . . Come home soon and don't provoke the desert robbers to leave you a naked model (without a shilling an hour) to the Pyramids.'

Halliday wrote at the same time that he found Millais' whiskers were becoming and further confirmed that the latter had been '. . . making two or three beautiful little studies of Annie Miller. He and I have been giving her a lot of work to do lately.'

It is interesting to compare Millais' pictures of Annie with Gabriel Rossetti's. She seems to have been '. . . all things to all men'. Mary Lutyens, who has made a minute study of Millais' life and work, first pointed out to me that Millais used these heads of Annie for *Waiting* and the *Girl in the Pink Bonnet*.[6] In his picture, with her hair tied back, she looks a demure little thing; but Gabriel Rossetti saw her as an absurdly seductive *Helen of Troy*. Swinburne described this painting as 'Helen with her Parian face and mouth of ardent blossom, framed in broad gold of widespread locks . . .' Certainly the spacing and proportion of the eyes, the nose and mouth are the same.

Lizzie Siddal was ill: she had been making jealous scenes about Annie and rather than compete with her in London had withdrawn to Hastings. Gabriel pursued her there and wrote to Madox Brown the same week: 'The Ruskin row seems to have grown into a roar in London but I suppose had not reached the wilds of Finchley. Mrs R will get a divorce it seems—her husband is—or not is—I know not what. There are other "solitary habits" besides those which you indulge in—more things in heaven and earth than are dreamt of even in Turner's philosophy.'

[6] In the possession of Kerrison Preston and hitherto known as *Effie Gray*, when Mrs Ruskin.

A letter from Stephens arrived about the same time. As usual poor Fred regretted that he could not repay Hunt any money. Like everyone else he was full of gossip. Mrs Ruskin had been 'proved undoubtedly a virgin. . . .'

'Ruskin seemed unconcerned with the publicity, having been seen several times out and about in Society.'

He, Fred, had enjoyed boating with Halliday last evening . . .

'Annie Miller was with us, she is about to sit to [Augustus] Egg. I believe she is a good girl, on my enquiring if any of our people had given her cause for complaint she said, we were a curious lot but none had been uncivil except one person who she had met at a studio, names she would not give. She has she says been sitting to none but such as you named except one person, whereupon I administered a lecture to her and seeing the Artist shortly afterwards informed him of the position in which you regarded yourself concerning her danger and put it pretty forcibly to him.'

From this moment there was no further mention of Gabriel joining Hunt in the East. He was not only offended by Hunt's lack of confidence, but annoyed by Stephens' interference.

According to Violet Hunt[7] (no relation), Annie Miller was all the rage that Spring. '. . . the Queen of the Artist's May, elected tacitly every year from some lady whose portrait adorned the walls' [of the Royal Academy]. At the Private View, she 'was pea-cocking about in a crocus gown in red and blue like a PRB painted picture . . . Her engagement [to Hunt] was practically acknowledged and she had taken care not to forfeit her position as the "Intended" of the painter of the picture [*The Awakening Conscience*] whose subject was for the first time the universal subject of discussion in these Islands, from one end to another . . . brewers, merchant-princes, manufacturers, shipping agents, contractors and iron-masters flocked round, shocked, puzzled

[7] Violet Hunt, *The Wife of Rossetti: Her Life and Death*, John Lane, London, 1932.

133

("Such things are, but why paint them?" And "the general colour is so odd one can't tell quite what to make of it at first . . ."—Miss Catherine Winkworth), but solid for Hunt.'

A great friend of Euphemia Ruskin's, Lady Eastlake, whose husband was then President of the Royal Academy, wrote a column as 'Corinne' in *The Quarterly Gazette*. Her description of the Pre-Raphaelite models at the Private View was not complimentary: 'Female horrors with thin bodies and sensual mouths, looking as if they were going to be hung, or dead and already decomposed. . . .'

The painting was scarcely flattering to Annie, indeed, the tortured expression on her face caused by her awakening conscience, was so hideously disturbing that some time after Hunt's return from the East, the owner Thomas Fairbairn begged Hunt to change it.

Hunt kept the picture in his studio for some time between 1856-57. At last Mr Fairbairn, who meanwhile had become Sir Thomas, insisted on his returning it in a hurry for some family party. I think that Hunt did more than change the expression, I believe he scraped out most of the head, instead of overpainting. X-rays show nothing underneath. The new face does not resemble Annie Miller in the least.

CHAPTER X

Whatever there is to know
That we shall know one day.
D. G. ROSSETTI

HUNT HAD no idea what courage it must have required for Annie to trot along Cheyne Walk and climb the whitened steps to Mrs Bramah's front door at 6 Lindsey Row.[1]

Maddock, the footman, admitted her and took her cloak. He was courting Mrs Bradshaw's maid Amelia. Widow Bradshaw was one of the few who permitted 'followers', but then she was in trade and took in the riff-raff—artists and their models. Soon Amelia would better herself. Annie was meanwhile still learning to read and write from Mrs Bradshaw's spinster daughter, Sarah.

Gradually Annie must have felt more at ease with Mrs Bramah, and learned when to shake hands or bob and how to sit down on a chair—hands in lap, knees and feet together.

She was probably no longer confused by the rich display of glass and silver and knew which shapes were used for what purpose.

Mrs Bramah grew increasingly fond of her pupil. How gay and pretty she was and often how artistically gowned.

She asked her own hairdresser, Childs,[2] who came of course to the house once a month, to wash, cut and singe Annie's hair. It was a thick cloak of rich gold cascading over her shoulders.

When Childs twisted it into ropes to form a dignified style the pins sprang out: she looked like a laughing Medusa. All three decided that on formal occasions Annie must wear a snood.

Mrs Bramah heard wedding bells and turned a deaf ear to her maids' catty remarks and the other servants' innuendoes.

Miss Miller's protector Mr Hunt, the religious painter, knew

[1] Whistler was to take No. 7 in 1861.
[2] Whose nephew, the young gasfitter, Annie's sister, Harriet, was hoping to marry.

that she posed as a model for certain artists. This was with his full approval. Only the other day, Annie had confided in Mrs Bramah that Mr Hunt was having her educated with marriage in view but had not actually proposed. Mrs Bramah's servants had plenty to gossip about.

Night after night the whole street woke up when Annie and her artists came home tipsy from larking at one of the many famous Pleasure Gardens. There were two hundred such amusement parks in or near London, but her favourite haunt was the Chelsea Cremorne. This was where the most *avant garde* artists and their models forgathered.[3]

While the band played popular selections from light operas, Annie and Gabriel Rossetti would have strolled across the lawns, between vivid geraniums, mock temples and painted kiosks—the Hermit's cave and the Fairy Bower . . .

Sometimes they might have sat under the elms, drinking sherry, lemonade or beer, watching the crowds and the hansom cabs come and go, and the beribboned penny steamers chuffing up and down the river.

When it grew dark, still full of energy, they would mount the great platform of a dance floor to waltz or polka round and round, as if for ever, under the glittering circle of gaslights.

Perhaps they were part of the scene which Hippolyte Taine[4] described:

'Towards eleven that night we went to Cremorne Gardens, a sort of *bal Mabille* where the day's madness was carried far into the night. . . . All the men [were] well or at least neatly dressed, the women were prostitutes, but of a higher rank than those in the Strand;—light-coloured shawls over white gauze or tulle dressed, red *natelets*, new hats . . . One of them was very gay and wild: I have never seen such overflowing animal spirits. . . .'

Gabriel and Annie must have made a spectacular couple. He

[3] It was here that Whistler painted *The Falling Rocket*, that controversial picture which caused Ruskin to accuse him of flinging a pot of paint in the face of the public.

[4] Hippolyte Taine, *Notes on England*, translated by Edward Hyams, Thames and Hudson, London, 1957.

was probably the most vital and attractive-looking painter there. The contemporary Bohemian fashion must have suited him well. It is easy to visualise them both, he with a flowing tie and a velvet suit and she the most successful model in town.

She was earning plenty of money: at least ten shillings a day, so she had ample to spend on pretty clothes. She wore no stays, just a few petticoats. Her dress usually had wide sleeves and was embroidered, clinging to her waist but casually flowing over the lines of her beautiful figure.

Mary Howitt, a Quaker, who published several children's books, also wrote articles advising well-bred young ladies how to make the best of themselves. She limited herself to advising:

'Only dress in the Pre-raphaelite style and you . . . will find that so far from being an "ugly duck", you are a full fledged swan . . . [The Pre-Raphaelites] have made certain types of face and figure once literally hated, actually the fashion. Red hair —once, to say a woman had red hair was social assassination— is the rage. A pallid face with a protruding upper lip is highly esteemed. Green eyes, a squint, square eyebrows, whitey-brown complexions are not left out in the cold. In fact, the pink-cheeked dolls are nowhere; they are said to have "no character"—and a pretty little hand is occasionally voted characterless too. Now is the time for plain women.'

Although it was rumoured that Gabriel was actually engaged to Lizzie Siddal, he blew hot and cold. No one, least of all she, knew where they were.

When friends called at Chatham Place they found Annie Miller very much at home. She behaved as if she not only owned the studio but Gabriel as well. It was fun posing, dressing up and acting as hostess. She fried sausages, cooked spaghetti and poured out drinks for them all. She made no pretence of being artistic or intellectual. She did not attempt to compete with that sickly so-called poet Lizzie Siddal.

Poor Lizzie sat neglected in Weymouth Street, miserable and resentful, while her women friends tortured her with sympathy, as women do, and with reports of her beloved's treacherous behaviour. She rarely felt well: now she was afflicted with the sickness of love. Theirs seemed a romantic, idealistic affair.

Certainly, she was a neurotic girl and had been obsessed with death since she was a child. The evidence implies to me that Annie enjoyed making love, but Lizzie was afraid to. The explanation may have been simply that the sexual frustrations she suffered, engendered by fear, made her ill.

Annie and Gabriel were seen everywhere together, not just at the Cremorne and the usual parties and exhibitions, but at the Crystal Palace and Madame Tussaud's, arm in arm strolling up Piccadilly to dance, eating shrimp teas and watching firework displays; they patronised all the jolliest chop-houses and rowdiest hop-shops—the Gun Tavern and Highbury Barn.

Even William Rossetti fell victim to Annie's charms; although he was meant to be courting Miss Rentoul, he 'entertained her on the river'. Not to be outdone by Halliday and others, Stephens took her out, first in a rowing boat, and then in a punt. Being a cripple he lost his balance, fell in, and was nearly drowned. Perhaps Annie pushed him after he stole a kiss. This incident upset him. How could he have been so weak? He begged Annie to forget it. In future he would behave as an uncle or godfather towards her. Sanneman, the Chelsea doctor, advised him against swimming after this.

While Gabriel was placating Lizzie, Annie was surrounded by beaux. Madox Brown recorded in his diary, 'they all seem mad about Annie'. Boyce too fell victim, but whenever she agreed to sit, at the last minute, she, or rather Gabriel, 'chucked'. Once he found a written excuse in Gabriel's hand stuck on the studio door: 'Dear Boyce, Annie and I have come with 1000 apologies, but really she *must*—do let her—sit to me tomorrow, and probably for some days to come. Pray pardon . . .'

Perhaps Annie divined that there was no future for her with Gabriel. Like most narcissistic men he was extremely attractive to women. He was flattered by the image of himself that he saw reflected in Lizzie—her water-colours and poems might have been his own.

But Annie loved a lark and Hunt's letters painted a minutely tedious picture of their future. Anyway, she had seen to it that Tom Diplock told no tales to his rich respectable aunt.

Tom Diplock, the surgeon, was now twenty-six. He knew Gabriel, the Brothers and their circle very well. He still lived in Sidney Street, and his aunt promised to buy him a practice in

Cheyne Walk with Dr Sanneman, a stone's throw away from Annie's yard behind the pub.

Diplock and Sanneman must have known better than most what was going on in the neighbourhood. Continence or abortion were the only sure methods of birth control. Dirty old women obliged terrified pregnant girls for a few shillings, and often made a mess of their job. Diplock had specialised in gynaecology at St Andrew's Hospital. His services must have been in demand if only to cope with the serious complications that ensued.

In the early '50s Lizzie Siddal probably succumbed to Gabriel's passion, with an unfortunate result. If she had a painful abortion it might explain her reluctance to accept Gabriel's physical love until she had marriage as a protection. To be married became an obsession: she waited for about nine years. His sonnet, *Nuptial Sleep*, written on his honeymoon, is not compatible with the initiation of a frigid, inexperienced girl. Another sonnet with the innocent title 'After the French Liberation of Italy' makes it clear that *sexually* Gabriel was sophisticated.

It seems that Annie preferred him to Hunt. Perhaps he was not only a better lover, but his eccentricities were more engaging and made her laugh.

Gabriel always preferred animals to children. Years later when he settled in Cheyne Walk he had to the annoyance of his neighbours his own zoo including salamanders, wallabies, chameleons and armadillos. (When Browning asked him why he wanted an elephant Gabriel said it would wash the windows!) As a result his landlord included a clause in all further leases forbidding tenants to keep peacocks and wombats.

Annie was aware of the jealousy she aroused in Chelsea. When not posing, or otherwise engaged with her artistic friends, she therefore decided to wander further afield. She made friends with an elegant courtesan in the West End. As James Laver wrote:

'Well-dressed prostitutes particularly frequented the arches of Nash's Colonnade, to such an extent indeed that the Regent Street shopkeepers protested. . . .'

(Presumably these included George Waugh, Druggist to Queen Victoria.)

The lowest rate charged by the prettiest West End tarts was a pound. If they provided accommodation the charge was far higher, of course. They often roamed in pairs, thus setting off each other.

'In Victorian times there were usually groups of girls outside the Athenaeum. Another favourite place of resort was the Burlington Arcade. This had the advantage of being under cover and much frequented at the close of the afternoon by men-about-town. Mayhew goes so far as to say that:

"All the men in London walk there before dinner," and it is recorded that even the city clerks, or at least those young ones among them who wished to ape their "betters", were in the habit of rushing from their offices to lounge for a few moments in these fashionable purlieus before going back to their homes in the suburbs.[5]'

[5] James Laver, *Age of Optimism*, Weidenfeld and Nicolson, London, 1966.

CHAPTER XI

The wan soul in that golden air.
D. G. ROSSETTI

BY MAY 1854 Hunt and Seddon had decided to leave Cairo
for Jerusalem. During the last two months Hunt had
struggled to learn Arabic. Now Seddon, as the better
linguist, took charge of the arrangements for the journey. He
bargained with the crew of a sailing boat to take them up the
Nile to Damietta.

Every day they bathed in the river, which was rash, because
the waters were infested with crocodiles and dangerous parasites.
Seddon kept near the boat, not being a strong swimmer. After
luncheon, they walked along the banks with their guns in search
of game. Hunt worked out the design for *Christ in the Temple*,
even drawing in the sand. On deck they both made water-colour
drawings.

One of Seddon's practical jokes marred the trip:

'One morning . . . we both dived into the river from the
stern, and swam about . . . at the end of ten minutes he went
to the side of the boat and by the aid of a sailor clambered on
to the deck . . . I saw that the boat was moving at a great rate
. . . I called out . . . laughter reached me. I saw him
gesticulating to the sailors to go faster . . . the boat disappeared round a distant corner . . . I had therefore to strike
out for the shore, and there almost naked to climb up twenty
feet of bank, overgrown with stinging thorns and thistles, and
on the top to walk along a rough path with bare naked feet
for half a mile, where the boat had been stopped. . . .'

The next day Hunt saved Seddon from drowning. Neither of
them ever referred to these two incidents to others.

On arriving at Damietta in the dark, they boarded a smack:
'laden with bags of rice nearly up to the gunwale, and without

a deck of any kind'. They were becalmed for five days. There were no cabins and many undesirable passengers. Completely self-confident, Hunt requisitioned the dinghy and installed himself with blankets, sketching and writing materials, guns and clothes; 'and a pleasant [cabin] it was, with the sea zephyr fanning us by day, and by night the deep violet sky spangled with stars for bed-curtains'. He was quite unaware that this high-handed behaviour was resented by passengers and crew alike.

The wind got up: they were off. Comfortably settled in the dinghy, towed along behind, Hunt began a sketch of the stern and the man holding the tiller.

'He observed me, and with much agitation commanded me to stop, assuring everyone that my act would be most unpropitious for our journey. As I laughed at this warning, he repudiated all responsibility and left the helm. Drifting as we were, a sailor at the mast-head assured us that we were within sight of Jaffa. I was busy, [writing to Millais or Annie Miller no doubt] and paid no heed. . . .'

He had already acquired this unpopular kind of independence. Nevertheless, they 'wafted into Jaffa, arriving at dawn, where we were greeted by the usual crowd of harbour loafers wrangling and screaming. . . .'

After some days, Seddon succeeded in procuring not only a couple of mules to take them to Jerusalem, but also transport for their crates of pictures and camping equipment. It seems miraculous that these survived.

The track was wild: there were no inns. Before sunset they reached the Monastery of Ramelah where the monks offered simple hospitality—'a diet of millet bread, beans, lentils and dates'.

They started off again at dawn, stopping only at occasional wells to water their mules, and exchange a few words of Arabic with muleteers on their way back to the coast. They had both grown beards in an attempt to look ferocious. Hunt was just twenty-seven and Seddon thirty-three.

Hour after hour, they picked their way over polished and slippery limestone. They were thirsty and hot, and heavily laden with unwieldy luggage and guns. Hunt wrote:

'Long desire and constant disappointment had dulled interest in the scenes we passed, and the eagerness of expectation was blunted. The hot stagnant air encouraged a mood in which all further calculations of being within sight of the end of our journey seemed futile; every step seemed to take us further into the wild away from any place of human life. . . .

'Suddenly and unbidden our beasts stopped, we raised our eyes, and there . . . a great landscape was spread out before us, and in the centre stood the city. Foursquare it was and compact in itself . . . except the enclosure round the tomb of David. . . .'

High above the valley of Jehoshaphat, domes and minarets were outlined against the Mount of Olives and the Hill of Offence, and in the far distance : 'azure and amethyst were the Mountains of Moab. The afternoon sun was already beginning to glow with the softness of amber, the breeze from the sea had awakened the birds, and the windmills turned with a music as of new life'.

Hunt turned to Seddon. He was 'leaning forward with clenched hands upon the pommel of his saddle, swaying his shoulders to and fro, while copious tears trickled down his cheeks. . . .'

Hunt's childhood dream was fulfilled at last. He entered the city, 'to the sound of savage music and shouting'. The defeated Arab soldiers were acclaiming the triumph of the Turkish Sultan. There was no hotel. Exhausted, he and Seddon goaded their mules through the tumult to the monastery recommended by the Consul in Cairo. On his advice, Hunt had already invested in another pistol and a double-barrelled gun. He hoped that he looked mature and forbidding. The monks offered them temporary refuge.

'I walked about the walls and up the Mount of Olives . . . the view was wild, barren, and diaphanous, like a vision of the surface of the moon.'

The next day, fully armed, they rode out to Bethlehem and explored the surrounding country. As usual Seddon wished to paint landscapes. Determined to avoid the disagreeable chore of housekeeping he wisely searched for a site to pitch the tent. Now they were both relieved to separate.

Hunt rented a furnished house in the city. He engaged two

143

servants who spoke a little French: an Abyssinian and a Jew. Both were idle and insolent. Whenever he clapped his hands to summon them it was in vain: they were lolling about the bazaar, smoking opium and drinking coffee.

All the same, his letters seemed happier once he had arrived in Jerusalem. He wrote to Mr Combe on 3 June 1854:

'I can't at all understand what is said of the unhealthiness of this city . . . the air is the most delicious I ever breathed. Timid precautions such as the avoidance of fruit and the like are laughed at. . . . After dining, all smoking our hookahs (the tobacco's so weak I still prefer a short pipe) and admiring the beauty of the scene, in Truth I believe this country could suit me better than any other in the world, and I think if I could have a few friends with me I should stop in the East altogether (I must take up serious study of Arabic) . . . when the absurd notion of the danger of this climate is corrected many English people will immigrate here instead of to bleak uninteresting places such as Australia . . . when I turn farmer I shall bring my mother and father and sisters here, and keep a flock of camels, and grow artichokes and palm trees.'

He admitted that he still missed feminine society and felt 'an increasing need of a wife'.

Letters from England began to arrive in Jerusalem, from Halliday, Stephens, Gabriel and Millais. Annie seemed fully employed between them. Millais seemed still only interested in Hunt's return: 'I am tired of waiting and shall forget you if you don't take care.'

There was not much news. Old Mr Rossetti and Lady Glyn had died.

No one wrote that Gabriel was staying with Madox Brown (who had lately married his Emma) and was painting a picture of a wall, a white calf in a cart and a prostitute. He was going to call it *Found*. He insisted that *he* had thought of this subject, the rescue of the fallen, ages ago—everybody knew: they had heard him discussing it. The sneaky old Mad had got in first with his version, *The Awakening Conscience*. Cock-a-hoop, he was reported to have said: 'Hunt stole my subject so now I shall steal his model!'

None of Hunt's friends had the heart to mention the situation between Gabriel and Annie (Lizzie was on the verge of another nervous breakdown). Nobody referred to the general reaction to Hunt's Academy pictures. The critics had murdered them.

Only his father felt that he should know the worst and enclosed 'all the press-cuttings'. One critic, Frank Stone, referred to *The Light of the World* as 'a most eccentric picture . . . a failure'. The lantern, which Hunt had designed, was a 'fantastic magic lantern of Greek design . . . the face of this wild fantasy . . . expresses such a strange mingling of disgust, fear, and imbecility, that we turn from it to relieve the sight'.

Christina Rossetti cannot have been pleased. Collinson's portrait of her shows a distinct resemblance to Hunt's use of her face as Christ's.

As for *The Awakening Conscience*: 'The author of *The Bridge of Sighs* could not have conceived a more painful looking face. . .'

Hunt read on. This picture was 'drawn from a very dark and repulsive side of modern domestic life. . . .' He skipped. 'It represents a lady . . . turning from a fast man who laughs fiendishly . . . a kept mistress . . . .' At times he found these reviews faintly comical: by now everyone knew that Annie, his future wife, was a beauty and a match for anyone . . .

Another critic referred to 'this absolutely disagreeable picture [which] fails to express its own meaning'.

Mercifully there would be no post for another ten days. He wanted to be alone, so against the advice of his friends, he set off on foot into the desert. They said that at least his servants should escort him but 'the Jew was a coward and the Abyssinian completely useless'.

The local *fellahin* believed that all Christians were legitimate victims for Moslems. Wherever he went he was pursued by beggars, who had preferred to mutilate themselves and hide in the hills rather than be conscripted for the Turkish army.

He ignored these pests and attempted to settle down and sketch; but he was shortly surrounded by a fierce gang led by the Sheik of Siloam. This was ironic. Having so recently changed the title of his picture from *Christ at the Door* to *The Light of the World*, he was particularly keen to visit the Pool of Siloam where the blind man was healed, and even to stand on the very rock on the Mount of Olives, where Christ had pronounced the magic words: 'I am the Light of the World . . .' St John 8 : 12.

'The Sheik of Siloam and his band mocked my movement with grimacing antics and shouted abuse of me as a dog, or a pig, of a Christian . . . when they threatened me with blows and caught hold of my traps . . . they counted too much on the forbearance of the last crusader.'

Being used to boxing and fighting fit, he was in control until one of his opponents produced a 'long horse pistol to finish the combat'. Hunt was distracted by the sight of his 'assailant shaking the powder into the pan of his flint-lock as he approached me'. Off his guard for a moment, the others between them succeeded in getting him down. He whipped out a cheap revolver bought with Millais on his last night in London. Cursing in limited Arabic, he now made it clear that he would shoot instantly unless they put up their hands and dropped their fearsome weapon. Bewildered they obeyed and he marched his enemies back to Jerusalem, where 'I procured the necessary warrants for their arrest, which I helped to execute myself'.

Later that night he went into his garden to try out the revolver. It was rusty and jammed and he nearly 'blew off two fingers of my painting hand'.

The friendly monks, with whom he had so recently stayed, eagerly recommended another of their 'innocent, non-political' guests, an experienced gunsmith.

This encounter with the brigands had various repercussions. He had much more respect not only in the city, but also in the surrounding country, 'where I was now able to walk about unmolested'. His reputation reached a young English surgeon called Sim, at the Christian Mission. They became great friends. Sim's servant happened to be the brother of the Sheik of Siloam and subsequently became Hunt's devoted servant.

Before beginning his picture, *Christ in the Temple*, he determined to study every detail of the background and costume. He first read the Old and New Testaments, then the Talmud and Josephus to discover the ceremonies prevailing nearly two thousand years before. He made himself familiar with the nature of principal feasts and fasts, with every aspect of Jewish ritual and with what stage the rebuilding of Herod's Temple had reached at the time of Christ.

Having resigned himself to the impossibility of finding Moslem models willing to pose at all—let alone in the nude—he asked Sim to introduce him to important Jewish families in Jerusalem. This Sim did: however, it proved impossible to persuade any one to sit for the same reason.

He desperately needed a model for the Virgin Mary, but when he discovered 'a nest of beautiful women, mother and sisters, they disappeared upstairs as soon as spotted'.

He even found a grandmother of under forty with a daughter of twenty-five, who already had a daughter of nine. Neither of the 'singularly beautiful women' would agree to pose.

One moonlit night, he climbed from his flat roof on to the top of a high wall to sketch the Mosque. His neighbour was indignant and accused him of spying on his harem. Hunt begged to be allowed to finish his innocent sketch. His neighbour insisted that Hunt should be screened from the view of his wives —it would disturb them to see a younger man.

At this stage of the picture he needed Jews to sit as rabbis. At last he succeeded in bribing a supposed Christian convert, enticing him to sit with ample supplies of sweetmeats, coffee and pipes. The Mission had set him up as a bible merchant. Surprisingly, he found a lucrative market for Old and New Testaments and copies of *Pilgrim's Progress*. He was 'sulky and fidgety' and soon admitted he did not believe.

However, he collected another Jew who agreed to sit as the water carrier in the picture. This model admitted that he 'used to go to the English church, but found it paid him better to belong to the Synagogue'. Hunt 'wished he could have served for other figures for it was tranquillity to paint a man with a mind so simply businesslike'.

But the picture was making slow progress, and he was short of money. Seddon was already talking of returning to England; he had a crateful of landscapes. He too was in love and hoping to marry on the proceeds.

It was essential for Hunt to produce another subject picture forthwith, independent of models, to pay his expenses.

When studying Jewish history for the Temple picture, he had become interested in the strange legend of Azazel. The ancient ceremony symbolised to the Jews the expiation of their sins: they drove a goat into the wilderness. At least a goat as a model would be easier to find than a man—and surely no literate person could fail to recognise the message of this awesome subject?[1]

For the background there was a rich choice of majestic scenery which he could paint within safe and convenient distance of the city. But Hunt was only attracted by extremes. His life became increasingly exacting, a self-imposed challenge.

The goat must be *white*. He must explore the wilds in search of the most sinister site. After examining the maps, he decided that this might well prove to be the salt-encrusted shore of the Dead Sea.

In vain, the consul and others pointed out the danger, folly and expense of such a journey. Syria was seething with political unrest. Patriotic feeling had degenerated into bloodthirsty feuds between the tribes.

Hunt was not the only one who felt in need of a change. Various other young men longed to get away. The small European community was divided; social life had become embarrassing because of the different sympathies aroused by the Crimean War. Hunt explained this: 'Till now I had believed that the Prussians and other Germans had kindred interests with the English, but . . . they were inspired with ill-feeling towards us, not excluding those in English pay, such as the Bishop and the Missionaries.'

Sim was a crack shot, and interested in zoology. He was fed up and due for leave. James Graham, a new arrival in Jerusalem, ex-director of a failed Glasgow bank, 'tall, fair and brawny, riding beautifully', was mad on photography. He was keen to take his modern camera into the remote parts of the Holy Land.

Seddon postponed his return to England. At any rate he must at least join the trial trip. Already there were plenty of others clamouring to take his place.

But Hunt, with the illustrations in his father's scrapbook so firmly imprinted in his mind, was the most enthusiastic. He resolved to go on ahead of the rest to reconnoitre.

Just before he left another post arrived. He read it hurriedly. Nobody bothered to mention the Crimean War. Everyone except

[1] He was tempted to write to Landseer with the suggestion that he should paint it.

Fred Stephens was preoccupied with his own and other people's affairs and an endless round of parties and dances.

Fred was still hopelessly in debt. It seemed that Annie was making more progress with her dancing than with her reading and writing. No letter in her hand was forthcoming as yet.

There was however good news from Hunt's father, who enclosed a wad of newspaper cuttings. Ruskin had come to the rescue again. He had written twice to *The Times*, at length, in defence of Hunt's Academy pictures which all other critics had condemned.

In his opinion, *The Light of the World* was '. . . one of the noblest works of sacred art ever produced in this or any other age'. The otherwise despised *Awakening Conscience* was minutely described and praised for its detailed technique and moral message.

Ruskin's action in writing these letters to *The Times* was hysterically resented by Euphemia Ruskin's friends. After the *divorce* (all referred to the annulment as this) they felt that he should retire from public life and hide his head in shame. Sir Charles Eastlake, P.R.A., was furious and revolted, his wife was deeply shocked by the 'disgusting farrago . . . on Hunt's odious picture', by this insensitive monster. Society considered Ruskin's failure, or reluctance, to consummate his marriage as positively wicked. Ruskin was reported as saying of Euphemia: '. . . it would be better that she was broken on the wheel than come between me and John Millais.'

Hunt stuffed these latest letters into his knapsack, resolving to read them again more attentively by the camp fire one night, to cheer him on his journey.

When Seddon arrived in London the Brothers and all old friends were keen for news of Hunt and eager to see Seddon's work. One of these reunions was described by Madox Brown: 'Hunt's father was there perorating curiously, a comical, brave old cock. . . .'

To him, Seddon was full of praise for the courage Hunt showed when face to face with 'assassins'. He was learning Arabic fast. The more research he had done and the more he had explored the Holy Land, the more passionate his interest in biblical history had become. His erudite interpretations and comparisons of the various ancient religious customs had involved him in long acrimonious discussions with Dr Gobat, the Bishop of Jerusalem, who had started his ecclesiastical career as a missionary in Abyssinia. He and Hunt were now conducting a feud.

When old Mr Hunt had gone home, the others gathered round Seddon for more news. The impression they formed was that the dear old Mad was madder than ever—and maddening too. He had expected Seddon not only to act as courier, but to keep house as well. He, Seddon, had had enough and gone off on his own. As for learning any painting technique from Hunt, the latter had taught him nothing at all.

Halliday, Stephens, Collins, Woolner and Diplock decided between themselves that it was high time the Mad came home —and for more reasons than Annie Miller. Seddon must have laughed. What a hope—the maniac was at present obsessed with a goat!

Halliday felt that perhaps Millais' plight would serve their purpose, and he pleaded with Hunt to return: 'I am terribly worried about Millais' depression. You are his only confident [sic]. He misses you so much and has got much worse.'

In March, Stephens sent news of Annie Miller:

'I have a visitor this evening who sits opposite turning over *Pendennis* with a quaint turn of the head this every now and then as I write particularly as I have just said, "Now Annie Miller, I am going to say something about you". Then she looks up. She seems rather more lively than usual tonight and I am about to make her put in this letter a few words about herself. She is I believe a good little goose enough, has been sitting to Egg lately and looks very well having very much reformed her hair-dressing. . . .

P.S. I have spent the last half hour in persuading the little goose above to write, and from some unaccountable funk she says she "can't write" so I must fill up by saying she hopes you are quite well and begs to be most kindly remembered.'

In April Halliday wrote again begging Hunt to come home on his own account. He confessed how much he was dreading Millais' marriage, he would miss him so. Halliday missed Hunt already:

'Come you and your traps here [to] Robert Street as my guest
—a hearty welcome and you can be completely your own
master. . . . I often see Stephens I encourage him coming
here for I have felt how much he must have missed you and
that he must have been left rather alone. . . . Gabriel Rossetti
has at last become as inaccessible as the Emperor of China, he
will neither be seen nor come to see anyone nor will he show
his own brother what he is doing so that he might as well be
dead—which is a sad pity. Collins is our constant friend and
he, Millais, Luard, Barwell and myself meet v. often.' Collins
was still fasting and 'looked like a half-starved ghost'.

Hunt received another disconcerting account of Rossetti in an
undated letter from Stephens:

'I saw Gabriel the other day with a great hunch on one
shoulder, dressed in a long flannel gown, looking altogether
something like a deformed enchantor.'

Millais' letters were not so frequent now: he posted a letter
dated May 22 but which had been written over a period of
several days: 'I have been such a correspondent with *Miss Gray*
that I have been kept by her from writing to you.' When he did
write, the letters were still full of Ruskin's iniquities—when
Hunt returned he would be amazed to hear what a 'vile fiend'
the man was. To return to the letter of May 22, Millais con-
tinues:

'Next month please God I shall be a *married man* . . . I am
going to be married so quietly that none of my family come to
the wedding—Good gracious, fancy me married my old boy,
I feel *desperately melancholy* about it which is rather different
to most bridegrooms, but callous to all results as it is quite
impossible to foresee the end of anything we undertake . . .
I take this fearful risk in desperation, I hate wasting my life,
and fretting away in *Bachelorism*, and cannot myself change
for worse (I may it is true make this girl wretched and so
increase my state) but it is worth the risk and you must pray
for me my dear old friend. . . .'

On July 3 he described his wedding day to Charley Collins:

'It happens to be a most lovely day which is a *great blessing*, but I feel feverish, and slightly out of sorts, an exaggerated sensation of going to an Evening party at fifteen years of age. How strange it is. I am only hopeful it may be the right course I have taken which can only be known from experience. I cannot promise to write again for some little time. I know I have all your prayers which is not a little comfort to me. This is a trial without doubt as it either proves a blessing or a curse to two poor bodies only anxious to do their best . . . There are some startling accompaniments, my boy, like the glimpse of the dentists instruments—my poor brain and soul is fatigued with dwelling on unpleasant probabilities so I am aroused for the fight.'

Effie wrote in her diary:

'I had to give him all my sympathy. He cried dreadfully, said he did not know how he had got through it, felt wretched; it had added ten years to his life, and instead of being happy and cheerful, he seemed in despair.'

The wedding was recorded among the Deaths in *The Leader*. However, it would seem that Millais stopped crying after his marriage: between them, Effie and Leech made a man of him.

Millais was not exceptional as a bashful bridegroom. Within a year or two, on the eve of his marriage, Burne-Jones confessed that he was very frightened, 'and shouldn't be surprised if I bolt off the day before and am never heard of again'.

Every letter Hunt received nowadays seemed concerned with the marriage or matrimonial intentions of someone.

Seddon had married his 'sweet and beautiful girl' in June and Madox Brown said 'he is a lucky dog'. Arthur Hughes was married to 'a little lady very meek and mute . . . He's immensely fond'. Gabriel 'was in Paris every day with his sweetheart, of whom he is more foolishly fond than I ever saw a lover'. Stephens wrote that Millais was 'gloriously happy and there is a rumour about that both the Rossettis are to marry—D.G. to a young lady, an artist. You will guess who'.

In Hunt's last letter to Madox Brown he had made it clear that he was uncertain whether or not Millais was yet married. Madox Brown replied in September:

'. . . Millais *is* married, your not being well aware of this fact strikes one with a painful sense of your isolation from polite society burried [*sic*] as you seem to be amid a heap of monomaniacs and people out of senses and out of elbows. He has *taken a wife* to himself in good earnest—construe the meaning of the sentence as you will—since which I am told that he writes from Perth his present residence, most feelingly on the forlorn condition of all unhappy young men not married, so you know what to expect. Collins has I believe received peremptory orders to marry himself forthwith and is I suppose going to do so. Gabriel Rossetti still prudently holds aloof from any measure of the kind likely to break in upon his artistic and poetic reveries, but there are rumours of William, that hitherto young man, having seriously taken some step or steps towards the estate, pronounced by Millais, now, to be of such "indiscribabble [*sic*] bliss". So you see that in coming home you are only hastening to a sort of maelstroom of matrimony round which you may describe a few convolutions more or less, but in you will plunge over ears for consummation with most inevitable summersault. The English are a marrying people and just at present it seems to be what they are most fit for, this and laying down electric wires which is a sort of geographical marrying, for since the last three months we seem to be in all else at a rather low ebb.'

Obviously this matrimonial epidemic inspired Hunt to propose, without further delay, in writing, to Annie Miller. Doubtless her Aunt Bess and her sister congratulated her on acquiring such a valuable letter. She also showed it to Mrs Bramah. Stephens wrote to Hunt on 14 November 1855:

'The enclosed is from Annie Miller, was sent to me at my invitation some time back. My last note to you expressed some nervous fears respecting her which I now think groundless. I was much pleased at her having declined to sit to some ladies, pupils of Mr Brown, on account of her promise to you.

[Lady Slade] She called upon me twice before this refusal but being from home it was not till afterwards that I knew of her resolution, with which I need not say I was much pleased, especially as she did so entirely on her own judgement, and she told me she had also declined sitting to Barwell, a painter, whom perhaps you know!

'She wrote to me some time ago to lend her some money as she had had 'some words' with her father. I was in a stew at this and wrote to her to come sit to me, when I learned that Papa had "borrowed" £2 of her and since refused payment. She was very particular. I of course counselled submission and gave her a sitting, praying for the same well in order to break the loss a trifle. I should have done more but was remarkably hard up at the time.

'I rejoiced she had not sat to the ladies who although harmless in themselves, I heard kept red-breeched flunkies and had swells hanging about the smallest of whom might have upset A.M. . . . Before receiving your letter which says you had written to Annie Miller recommending matrimony, I had endeavoured to point out the advantages of this holy institution in a jocular way so that she might think of it seriously. (What vanity of mine, as if a girl of that age could keep it *out* of her head). It seemed to have some effect. She is, I believe, safe and good at the present time, *calls me her Godfather, and though I purposely see little of her, I have endeavoured to act as such.*'

The italics are mine. It would seem that Stephens was as susceptible as others to Annie's charms. A fact which alarmed him as a challenge to his loyalty to Hunt in his dealings with Annie.

CHAPTER XII

Alone, and in a land of sand and thorns.
TENNYSON

IN NOVEMBER Hunt determined to leave Jerusalem in search of his background for *The Scapegoat*. He hoped to find the suitable spot with a view of the Mountains of Moab from the shores of the Dead Sea.

His description in his memoirs of this expedition is in vivid prose which if quoted at length would be excessive here. I have selected some passages and linked them as best I could, trying not to spoil the continuity of the melodrama by using my own style.

Everyone knew that the roads were impassable and that this whole area was in a turmoil of tribal wars. It was therefore with difficulty that he succeeded in recruiting porters and muleteers to accompany him 'into the wild, desolate regions infested with a roving population of cut-throats and brigands. . . .' Only the most miserable horses and mules were for sale or hire—those thought already moribund by their owners. Neither men nor animals were expected to return.

Hunt's personal bodyguard seems to have spent most of the time 'in tears, quaking with terror'.

Hunt referred to the men as 'a sullen lot of outcasts', with nothing better to do than join in this unpromising escapade with the strange young Englishman whose antics were already a byword. They were victims of 'frequent attacks from savage desperadoes', who tried to steal their equipment, weapons and ammunition. They were 'pelted with missiles, and defrauded of sleep by deafening thunder'. They ran out of opium almost at once and were dependent on Hunt for tobacco. He slept well thanks to massive draughts of arrack.

'The wretched men and their skinny beasts huddled under rocks or trees for shelter. Boulders dislodged by torrential rain

155

crashed about and huge branches were torn off by the savage winds . . . the sky was blood red'.

They were convinced that the expedition was doomed. 'In vain they wailed that the *ghouls* and *effreets* who lure travellers over precipices to eternal damnation were actually visible in the storm.'

The decrepit mules were totally unfit to negotiate such treacherous paths. Being overloaded, the strongest animal slipped and fell into a ravine. Hunt's horse, mercilessly heeled to climb an apparently endless mass of scree, overbalanced and rolled down in a rattle of stones. Hunt threw himself clear of the high Arab saddle. His loaded gun, happily, did not explode. The horse was just able to get up and Hunt was badly bruised.

When they were completely lost and without food, Hunt's dispirited servant begged him to lead them back to their tracks to Jerusalem. But Hunt 'had no intention of giving up the scape-goat project, cost what it might . . . I could not risk losing my character for firmness, and insisted on the original plan. I would not relent . . . and affected to despise their pleadings'. Pointing to his gun he rode to the rear of the cavalcade and forced it to continue.

He had acquired an obstinate determination allied to courage and pride during the struggle of his youth.

The thorny path was familiar: he chose it rather than any other. When the way ahead looked clear, he felt compelled to create real or imaginary obstacles.

While he lay in a raging fever, drugged with hashish provided by Suleiman, a devoted young Arab, whom he had adopted in the desert, the huge, hairy devil appeared to him once more in his delirium. Probably this time in the guise of a hyena or a greedy and inquisitive goat. He suffered hallucinations and

'asked for unseen ones, they appeared. I had much to tell and not less to hear; many there were whom I took by the hand and grasped by the shoulder. It was satisfaction almost to pain. While still eager to debate a force of separation came between us, I held out my arms as it seemed, but I was torn backwards across the round dark sea and over the wind swept hills, and waking, I found myself again in the lonely tent . . . with

Self-portrait of WILLIAM HOLMAN HUNT, aged 14, 1841.
Owned by the author.

J. E. MILLAIS as the dying boy in *Rienzi* by William Holman Hunt,
1848. (Detail)
Reproduced by kind permission of Mrs E. M. Clarke.

LIZZIE SIDDAL by Rossetti.
Reproduced by kind permission of the Trustees of the Victoria and Albert
Museum, London. 'Victoria and Albert Museum. Crown Copyright.'

EMMA WATKINS as the Shepherdess in *The Hireling Shepherd* by
William Holman Hunt, 1852. (Detail)
Reproduced by kind permission of the Trustees of the City of Manchester
Art Galleries.

J. E. MILLAIS by William Holman Hunt, 1853.
Reproduced by kind permission of Mrs Elizabeth Burt.

DANTE GABRIEL ROSSETTI by William Holman Hunt, 1853. Original untraced. Reproduced from the second edition of *Pre-Raphaelitism and the Pre-Raphaelite Brotherhood.*

Edith Holman-Hunt added the following footnote:
'This portrait of D. G. Rossetti, attributed to his pen by F. G. Stephens in his memoir of Rossetti in the *Portfolio*, was a hasty scribble made by Holman Hunt in the Cleveland Street Studio, and the unconsidered trifle was given by Rossetti to A. Munro, who gave it to Arthur Hughes, who gave it to W.H.H.'

WOOLNER by Rossetti, 1852.
Reproduced by kind permission of the Trustees of the National Portrait
Gallery, London.

ANNIE MILLER by Rossetti, 1860.
Reproduced by kind permission of the Trustees of the Birmingham Museum
and Art Gallery.

The three Waugh sisters by William Holman Hunt, 1864. Original untraced.
Reproduced from *Pre-Raphaelitism and the Pre-Raphaelite Brotherhood*.

FANNY: *Isabella and the pot of Basil*, by William Holman Hunt, 1866–67.
Reproduced by kind permission of the Trustees of the Laing Art Gallery and
Museum, Newcastle-upon-Tyne.

The American girl: *Bianca* by William Holman Hunt, 1868.
Reproduced by kind permission of the Trustees of the Worthing Museum and
Art Gallery.

ALICE WOOLNER, nee Waugh, by Arthur Hughes, 1864.
Reproduced by kind permission of Commander Woolner.

EDITH HUNT, née Waugh, by William Holman Hunt, 1876.
Reproduced by kind permission of Mrs Elizabeth Burt.

CYRIL BENONE HOLMAN HUNT by William Holman Hunt, 1876.
Reproduced by kind permission of Mrs Elizabeth Burt.

The Awakening Conscience by William Holman Hunt, 1853.
Reproduced by kind permission of Sir Colin Anderson.

William Holman Hunt's sketch of himself in a letter written to
Thomas Combe from Cairo in 1853.
Reproduced by kind permission of Mrs Elizabeth Burt.

The Afterglow in Egypt by William Holman Hunt, 1853-63.
Reproduced by kind permission of the Trustees of the Southampton Art
Gallery.

ANNIE MILLER as *Helen of Troy* by Rossetti, 1863.

ANNIE MILLER as *The Girl in the Pink Bonnet* by J. E. Millais, hitherto
known as Effie Gray, when Mrs. Ruskin, 1853.
Reproduced by kind permission of Kerrison Preston, Esq.

F. G. STEPHENS by J. E. Millais, 1853.
Reproduced by kind permission of the Trustees of the National Portrait
Gallery, London.

EMILY HUNT by William Holman Hunt, 1857.
Reproduced by kind permission of the Trustees of the National Gallery of
Victoria, Melbourne.

Annie Miller's father, HENRY MILLER: *In Chelsea Gardens* by Francis
Moody, 1859.
Reproduced by kind permission of Mrs E. W. Wheeler.

the creatures of the wilderness screaming and howling from above and below, aggrieved that our fires barred the way between them and the salt water. . . .'

He read and reread all his friends' letters during this solitary time in the desert. Halliday's enclosed patterns for shirts and a new suit from the tailor, Poole. Hunt used the envelopes as cigarette papers.

Throughout the expedition most of the sheiks were aggressive, demanding preposterous sums for safe conduct through their territory. Rather than succumb, Hunt was sometimes obliged to retreat or take a longer way round.

His method of dealing with 'unscrupulous natives to whom murder was a mere pastime' was typical of Englishmen of the day.

On several occasions when surrounded by horsemen 'livid in the face with hatred, blackened with powder, with blood-shot eyes, worn with long watching and strife, carrying spears, guns, swords and clubs', he behaved in the same way:

'I continued placidly conveying my paint from palette to canvas, steadying my touch by resting the hand on my double-barrelled gun. I knew that my whole chance depended upon the exhibition of utter unconcern, and I continued as steadily as if in my studio at home.'

On one occasion when a gang of robbers confronted him:

'. . . the leader thundered out, "Give me some water." I turned and looked at him from his head to his horse's feet, and then very deliberately at the others, and resumed my task without saying a word. He stormed again, "Do you hear? Give us some water." I replied: "I am an Englishman; you are an Arab. Englishmen are not the servants of Arabs; I am employing Arabs for servants. You are thirsty—it is hot—the water is there—I will out of kindness let you have some, but you must help one another; I have something else to do," and I turned again quietly to work.'

Again, when attacked by some bandits, who boasted of killing a party of Americans, he retorted: 'I daresay, but I am English

157

so you'd better be careful', and continued to sketch apparently unconcerned.

When bullets were whistling round their heads, his so-called bodyguard was, as usual, possessed with violent paroxysms of sobbing and warned that the sheik of this particular tribe was once imprisoned by the English consul. If Hunt admitted to being English they could expect no mercy. 'Pray say that you are American or German,' he implored, 'or we will'. Hunt replied that if any of them said anything of the kind, he would ask the enemy, as a special favour, to kill them first.

When another sheik held up the cavalcade and shouted: 'Dismount!' and instructed his men to seize the mules, Hunt rode straight up to him and quietly announced that the moment anyone touched a bridle he would shoot him dead. Then, bowing politely from the saddle, he watched his men file safely past the Arabs.

Hunt's chief concern was the safety of that rare specimen, the white goat. Instead of leaving this treasure safely tethered in his Jerusalem garden, to be tended by the two idle servants whom he was paying anyway, Hunt insisted on taking it along. Other models, such as Emma Watkins and Annie Miller, had posed in comfort in his studio against backgrounds already painted out of doors. Not so the goat. It walked or was carried in turn by protesting porters.

Bitten by poisonous insects and parasites, its pathetic bleating attracted unwelcome attention from howling pariahs and hyenas. Whenever unsupervised, the goat invaded Hunt's tent and devoured anything it could find. It did not even succeed in fulfilling its mission. Before the picture was complete, 'the poor goat was suffering and too weak to walk, so I had him lifted on to the picture-case and carried, but the sun soon distressed him. Then we took the poor beast down, but it was of no use, the ominous vultures could be spied from afar. I poured water into his mouth, but nothing availed to save him.'

Eventually Hunt's party reached the end of the journey—the province of Oosdoom (now spelt Uzdum) on the shores of the Dead Sea—'a God-forsaken area of awful and silent solitude, a Dantesque desolation shrouded in mist'.

The thirsty men rushed to drink from the rivulets of brine. Hunt went on foot in search of fresh water or some sign of life.

He nearly disappeared in the slimy, salty quicksands, and only survived by throwing himself full length on the wobbling surface to distribute his weight. He crawled out just in time clinging to a protruding rock.

The consul had warned that it was impossible to survive in this sinister place without protection from the local sheik who was notoriously hostile to travellers. He also 'advised extreme caution in dealing with this villain' and had given Hunt a scarlet cloak to drape about the man's shoulders while chanting formal messages and compliments in Arabic.

On spotting plumes of smoke, Hunt discovered the camp, but he 'feared to embrace the sheik in Arab fashion because he was so filthy'. The sheik grabbed the cloak, bundled it up and sat on it. 'He stank and had a long face like a mule with projecting teeth.' Ferocious-looking retainers formed a circle about him and veiled women peered between the hangings.

Having exchanged the minimum of greetings, without further preamble Hunt declared that he wished to spend several weeks in the vicinity, painting a picture. He would need food and water and a guard. How much should he pay for provisions and protection?

The sheik solemnly replied that, by Allah, what the traveller asked was. no light matter! The place was dangerous; he must send down at least a hundred of his men as guards. He would do his best to persuade them to be satisfied with five hundred English pounds. Upon which all the men within hearing cried out: 'By Allah, no, never, impossible.' Hunt replied that he was not an English lord, but more like a dervish or a monk: he could guard himself. The most he would pay for protection was seven pounds. He then stalked out amid growls of annoyance.

The sheik called at Hunt's tent when it was dark. After prolonged haggling Hunt beat him down to £3.

The animals he bought for food were delivered to his camp with their legs tied together, by 'hideous boys, black and naked, with crowns shaven save for one central tuft of hair'. Hunt caught them screeching like demons, 'directing scorpions up to the helpless fowls, and provoking the creatures to sting them'. Furious, he lashed out and scattered them with his *corbash*.[1]

---

[1] A *corbash* or *kurbash* is a Turkish word for a whip which in those day• was used indiscriminately on mules and Arabs.

The next morning the cavalcade set off for the shore of the Dead Sea. Hunt rode ahead. A good-looking young Arab, aged perhaps eighteen, came up and kissed his hand, introducing himself as Suleiman, the sheik's nephew. He had been fascinated, watching Hunt at yesterday's parley, and now asked to be his 'son'. Hunt agreed to take him to the sea with him where he would do his 'writing'. Although there is an Arabic word for painting, Suleiman did not know that such a technique existed.

When Hunt settled down to work, the boy sat in front of him 'staring intently . . . with utter bewilderment'.

Suleiman went with him to the shore every day. One evening near sunset, Suleiman insisted that it was high time they returned to the base. It grew dark and they might be attacked by robbers or even murdered. By now it was bitterly cold. Having sat still all day, Hunt—to get his circulation moving—began to dance. When he stopped, Suleiman 'seemed like one possessed of a terrible secret'. He approached with uplifted arms and flung them round Hunt's neck, crying: "You are inspired: you dance like a dervish—you are one! Can you do it again?" Away Hunt went, 'a second and a third time, indeed often', waltzing with his gun as a partner.

That night, while the sheik's and Hunt's men sat round the fire, Suleiman entertained them with accounts of these antics. From his tent, Hunt could hear yells of delight. Later, accompanied by the sheik's nephew, the Arabs requested a formal interview. After the usual salutations, Hunt offered them tobacco to mix with the chopped herbs that they grew in the few fertile patches available. They were ferocious smokers of hashish and were still known as *hashashines* (assassins). The courtesies being over, an elder asked Hunt as a favour to dance for them. He declined, and the company retired greatly disappointed.

Suleiman divulged an inspired plan for his and Hunt's future which had the prior approval of the tribe, who were clearly fed up with their smelly sheik. Suleiman was his nephew and heir. The sheik had countless wives, but was by now presumably sterile. All the same he had a daughter the right age to be Suleiman's bride and was keen on the marriage. However, Suleiman was not interested in girls. Hunt must marry her and become sheik before him. Presumably Allah would dispose of the old sheik somehow and his brides would prove barren. Hunt and Suleiman would then lead the tribe on their raids and battles: 'and when we are at peace and encamped, you shall be our dervish and dance. We have arranged it: so let it be'.

Hunt's reaction was non-commital.

Shortly after this, as Suleiman had predicted, a band of robbers appeared. Hunt continued to paint. Suleiman told them that a hundred tribesmen were guarding the camp, and that the stranger was a holy man, a dervish, who spoke at length about the Prophet.

Suitably impressed the intruders left them alone. That night, in public, Hunt 'danced more from prudential motives than from lightness of heart'.

Soon after this, the background of the picture was finished. The model was dead: it was time to go home.

Uncomprehending servants were ordered to load the tottering mules with chunks and bags of salt, odd bits of rock, and bones from the Dead Sea shore. How these props, the picture and the cavalcade survived the journey through an increasingly dangerous theatre of war, especially as they were involved in fierce battles themselves, is indeed miraculous.

Once safely back in Jerusalem, Hunt's chief concern was to find another white goat; it does not seem to have occurred to him to bleach one. He rode far and wide:

'. . . but it turned out that such a beast could only be found at a great distance. Having until January searched in vain, I sent a man beyond the Jordan to find one, he delighted me after two or three days by appearing with a model which was nigh perfect; the price was a fancy one, the animal was tired with his journey, and it was petted in every degree as a precious possession, but the next day it died before I could do a touch from it. I then had to send off two venturesome lads for another, and in a week, in the middle of February, they returned with a kid without a trace of brown or black on his coat.'

This precious specimen was tethered to a post in the garden with its hooves embedded in the Dead Sea salt, carefully spread on a large tray; in case of rain this could be carried under cover.

For added realism Sim obligingly produced some wild goats' skulls of which 'he had a large collection by happy chance'.

The picture was finished by the middle of October, when it was crated and dispatched to Combe, with an explanation of its significance.

As winter approached, to amuse himself in the evenings, Hunt made some drawings, so meticulous that they resembled engravings, of imaginary Russian secret weapons including 'a new gun; it carried a bomb and had a seat for an intrepid aeronaut[2] near the muzzle'.

With the connivance of Sim, these 'engravings' were infiltrated into the German Colony with excellent effect. Hunt and Sim found this joke vastly amusing, 'as it was impossible to ignore that the German Colony, instead of having a fraternal feeling, which I had thought existed on either side, entertained a settled captious jealousy of the English'.

Hunt and Sim with their photographer friend, Graham, now enjoyed and endured many expeditions of quite extraordinary variety and interest. Descriptions of these in Hunt's memoirs make good reading.

His character had much matured since leaving England; he had found no wives, or even lady-loves, although when alone in Damascus he was clearly intrigued by the famous Jane Digby to whom he refers as Lady Ellenborough:

'I refrained from indulging in the common curiosity to visit the lady, but in my strolls I met her in the streets. She was tall and slim and must have been attractive in early years, she evidently wondered at the presence of an English stranger in the city of her adoption so late in the season, but so our mutual glances ended.'

Although he was still in his twenties, he had until now always been attracted to women younger than himself. Jane was described by conventional European visitors as 'a one time beauty, with four husbands still living and now married to a black'. She was in fact now forty-nine, the favourite Moslem wife of Sheik Mezrab. Isabella Burton said that even in her sixties, she

[2] i.e. balloonist.

162

looked no more than thirty-five as she wandered through the bazaar wearing oriental dress, with her beautiful hair in two long plaits to the ground.[3]

In spite of the lack of effective remedies and ignorance of antiseptics, Hunt had remained remarkably healthy, surrounded as he was by cholera, parasites and foul diseases of all kinds. This was due to his scrupulous attention to personal hygiene and his insistence on bathing or thoroughly washing himself in boiled water whenever possible.

On one fearsome expedition in Syria such eccentricity provided entertainment for the locals.

His servant Issa, having put up the tent, brought him two large buckets of water and:

'. . . soon I was busy . . . rubbing and scrubbing . . . I heard a boisterous altercation going on between Issa and . . . strange voices. Abating my stamping, and brisk towelling, I called out to him. . . .'

Issa explained:

' "Why, these people are so unreasonable . . . hearing that you were having a bath all the men, women, and children came out to look through a hole in the tent. But they can't all see at once, and I want those who were here at the beginning to go away, and make place for others, but they won't; and those behind are laughing and quarrelling with those in front, and I threaten that I will turn them all away if they can't agree." '

But now at the end of 1855 he fell victim to malaria—'Tertiary fever, an ague'—as it was then called.

Apart from admitting the fevers and deliriums experienced when painting *The Scapegoat* in Uzdum, he insisted that he was perfectly well, and continued to ride forty or fifty miles a day

---

[3] When I was a child, my grandmother made frequent contributions to my 'museum'. The phial of kohl with which she presented me one rainy day, together with a bundle of Lord Kitchener's letters was, she explained, used by Eastern women and, of course, *Lady Ellenborough* 'to paint their eyes'. Not wishing to appear stupid, I often had to accept such mysterious scraps of information without question.

and to 'live rough'. He was forced to give in at last; Dr Sim wrote privately and urgently to Halliday, who he understood was counting the days until he and Hunt could share a studio together in England. As a result, Halliday travelled as far as Pera[4] to fetch him home.

[4] Near Constantinople.

CHAPTER XIII

'It is no wonder,' said the lords,
'She is more beautiful than day.'
TENNYSON

WHILE HUNT was dancing in the desert, alone or with a gun, his beloved Annie was waltzing in London with her latest admirer, the 7th Viscount Ranelagh. Fashionably, he drank champagne from her slipper at Bertolini's, then one of the smartest restaurants.

She may have picked him up in the West End, or nearer home. His seat was Ranelagh House in Fulham, and he owned various properties in that neighbourhood. He knew Chelsea well, having attended Dr Roberts' School in Whitehead Grove.

After his father died, his mother, Caroline Louisa, Lady Ranelagh, spent much of her widowhood in Sussex. She came and went as she chose, and was financially independent: a full staff of servants was kept at the London house all the year round. Her background is important to this story.

In 1804, her husband had first married the illegitimate daughter of Sir Philip Stephens. The following year she died at Admiralty House, aged thirty-three, giving birth to a stillborn child.

Six years later, he married Caroline Louisa, the mother of Annie's beau. She and her brother, Thomas Jones, were the illegitimate children of Colonel Lee of Yorkshire and a Miss Thompson, whose maiden name the children bore. Curiously, the Ranelaghs and Thompsons had been connected in the past, which explains why the boy was given the Christian names, Thomas Jones.[1]

Colonel Lee and the Thomsons, who by this time had dropped the 'P', were delighted when Lord Ranelagh actually. married Caroline Louisa, four months before the son and heir was born. Perhaps he had been tempted by the ample dowry to which both Colonel Lee and the Thomson family contributed. When

[1] *Jones* was originally *James.*

165

Lord Ranelagh died he in turn left numerous illegitimate children, whose Christian names he could not recollect. Many were provided for in his will. The bewildered solicitor referred to most of the boys as Thomas, and they were eventually identified through their mothers, whose names his Lordship fortunately remembered.

When Annie and the successive Lord Ranelagh met, he was thirty-five and she was twenty. Later, Hunt and others referred to him as 'that notorious rake'. However, as an officer in the Life Guards, he certainly cut a dashing figure and, whatever his morals, he was brave. In his youth, he had served at the Siege of Antwerp and afterwards as a volunteer in the Spanish War of Succession.

Not only was Annie impressed, but her father, being an old soldier, must have boasted of his daughter's latest conquest to the other pensioners at the Royal Hospital, Chelsea.

Lord Ranelagh was not only charmed by her beauty, but also, probably, by her expert dancing, gracious manners and pretty voice—assiduously cultivated by the charitable Mrs Bramah, at Hunt's expense!

Annie was the notorious model of last year's most sensational Academy picture, the toast of the most *avant garde* painters of the day. He was proud to be seen with her. Perhaps he and his friends felt that if Holy Hunt were such a fool as to leave this light of the world to her conscience, he deserved to lose her anyway.

Ranelagh House was very comfortable, but his mother came and went at the most unexpected times. He therefore shared rooms in Mayfair with brother officers at 7 New Burlington Street. It was here that Annie met his first cousin, Thomas Ranelagh Jones Thomson. His father was Lady Ranelagh's brother, who had married money and drank more than was good for him.

Thomas Ranelagh Thomson was twenty-seven, a few months younger than Hunt. When he was nineteen he had bought a commission in the infantry—the 89th Regiment of Foot. By the time he and Annie met in New Burlington Street, he had bought himself out of the regular army and was an officer in the Royal East Middlesex Militia.

Being already Lord Ranelagh's mistress, Annie did not pay much attention to Thomas Ranelagh Jones Thomson.

Her lover's carriage was a familiar sight in Chelsea, bowling down the Fulham Road to Ranelagh House or grandly driving Annie home to the Cross Keys. The Chelsea neighbours, so critical of her hitherto, now changed their minds. When the liveried footman jumped down to open the carriage door, glistening with the Ranelagh coat-of-arms, and doffed his cockaded hat to her, they all were agreed that Annie had made good.

Harriet had left the Cross Keys a year ago for a situation in private service in King Street, Kensington, so that she could be near Henry Childs, the gas-fitter, who had moved to live and work there. He was only twenty, and Harriet a year older, when he eventually married her, in pregnancy. Both were illiterate. On the marriage certificate, they and the witnesses all signed by mark.

Whatever gossip Halliday had heard about Annie Miller, he repeated nothing to Hunt on their journey home. Nor did he refer to Gabriel Rossetti and George Boyce both being crazy about her the previous year. He admitted that no one knew where they were with Gabriel and Lizzie Siddal. Sometimes she was his fiancée, at others simply his talented pupil.

There was plenty of other news. Millais was in Scotland, painting better than ever, but having a fearful struggle to make ends meet. Effie was expecting a baby. Tom Diplock was engaged. Charley Collins was courting one of the Dickens girls and eating more, but Wilkie Collins was living in sin, shamelessly. Madox Brown was pitiably poor and had been reduced to pawning his last few spoons, even young Emma's shawl. They were married at last and had had an infant prodigy called Oliver. Lucy, his daughter by his first wife, was a big girl now.

Finally Halliday confided that he himself was wildly in love with a stunner called Jemima. Marriage seemed a long way off, however. Anyway, he and Hunt decided to share a London crib, together with Hunt's former pupil, Martineau. Hunt must have felt uneasy on hearing that Fred Stephens was still in debt.

They arrived in London at 3 a.m. at the end of January 1856. Halliday went off to his old crib and Hunt went straight to Millais' studio. Lowes Dickinson opened the door and gave him a warm welcome: Hunt had been away for two years. When he left England he was clean-shaven except for side-whiskers. Now he looked far more mature and had grown a beard.

Millais at once wrote from Scotland describing his own appearance:

'I think when you see me you will find me most altered of the lot as whiskers have taken possession of my cheeks, and I fancy I am stouter (however this may be a delusion) . . . I cannot help touting for matrimony it is such a healthy, manly, and right kind of life—After all a man by himself plays but half his part in the World, and is absolutely ignorant of much which he should know. I cannot enumerate the advantages now—*Man was not intended to live alone.* . . . I know that Halliday with the slightest encouragement will leave you for *Jemima*, which would put you out just now after your great arrangement to live a while together. Marriage is the best cure for that wretched *lingering* over one's work, which seldom betters it, and racks the brains and makes miserable. I think I must feel more settled than you all. I would immensely like to see you all *married* like myself and anchored, you will have got the restless liking for travel now and we shall never be safe from hearing of your starting off again, only that this time I will not help you to get away.'

In another letter written shortly afterwards:

'How delighted old Stephens must be at your return, surely you will never be so heartless as to leave him behind again? . . . I should like to hear of your settling down in Martin's old house if it was only to ensure your remaining in London— then, if ever you wanted to marry there would be house and *nursery* room—and Halliday would pack and do the like, and we would then have a pleasant society, if our wives wouldn't quarrel—still harping on wed-lock. You will forgive, and understand this when you think how natural it is to desire a friend to take even a showerbath after you if he has never experienced such a luxury.'

It is obvious from these letters that Millais thought it inconceivable that Hunt still intended to marry Annie Miller.

Within a week or so, as arranged, the three friends, Halliday, Martineau and Hunt, all moved to 14 Claverton Street, Pimlico, round the corner from Stephens.

Gabriel said that the house was 'very nice except for its dismal situation'; but for the time being it suited Hunt very well as it was only a penny steamer away from Annie, who still lived in the yard between Justice Walk and the Cross Keys.

According to Violet Hunt, the Mad was:

'still besotted on Annie. Halliday and Martineau . . . found him a thorough nuisance. She would call in, "looking more syren-like" to ask about something or other, saying she couldn't stay, just when they were sitting down to dinner, and Hunt would jump up and keep them waiting while he put her on a boat to go home to Chelsea. . . .'

Hunt set about finishing *Christ in the Temple*, hoping it would be ready for the Royal Academy May exhibition. He engaged models from a Jewish school and continued the background at the Crystal Palace Alhambra.

He had a great deal to do. His father was ill, still involved in interminable lawsuits. The work he had sent back from the East must be sold. There were engravers to see and Moxon, the printer and publisher, had commissioned him, Millais and Gabriel Rossetti, to illustrate Tennyson's poems.

The pictures were not well received. The dealers clamoured for replicas of his early work which they and the public had formerly despised.

When he visited the Combes at Oxford, his 'guardian and mentor' strongly advised him to abandon *Christ in the Temple* and to raise money quickly with ' "potboilers", so called because they keep the kitchen range alight'. Combe pointed out that Hunt's bank balance was alarmingly diminished: it would be folly to sell out his few remaining long-term investments. He should apply at once for election as a Royal Academy Associate.

Even *The Scapegoat*,[2] which had cost him so much to paint, had a mixed reception. The Belgian dealer, Ernest Gambart, was at pains to conceal his horror at and disappointment in the long-awaited picture which, mysteriously, young Hunt called *Le*

[2] Over a hundred years later, Graham Reynolds, (*Victorian Painting*, Studio Vista, London, 1966) called it 'one of the most conspicuous eyesores in nineteenth century art'.

Bouc Expiatoire. He had never heard of such a creature. Tactless and indignant, Hunt declared that this ignorance was due to typical French neglect of the Talmud and the Bible. The legend of the scapegoat—the ram in the thicket—was well-known to *all* educated English people. Gambart, seeing his pretty young English wife chatting to a friend outside the window, beckoned to them. He would like to hear their opinion of Mr Hunt's picture.

Leaning on their parasols, the two English ladies exclaimed: 'Oh, how pretty! What is it? . . . a peculiar *goat*, you can see by its ears, they droop so. . . . Are you intending to introduce the rest of the flock?'

The Royal Academy Hanging Committee thought the animal suitable to hang on the line near a handsome stag.

It was sold, when the exhibition closed, to Mr B. G. Windus, for 450 guineas. But for months, in castle or cottage, its merits and defects were the most fashionable, if acrimonious, topic of conversation.

The Times' art critic considered it an excellent portrait of Lord Stratford de Redcliffe. The same paper gave the picture an independent leader, and Lord Palmerston made it the principal subject of his speech at the Royal Academy dinner.

During this spring, Hunt met Gabriel at a private view in Charlotte Street. Lizzie Siddal had contributed what Gabriel called some stunning drawings. Hunt was full of praise, but tactlessly, remarked that had he not known they were hers, he could have taken them for Deverell's. Once more he had offended Miss Siddal. Gabriel was annoyed and retorted that they were superior to anything Deverell had ever done.

Hunt states in his memoirs: 'I did not realise any special interest Gabriel felt in Miss Siddal'. This is of course nonsense: he knew well from endless letters, not only Madox Brown's, that they were deeply involved.

Hunt and Gabriel seem to have been on good terms during 1856 apart from this one encounter, perhaps exaggerated by Hunt in retrospect. The same year Gabriel took him to dine with his friends, the Brownings—Robert and Elizabeth. Although Hunt was suffering from a severe attack of malaria he accepted. He and Gabriel were obviously still friends.

Madox Brown took an acute interest in the emotional affairs

of the original Pre-Raphaelite Brothers. This curiosity was fed with gossip, often stale and inaccurate, by his young wife, Emma.

In September of that year he wrote in his diary that the trouble between Gabriel Rossetti and Hunt had 'all blown over . . . Hunt and he seem all right again : Gabriel has forsworn flirting with Annie Miller it seems. Guggums having rebelled against it and he and Guggums seem on the best of terms'.

Presumably Madox Brown and everyone else assumed that by now Hunt knew of Annie Miller's intrigues with Gabriel, Boyce and others. They supposed that all was forgiven.

Gabriel's letter to Allingham plays down his affaire :

'My *rapports* [sic] you ask of with that "stunner" stopped some months ago after a long stay away from Chatham Place, partly from a wish to narrow the circle of flirtations, in which she had begun to figure a little; but I often find myself sighing after her, now that "roast beef, roast mutton, gooseberry tart," have faded. . . .'

It seems Annie was a good cook.

If Hunt had indeed known of Gabriel's betrayal then, the scene described by Burne-Jones that summer would be scarcely credible.

Edward Burne-Jones was then only twenty-two and like his contemporaries, William Morris and Swinburne, infatuated with Gabriel Rossetti, just as Hunt had been a few years earlier : 'One glorious day . . . at Chatham Place, there entered the greatest genius that is on earth alive, William Holman Hunt . . . a splendour of a man with a great wiry golden beard and faithful violet eyes. . . .' The pattern of Gabriel's magic carpet was simply repeating itself.

Professor Doughty's description of the occasion,[4] quoting further from Burne-Jones, serves well enough : although he refers to Hunt's 'majestic red' rather than 'wiry golden' beard : 'Perhaps Hunt, dropping in on Gabriel and finding Morris there making drawings, and Jones painting, somewhat resented their presence, regretted their [his and Gabriel's] lost intimacy; but

[4] Oswald Doughty, A *Victorian Romantic: Dante Gabriel Rossetti*, Muller, London, 1949. Second edition, Oxford University Press, London, 1960.

Gabriel sat down and played with Hunt's majestic red beard, passing his paint brush through it, and talking continuously all the evening. "Most gloriously," thought Jones, lost in adoration of the two Pre-Raphaelite stars, "such talk as I do not believe any man would talk beside him [Rossetti]." '

CHAPTER XIV

Let us see these handsome houses
Where the wealthy nobles dwell.
TENNYSON

IN 1856 Hunt's attempt to be elected an Associate of the Royal Academy once more failed. He received only one vote and was deeply hurt. He never applied again nor did he ever forget this humiliation. He had exhibited there regularly since 1845, with the exception of two years.

Worried and overworked, his health grew worse. Sir William Gull, the physician at Guy's Hospital who had succeeded in curing his fever, Dr Acland[1] at Oxford, as well as the Chelsea doctors, Sanneman and Diplock, advised him to move from damp, low-lying Pimlico to higher ground. In consequence, he and Halliday and Martineau rented Tor Villa on Campden Hill. It was because he moved to Kensington relatively far away that he wrote Stephens so many letters.

Stephens still lived conveniently near Annie Miller. He had admitted that he had 'been obliged to borrow' from the fund established for her education; but she never once complained of being in want, she was so much in demand as a model—scarcely ever at home, according to her aunt. She could read very well, write legible notes and make simple calculations. Mrs Bramah was delighted with her progress.

He, Fred, would redeem the trust he had betrayed, he would atone and 'find something which I could do to assist you and lighten the weighty pecuniary obligations I am under to yourself'. If he could be of any service in the future, Hunt had only to ask. He also wondered if Hunt thought that Millais was good for a loan of twelve pounds. 'I should not like a refusal but I know he helped Deverell once.' In fact Millais was very hard up. Hunt succeeded in selling the picture they had bought together for ninety guineas to help Deverell two years before,

---

[1] Henry Wentworth Acland, 1815-1900. Famous physician in Oxford and friend of Ruskin.

and Millais was grateful to receive his share of forty-five guineas. Ever meticulous, Hunt sent the profit of ten guineas to Deverell's more needy relations.

In May Effie gave birth to a son. Millais longed to see Hunt. He sent game and salmon that summer and wrote begging him to come up north: 'Writing is such a dreadful substitute for talking.' He was horrified to hear from Halliday and Charley Collins that Hunt was still involved with Annie Miller. He hoped to produce a suitable substitute: 'Come and stay . . . you will find us very jolly and some very lovely little girls for neighbours'. He praised Effie's expertise 'in the procuring of models . . . going into strange habitations and seizing adults and children without explanation and dragging them here, and sending them back to their homes with a *sixpence* when I should have been doubtful between a sovereign and thirty shillings.'

Being a loyal friend, he cited Wilkie Collins's situation to warn Hunt of such undesirable relationships:

'I had a long letter from Wilkie Collins the other day in answer to some advice I ventured to give him respecting a certain lady in his possession . . . I see *nothing* to prevent him from getting rid of this disreputable kind of secret connection, and finding a wife, except that his taste is so *unhealthy*. . . . I think that you would have now the most influence over him—I am married and am inclined to think from his manner . . . that he imagines I have in consequence a little degenerated . . . why should this stupid fellow go and tie himself to such a woman? You must clearly see the folly of such a *liason* [sic] . . . ?'

Anything Hunt could say in defence of such dastardly and foolish conduct would be 'all bosh!'

Bosh or not, Hunt was too busy to get away and uninterested in sixpenny models and little Scottish stunners. He was still in love with Annie Miller.

Nevertheless, however infatuated he was during that spring and summer, he seemed in no hurry to marry her. He was not unaware of the implication in Millais' letters and she had not made the progress with her education for which he had hoped. She still had 'objectionable habits'. Perhaps she was more relaxed in a studio atmosphere with him and her old painter friends than she was in a more aristocratic milieu, or with Mrs Bramah.

Anyhow, she still had much to learn. In the meantime, he too had a great deal to do.

That winter the news came from Cairo of Thomas Seddon's death. Hunt's father also died. Hunt promised him, on his death-bed, to take care of Emily and to resume teaching her to paint. Evidently, old Mr Hunt had become disillusioned with 'sober business'. He left very little money, but his widow's rich brother, William Hobman, contributed to her keep. Much to Annie's dismay, Emily moved her easel into Tor Villa.

Annie had well understood how busy Hunt was, but now she became anxious about the future. After all he had proposed to her in a letter from Syria over a year ago. Her aunt Bess, her father and her sister, not to mention Mrs Bramah, Lord Ranelagh and all her other admirers, kept asking if she were engaged to Hunt or not?

Until she had a wedding ring on her finger, she dared not risk losing the other strings to her bow. Hunt was often away paint-ing portraits or backgrounds, and in the evening she must amuse herself.

During the first week of December, she decided to have it out with Hunt. When would they be getting married? Why wait?

He was prepared, and replied that her education was not complete. *The Times* of those days was full of advertisements of academies for young ladies. He would be pleased to pay the fees, on her behalf, of some such reputable establishment. The pupils lived in, attended lectures, visited museums, studied the history of art . . .

Furious, she refused.

Characteristically, Hunt stood his ground. It was his last word: she should think it over. Within a week he must hear a straight answer. He was off to the country now. If she disliked the effort of writing a letter, she could tell Fred her decision. He, Hunt, had many other things to think about. She and Fred could talk it over.

Before leaving to paint at Upper Norwood, he called on Stephens to apprise him of the situation. No doubt Annie would visit him in a day or two. She knew various other artists in

Pimlico such as Moody. Fred was not to commit Hunt to matrimony, only persuade her to take this first step towards the altar by going to school.

All the same, when no answer came he was much concerned and wrote Stephens an undated letter (probably on December 5) from Sydenham:

'I am anxious to hear whether the young lady came yesterday and if so what her determination is. She must indeed be most uncomplimentarily indifferent about a certain individual's interest, or must be a heroine in self-denial in stopping away from him—more so than the hero if his present foolish wish were weighed—conceived at the side of a melancholy grate in a room in whose dismal solitude there is no thought of life but in a flat whispering from a back room. To be at all anxious about her decision is very stupid—whether "yes" or "no" I am convinced that it will be fruitless to persevere but I will go on for years against all conviction rather than be the first to give up the attempt—which might have such a happy issue if she would determine to give up a wretched false pride, and a fatal indolence.'

On Friday, December 9, Stephens replied:

'Miss A.M. came to me on Sunday and I represented the case to her; of course only as relative to her own worldly advantage, not being at liberty to enlarge upon your own feeling in the matter. I represented you a most anxious and sincere friend who was desirous of benefitting her so that she might be able to obtain a happier position from her own exertions. All this she treated as a thing which was of no importance, and of little interest to either you or myself.

'I offered my own services (making neither of us ostentatious in doing so) because she seemed to have a pique with *you*, and no one would be more willing to aid her than myself. I know of course that you would sanction and assist in this, if her pride would not allow her [to receive] assistance *directly* from you. The reply from A.M. was as before she "did not care". I even argued *moderately* your claim to her gratitude for what was already done and your goodwill—to no effect.

'However knowing the beneficial effect a cup of tea has upon the female mind, I got her to stop for this, and afterwards renewed the attack, she then promised to write to me on Wednesday as to her determination, and if she could think of anything in which either of us could forward her views. I presume she will do this, or call, and I will let you know the result.

'Do not imagine that I made your desire to serve her in a manner which could pain or insult her in anyway—it was not the case I assure you. If she had been my own sister I should not have been half so delicate with her.

'I confess that, although I did not show it, I was immensely disgusted with the hardness she exhibited. It pains me to say it, but I really cannot think for a moment that she has any regard for you, beyond what has hitherto flattered her vanity. You will know of course that I could not allude to any feeling of yours beyond a hope of serving her.

'Your note makes me uneasy about you; it is useless, I am sure to warn you against the utter hopelessness of your entering into a more serious engagement with her unless she shows some sort of stability of character. There cannot be the slightest prospect of happiness or even a *peaceful house* with such a person who will not control herself in any way. She said that she did not care about painting and never did, and had told you so long ago.

'You will have cleared yourself of all responsibility by your efforts to serve her, and are bound to consult your own happiness and duty *as well as hers* by breaking off with her at once in case she persists in refusing your offers. You cannot of course hold yourself out to her as a prize for exertion on her part, and I cannot see any other way of guiding her even if this sufficed which I do not think it would.

'Should I hear from her tomorrow I will either write or *if possible*, walk over tomorrow in the evening and let you know what she says, for I should like to talk to you on the subject and even more fully about what occurs than I can write it.

'I trust she may come to her senses tomorrow, but am compelled to think that her feelings are so shallow that she will never feel deeply enough to be worthy of the position in which you wish to place her. I told her that you would always be her friend in any case but that you hoped she would exert herself.

'I even *entreated* her to consider the chance she was throwing away for her own happiness here and the duty she owed to others and her family etc., this she almost laughed at. I entered upon higher grounds, but that was clearly incomprehensible to her.

'I spoke of myself, and how much I regretted the opportunities I had thrown away. In short I pleaded with her against herself, to little purpose that I could see.

'She was piqued against you it is clear, but would state no grounds for it but what you had said of the folly of her continuing to waste her Time as hitherto. In fact, I *fancy* she expected the golden apple was going to drop into her mouth and that you would marry her without further trouble or interest on her part, this for you to consider if you do this on account of your own feelings, unless you are bound to her I sincerely hope you *will not* [anticipate] great change on her part.'

This letter upset Hunt so much that he found himself quite unable to paint. He knew that Stephens must think him a fool to persist, and thought he might succeed in persuading Annie to go to a finishing school if he took the line that his interest was purely altruistic. He replied on December 10 by return of post:

'Of course I expected to hear what you said—perfect indifference on her part either in refusing or accepting an offer of assistance.

'I wonder what particular sin of mine it was that brought me into contact with such a girl. That wretched indifference is the most hopeless of all states. Her final answer will be the same so that either yes! or no! would be of equal worth. When I spoke to her last week and induced her to break silence by about five minutes assurance of unlimited—unended interest in her good she said first "I wish I were dead!"

'I am afraid that she does this at every fresh annoyance— she must either have life without the control of one vanity, or would not have it at all.

'On Monday after writing to you I wrote her a long letter —you will not mind this interference with your deputyship when I say that the letter was exactly in the same strain as the advice tendered by you. I asked her to answer—yet there is scarcely time.

'I give up all profession of personal love as a bribe to her success and between you and me I no more entertain the idea as I once did of declaring such as the ground of my exertions in her behalf. I merely said that I was determined that my hope of placing in an independent and honourable position should not fail through want of reasonable patience on my part. There is nothing else you need be bothered with tonight except a request to let me know at once if she communicates with you. This is not far from Little Norwood to where the omnibuses come—and nearer still to the Sydenham Station— so you could easily come.'

Stephens approved of Hunt taking this new tack. At least it did not commit him to marriage. He wrote at once:

'I am delighted that your resolution is as stated. I am sure this is the best. I have had neither written or spoken word from A.M. and this is late Thursday evening.'
He added a P.S.,
'The enclosure has this instant come.'

Annie's note has not survived. She probably made excuses for the delay, was not sure what her aunt would feel about being left alone, and so on.

Hunt was utterly distracted and totally unable to concentrate on his chosen background for *Christ in the Temple*, the Crystal Palace Alhambra. He came up to London again just for the day and wrote on his return that night from the Langton Hotel, Sydenham:

'I did not find Annie at home on Sunday, but found her Aunt who seemed a reasonable woman, and professed great interest in the hope to educate her niece. She told me that Annie had been fretting very much but seemed ready to do anything that I should recommend.

'I enclose you a note sent since, if written by Annie, which it is not, I should regard it as highly hopeful—her desire to be merely a *day* pupil may remove the difficulty you apprehend to find on Sunday.'

As the note was not in Annie's hand, and her aunt was illiterate, it was probably written by Hughes, the impoverished clerk, who lived with the laundress and the chimney-sweeps.

At any rate, everyone seemed to agree that Annie should accept Hunt's offer of further education. If she went to school during the day only, she would be free to amuse herself during the evenings. Lord Ranelagh and his friends were after all unlikely to offer marriage. Annie undoubtedly was afraid of what might lie ahead if she slipped back: whores hung about the dark yard behind the Cross Keys, but not too near the lamp because they had lost their teeth. It was not only for vanity's sake that women endured agonising toothache: the loss of front teeth prevented them from earning a living. In the last resort Childs, the Chelsea barber, wrenched the stumps from their jaws with an old pair of pliers.

Reading of the hectic social life Hunt enjoyed without her, it is no surprise that Annie continued to consort with Lord Ranelagh and others at night. Hunt's memoirs are full of references to 'sumptuous smoking parties'.[2]

On Campden Hill, in Kensington, his neighbours were very grand: the Hollands, the Butes, the Argylls, the Airlies, Lord Macaulay, the Leslies.

Woolner had always been a social success. Still bachelors, Hunt and he were inundated with invitations from the lion-hunters and the great. Lord and Lady Holland had virtually, not virtuously, adopted Watts whilst he was in Italy.

Now they leased Little Holland House to a Mrs Prinsep, an ambitious and gifted hostess. Determined to found a salon, she succeeded brilliantly.

When Watts returned to London thinking 'very seriously of

[2] One famous host, Arthur Lewis, moved to nearby Moray Lodge. Hunt referred to his parties as 'Bohemian', as they included such varied guests as 'Mr Poole the tailor, and Mr Tattersall the horse-dealer, together with Thackeray, Trollope, Yates, Millais, Leighton, Leech, Halliday and du Maurier to quote just a few.'

Prussic acid!' she gave him a studio in Little Holland House and looked after him like a possessive, protective elder sister. His presence was just what she needed. Her parties became 'the rage'. Hunt wrote in his memoirs:

'Aristocrats there were of ministerial dignity, and generals fresh from flood and field appearing in unpretending habit, talking with the modesty of real genius adding an interest to life which nothing else could give. . . tea was served under shady elms, bowls and croquet were played on the lawn at hand, and on summer evenings the dinner tables were brought out for the welcome guests who lingered late. . . . Children romped over the lawn, diverted from their play when a certain peer came in followed by a string of twelve French poodles, his own hair curled to match their fantastic coiffure.'

Hunt wondered if she and other hostesses would be reluctant, or even refuse, to receive Annie as his wife? What would the lovely Lady Constance Leslie think of such a marriage?

Annie must persevere if she were to be acceptable in such company. In England, painters had been accepted at court for hundreds of years—but not *models*, the very word was synonymous with. . . .[3] Although Effie had never been a professional model, just because she had sat for Millais, a friend of old Mr Ruskin's had declared 'that the woman who was made an Academy Model could not be a virtuous woman'.

Hunt and Millais introduced Gabriel Rossetti to Mrs Prinsep. For a while the house and its atmosphere enchanted him. He had always been a collector. It was through him that Hunt developed such a passion for oriental pottery and domestic utensils, with a prejudice against European fashionable china. Mr Gladstone was quite put out when Hunt criticised his precious Sèvres, although interested to hear his views.

When Hunt moved into Tor Villa, he began what was to become an important collection of furniture and *objets d'art*. His first acquisition was a large Regency sideboard presented by Augustus Egg in appreciation of a past favour. It came from Kensington Palace and is now at Old Battersea House. My

[3] When Watts eventually married the pretty young actress Ellen Terry, Mrs Prinsep's behaviour towards her was odious.

181

grandmother often made me polish it; she draped its legs with a curtain. Reference books were kept beneath, in which I searched for the Facts of Life, in vain.

The first important piece of furniture that Hunt bought was an ivory cabinet, which became my christening present. It is now in the Victoria and Albert Museum.

Hunt next picked up an old chair which he carved with his initials and scrolls. Soon afterwards, he designed some chairs based on an Egyptian stool at the British Museum. These were so much admired that Madox Brown designed a table to go with them and gave it to Hunt. Thus the craze began, which led to 'the firm' started by William Morris.

In 1857, the expense of furnishing his and Emily's rooms at Tor Villa, sending Annie to school, and dressing in Savile Row, was a strain. He was obliged to continue painting portraits and 'pot-boilers' and to accept ill-paid jobs, illustrating second-rate magazines and newspapers.

Christ in the Temple had been face to the wall for a year.

Word soon got round amongst important patrons and collectors that Hunt had failed to become an Associate of the Royal Academy and they were reluctant now to invest in his work.

During the past few months, the project of founding an artists' colony had often been discussed by old and new Pre-Raphaelite friends—a group of separate studios 'with a common room and a general dining-room', and perhaps two servants living in— there was sure to be a basement suitable for them. The members need only contribute two pounds a year each for the wages and keep of a cook and maid.

Millais and Effie wanted a London *pied-à-terre* with Hunt: Martineau, Halliday and Charley Collins might be included. They would all get on famously; although, of course, he hoped that 'all of them would soon be *happily married*'. This scheme did not include Gabriel Rossetti and *his* new friends.

Hunt liked Millais' idea, but they both wondered if 'the lady members might not exercise themselves in getting up quarrels?'

For once optimistic, Madox Brown pronounced himself confident 'that no such calamity need be feared . . . with ordinary women such might be the case, but our sisters and wives would be truly superior. . . .'

Gabriel was enthusiastic. *His* plan did not include Millais: as well as the Mad, Burne-Jones and his lovely Georgie[4] and William Morris must all join in. What fun they would have!

Had he and Hunt, as has been suggested, been on bad terms already, he would hardly have proposed this, especially if he had thought there was the least chance of Hunt producing the controversial Annie. So far the whole idea was very vague, but Burne-Jones agreed that Tudor House in Chelsea might prove suitable although the accommodation was somewhat limited. Hunt, being older than the rest, should have first choice. No one seemed to know if he would move in alone, or with his sister. Of late, the Mad had kept very quiet about his private life. Rumour had it that everything was over between him and Annie.

When Gabriel spoke casually of the plan to Lizzie, she seemed quite keen. Perhaps at last she would be married.

However, as soon as she heard that Hunt was to be included, she flew into 'one of her terrible white rages'. According to Madox Brown's diary and other accounts, in her strident voice, she screamed objections and reproaches. Hunt never ceased trying to make a fool of her! Due to Allingham's sister and Emma Brown, Lizzie's information was up to date. Hunt and that detestable Annie Miller were again as thick as thieves, in spite of all the trouble she had made. He would be sure to bring her with him. Poor Guggums went home sobbing.

Although accustomed to her scenes, Gabriel was amazed at the violence of her feelings, and wrote to Madox Brown on 26 February 1857:

'She now says that she . . . would strongly object to the idea of living where Hunt was, of which objection of hers I had no idea to any such extent. . . . However, my wishes as to this scheme would entirely depend on hers, supposing that it would really affect her happiness; in which case I should cease to care for it or think of it.'

It is clear from his letters to Stephens that Hunt demanded an explanation from Annie. What *had* gone on, while he was away, between her and Gabriel, his trusted friend? Without mentioning any of her other lovers, she admitted that perhaps she and

[4] Georgina Macdonald married Burne-Jones in 1860.

183

Gabriel had been indiscreet. They had met by accident in George Boyce's studio. Stephens was short of tin and she had needed work. It was all Gabriel's fault: she was lonely and missing Hunt: Gabriel had swept her off her feet. . .

I think that at this stage Hunt, trembling with jealousy but controlled, pointed out that her conduct was not only dishonourable but extremely *risky*, she might have become pregnant. It was then that she probably made a fatal mistake by saying that 'procuring abortions'[5] was an everyday amusement for Gabriel Rossetti.

She had said enough to ruin Hunt's nine-year friendship with Gabriel. William Rossetti refers to this sad end, in his biography of Gabriel:[6]

'I understand perfectly well what it is that Mr Hunt terms "the offence" . . . but if my reader chooses to ask the old question, "Who was the woman?" he will . . . chance to remain for ever unanswered. . . . It behoves me to say that Mr Hunt was wholly blameless in the matter; not so my brother, who was properly, though I will not say very deeply, censurable.'

Violet Hunt adds to this that:

'Grant Allen saw "the makings of a novel in the whole affair", but never wrote it. Annie Miller is the one Pre-Raphaelite heroine who has, perhaps out of consideration for those two great men, been "kept dark" . . . tho' in the 60s and 70s her name was on every tongue.'

Hunt headed this chapter of his life in his memoirs, 1856, with the quotation: 'It is said that Jealousy is Love, but I deny it; for though Jealousy be procured by Love, as Ashes are by Fire, yet Jealousy extinguishes Love as Ashes smother the Flame. (La Reine de Navarre)'

In time Hunt and Annie were reconciled. A scapegoat had been found. They were happier together during the following

[5] See page 286.
[6] William M. Rossetti, *Dante Gabriel Rossetti: His Family Letters with a Memoir*, Ellis, London, 1895.

summer than they had been since his return from Syria.

They agreed that one day she would move from her room in Cross Keys Yard to respectable lodgings. She need not go to school any more. He would pay for a governess, a duenna, to live in the same house. In this way Annie could continue her education at home so to speak. She would go on sitting to him, but could earn pin money from a few reliable friends: Augustus Egg, Millais and those splendid fellows Martineau and Halliday who already lived at Tor Villa, and of course she could pose for Emily and her class of girls.

Emily was terrified that her brother would be 'caught'. In mixed company she never painted from the nude. If she met Annie on the stairs she ignored her. Emily complained to her mother that Hunt rarely entertained or took her out to parties. After all, he was famous now and she would like to go to Little Holland House.

Although Emily was so pretty and talented Martineau and Halliday must have found her presence at Tor Villa oppressive. They were thankful when she took herself off to paint backgrounds at Ewell and visit her uncle Hobman.

CHAPTER XV

And round his heart one strangling golden hair.
D. G. ROSSETTI

IN THE summer of 1857, when Hunt visited the Combes, he found that Gabriel Rossetti had taken Oxford and the University by storm. He, Millais and Charley Collins deeply resented this.

Ruskin had transferred his patronage to Gabriel and his admiring circle, but avoided Hunt knowing that he and Millais were still intimate friends. John Woodforde, the architect, was impressed by Gabriel Rossetti's talent and originality. It was largely through him that Rossetti and William Morris were commissioned to decorate the Union Club, in any manner they wished. Rossetti determined on frescoes.

Ten painters assisted: Burne-Jones, Arthur Hughes and others including young Val Prinsep, who forsook Little Holland House until he was dragged back at his mother's request and with Ruskin's help from the 'undesirable influence of Rossetti'.

Undergraduates, notably Swinburne, aged twenty, joined in and climbed the scaffolding with paint and brushes; each contributing their bit, squirting each other with soda-water and dropping paint all over the place. Wombats and caricatures appeared at random between marigolds and knights in armour.

Madox Brown, penniless as usual, was horrified at this squandering of tin. When Gabriel 'from the top of a ladder upset a potful of priceless lapis-lazuli, ground into real ultramarine, he merely remarked: "Oh, that's nothing—we often do that".'

Respectable members of the University, on entering the building to see how the work was progressing, were aghast at the chaos, ribald jokes and roars of laughter.

Hunt and Millais exchanged disapproving letters. Ruskin was largely to blame, according to Millais:

'I can scarcely trust myself to speak. Ruskin who certainly
186

appears to me (now that I know *all* about his treatment of my wife) to be the most wicked man I have known in my life. This I say without hesitation and methodically.'

Hunt and Millais were both jealous and bewildered by Gabriel's success and resented rather than rejoiced at the fresh green shoot which sprouted from the half-dead root that they had originally planted. Contemporary diaries and letters show no evidence that Gabriel Rossetti claimed to be the true founder of Pre-Raphaelitism. This presumption is only alleged in Hunt's memoirs, written (in retrospect) nearly fifty years later.

Mr and Mrs Combe felt intense sympathy for Hunt during this trying summer. Combe lent him £300 to finish the long-abandoned *Christ in the Temple*. The time for pot-boiling was over.

Hearing what was going on at Oxford, Annie played truant. Gabriel had picked a new stunner, Jane Burden, the daughter of an Oxford groom, spotted in church and obligingly introduced after Matins by Combe.

Annie wanted to join in the parties on the river or at the theatre. She went down to join in the fun, pleading illness as an excuse for being away from school.

John Hughes, the scrivener, wrote a letter to Hunt for Annie's aunt Bess stating that her niece had been unable to pose at Tor Villa for the last two days because she was 'ill'.

Stephens was at once dispatched to take her to consult Tom Diplock, or Dr Sanneman, his senior partner, who had seen Annie as a child roaming the Chelsea streets barefoot.

According to the aunt's dictated letter, Dr Sanneman had a poor opinion of Annie's health. She might even be consumptive.

Hunt was much concerned, and although Stephens offered to take her to a specialist, Dr Eliotson, Hunt actually found the time to take her himself. He reported to Stephens: 'I am happy to say that Dr Eliotson gave a very favourable verdict . . . her lungs are weak but not diseased—the letter which he wrote she took home with her to give to Mr Sanneman'.

About the same time, he wrote a grateful undated letter to the Combes expressing his delight at being able to resume *Christ in the Temple*, adding:

'Millais is the only happy man of our party seeing that he had some relief from the toil of painting in a wife and child. I shall come next to consult you seriously upon the subject of matrimony and decide one way or the other for good—beg Mrs Combe not to be alarmed at this notion. I have not committed myself. . . . Some of the portraits of all times are so lovely as to send me quite crazy—I am hopelessly in love with several ladies painted by different painters down to Gainsborough and Reynolds.'

The latter's paintings of women inclined him to 'vow that I will have no other and so escape living Syrens, and die an old bachelor'.

In the autumn of 1857, Stephens succeeded in finding what he and Hunt thought a respectable boarding house for Annie near Lupus Street, Pimlico—11 Bridge Row.[1]

The landlady was a Mrs Stratford whose husband was a minor civil servant, an Inland Revenue messenger. (One of Hunt's Hobman aunts married a Stratford, but investigation shows no connection between them.)

This particular place was probably recommended by Mrs Bradshaw, Hunt's former landlady, who still kept the stationer's shop in Chelsea. Miss Bradshaw, her governess daughter who had first taught Annie her ABC, had a friend who lodged at Mrs Stratford's—Miss Prout, a retired schoolmistress. Thinking that Fred had for once produced the perfect answer, Hunt took the best room in the house for Annie. Miss Prout was engaged to give her regular lessons for a modest fee.

This arrangement was not entirely to Annie's taste. However, if she spent the night with Lord Ranelagh at New Burlington Street, she could always say she had stayed with her sister, Harriet, in Kensington, or with her aunt in Chelsea. The free board and lodging were preferable to the warren behind the Cross Keys. Both her aunt and sister had to be sweetened with a sovereign or two now and then. She had lately introduced her father to the Pimlico artist, Francis Moody, who painted him in Royal Hospital Garden, against a background of children and flowerbeds.

[1] Demolished in 1868. This site now forms part of Buckingham Palace Road.

When Annie entertained her lovers at home both Mrs Stratford and Miss Prout were at first prepared to turn a blind eye in return for the gentlemen's tips. These bribes, added to what Hunt was paying them for his protégée, made Annie a welcome guest for a time. Neither Hunt nor Stephens suspected that she was making a fool of them.

On 21 January 1858, Hunt and his friend and pupil Martineau visited George Boyce, who recorded in his diary:

'Hunt and Martineau called. Hunt introduces theory in prospect to *marry* Annie Miller, and after that her education both of mind and manners shall have been completed, how instead to destroy as far as was possible all traces of her former occupation, viz. that of sitting to certain artists (those artists however, being all his personal friends, Rossetti, A. Hughes, Stephens, Egg, Holliday [Halliday?], Millais, Collins and myself and as mine was the only direct study of her head, as it was, he would hold it a favour if I would give it to him and he in return would give me something of his doing that I might like. At first I resisted stoutly, but finding that it was a serious point with him, and that my refusing would be in some degree an obstacle in the carrying out of his wishes with regard to her (which it would be both selfish and unkind and foolish in the remotest degree to thwart) I at last reluctantly assented to give him the study, the most careful and the most interesting (to me) and which I prize the most I have ever made. He thanked me heartily for my compliance. He gave me real pleasure to telling me that she says I always behaved most kindly to her.'

Hunt spent the next two months preparing his family and more conventional friends for his imminent marriage to a mysterious lady.

CHAPTER XVI

Whose speech Truth knows not from her thought
Nor Love her body from her soul.

D. G. ROSSETTI

ONE MORNING a few weeks later, Hunt suffered a terrible shock from two letters which arrived by the same mail. My grandmother left me her written explanation of this 'thunderbolt':

'Emily, Holman's sister, wrote him a furious letter saying "*Everyone* knows your character now. Uncle Hobman has read in *Household Words* the DISGRACEFUL story about you and your model, who is called the Calmuck in the article. . . ." Wilkie Collins also wrote describing the article as "an abominable libel", urging Holman to write at once to [Charles] Dickens.'[1]

Hunt rushed out to buy the current issue dated 3 April 1858.

With mounting horror, he read the story entitled *Calmuck*, a thinly disguised satirical account of his affaire with Emma Watkins, the fieldgirl whom he had picked up at Ewell, and painted as the shepherdess in *The Hireling Shepherd* six years before.

His name had been changed from Holman Hunt to Mildmay Strong, a hard-working and dedicated artist, 'one of a turbulent and firebrand race of young painters', who would travel thousands of miles in search of accurate backgrounds, local colour and authentic props. Had Mildmay Strong wished to illustrate an arctic expedition, 'his address would be Number One, the North Pole'.

His devoted followers had no time to do any painting themselves, being obliged to pose in tortuous positions as his unpaid models, until drenched to the skin or stiff and numb with fatigue.

---

[1] Dickens was both owner and editor of the periodical.

He would sit up all night painting and begin working again at dawn.

After painting the background for *As You Like It* near Sevenoaks, Mildmay Strong succeeded in finding a suitably repulsive-looking girl to sit as that unattractive Shakespearean character, Audrey, the country wench.

He installed himself and her in a cold and miserable attic, where he was discovered by his followers. They nicknamed his companion the Calmuck: her features 'bore some resemblance to the Tartar-type'.

After a while, the wretched creature, wishing to escape the rigid and punishing tasks imposed by Mildmay Strong, announced that she was already married to a violent-tempered, jealous sailor: he was expected back from the sea any day now and if he tracked her down . . .

Strong's disciples, irreverent now, were delighted to anticipate the melodrama. They banged on the attic door with their sticks, shouting threats, 'counterfeiting rough weather-beaten voices'.

Throughout these disturbances Mildmay Strong calmly continued to paint and not until he had done with her did he send the Calmuck home in disgust.

When mocked and accused of cowardice by the rebellious students, he declared that he could not risk injuring his hands until he had completed a new composition for an Eastern subject. If he were to hit the maddened sailor 'a straightforward right-hander in the face, I might dislocate the meta-carpo-phalangeal articulations of the fingers and not be able to hold a brush for months'.

Everyone knew that Hunt was a keen amateur boxer.

Furiously indignant at this caricature of himself, he sat down and drafted several letters to Dickens. One of these I found with my grandmother's notes, together with one empty grey silurian envelope in Dickens' hand.[2] I sold Hunt's draft and have been unable to trace it. Dickens replied:

[2] When I was a girl and my grandmother had been run over by a truck and was dying at St Mary Abbott's Hospital, apart from a grief-stricken servant, I was alone in the house. Every day my terrifying aunt, who was 6'1" in her stockings, appeared and removed taxi-loads of portfolios and papers. Dickens' letters to Hunt survived, thanks to her adopted daughter, Mrs Elizabeth Burt, who has kindly allowed me to quote them together with such papers of mine which still exist.

Tavistock House, Tuesday April 13th 1858

'My dear Sir, I am pained and shocked by the receipt of your letter, referring to a story called "Calmuck" lately published in *Household Words*, and which has been *a very long time in type there, unused*. [The italics are mine.]

'When you use the words "the extremely objectionable nature" of that article, I am quite sure you use them in reference to your own knowledge of some allusions in it, and not to mine. If I could have had any reason for deeming it objectionable, I need not say (I hope) that you would never have found it in print under my auspices.

'I have too great an interest in, and too high a respect for, your calling and yourself, to be otherwise than anxious to understand your cause of complaint, and to remove it, if I can, in the frankest and fullest manner. If it should suit your convenience to call upon me here on Friday at half past twelve, I have not the slightest fear of our going wrong, because I have a perfect faith in our both equally desiring to do right.'

Dickens was certainly feigning innocence. Perhaps hearing that Robert Brough (who wrote the story) and his family were in desperate financial need, he exhumed this contribution which had lain on a shelf for years unused, and published it without paying enough attention to its contents; for it was obvious to everyone that it was Hunt, famous now, who was ridiculed—to make matters worse the story ended with the words 'it is thoroughly true'.

Hunt was by no means satisfied with the interview. He was bombarded with abusive letters from disillusioned admirers. But his greatest fear seems to have been that his old enemy, Dr Gobat, the Bishop of Jerusalem, should come across it, identify him with the disreputable character, and use this as a weapon to prevent his return to Syria.

When Hunt defended himself before his family and others, they advised that if indeed the story was an infamous libel, then he should insist on the withdrawal of all copies, and demand an apology in the next issue.

He wrote to Dickens again, and received the following answer on Tuesday, April 20:

'I feel it to be useless to express my astonishment that you and your friends can possibly conceive the Bishop of Jerusalem to be, by any remote contingency, between the centre of the earth and the centre of the sun, in any danger of associating you as a responsible and individual gentleman, with the hero of this story. I believe with much confidence, however, that he could never have come to *be* the Bishop of Jerusalem, if he were in the least hazard of so committing himself.

'My judgment is unchanged. It is altogether against the insertion of a contradiction. I have not a doubt that it would suggest to the public what they have not the faintest idea of, and that its effect would be exactly the reverse of your desire.

'But as it is quite out of the question that the text of the article can be altered in future copies (for it is printed and stereotyped and done with), I must ask you to decide whether there shall be a contradiction or no. If yes, I will care to make it complete and plain.'

My grandmother's explanation of the affair continued:

'Dickens offered to put in an apology but advised from his experience that any attempt to refute a slander only gave it dimensions, and to let sleeping dogs lie. Therefore Hunt asked Dickens to write another letter which he could show to his family, repeating his, Dickens', dismay even more *forcibly* to reassure them that the article was fiction.'

Dickens complied with this request and wrote again April 30:

'With the sincerest desire to do what is right, and what is best calculated to remove any disagreeable association that anybody may have made between you and that preposterous story of Calmuck, I have considered and reconsidered the question of inserting an explanation in Household Words to the effect that you have no more to do with it than I have. But I am quite sure and certain that such a proceeding (however carefully your name might be detached from it) would defeat its own object, and would instantly set all sorts and conditions of people speculating on who the artist may be who is not to be connected with it ! ! And thus, the very association, however ridiculous and baseless, which we wish to avoid, would be got into numbers of heads which are as innocent of it as my own was, when you first wrote to me. As I have already told you, I never liked the story, and it has been lying at the office, unused, a long time. I am sorry now, that I did not strike out of it the pretence that it is true. But that is so common a pretence, that it really did not attract my attention or make any impression on me. I assure you that I had no idea there was such a statement in the paper, until I looked for it expressly.

'It seems such a superfluous proceeding to tell you, "I know it is *not* true," that I really hesitate to write what I should suppose all reasonable human creatures must already be convinced of. But I do it nevertheless. Rest satisfied, I beg, that I accepted the story, with much doubt, as a very weak fiction— that it *is* a very weak fiction, and nothing else—that if I could have contemplated the possibility that anybody (not to say you but anybody) could be absurdly and wrongfully associated with it in the least particular, nothing would have induced me to print it—and that I am heartily sorry I ever did print it, seeing that it is an arrow, with anything but a sharp point, shot vaguely over a house-top, and glancing off, in a manner wholly unaccountable to and unforeseen by me, against a brother-artist.'

Mrs Bradshaw must have been indignant at the uncomplimentary description of her lodgings. She and Emma Watkins, the original 'coptic', had remained friendly and after Emma's marriage, the girl came to stay now and then, when her husband was at sea.

This scandal was bad enough, but there was even more trouble to come.

Every month Hunt supplied Stephens with money so that Annie could pay the Stratfords and Miss Prout. But Annie spent it on fripperies instead of settling their accounts.

Annie must have resented the satire in *Household Words*. Most people she came across were aware that the *Calmuck* was out of date and referred to Hunt's previous model, Emma; but Annie was known as his model now and had been for years. She surely complained to Hunt that the story had done her no good and that she feared that the less-informed readers of *Household Words* would identify her with that 'ugly girl'. She would not of course have added that even Lord Ranelagh teased her now and was not as generous as before. Nor did she explain or excuse her financial embarrassment to Hunt. She went to work, but even so failed to earn enough. By the beginning of June 1858 she still owed Mrs Stratford a tidy sum, and the latter threatened to write to Mr Hunt unless she paid up.

After a row, Mrs Stratford called Annie's bluff, and went round to the police station in Rochester Row. The inspector there was a friend of her husband's. When the 'peeler' called at the boarding-house and asked for her, Annie told him that Mr Stephens managed her affairs. He lived close by at 96 Lupus Street. When the sergeant knocked on his door, Stephens was aghast, and accompanied him back to Rochester Row, where he gave Hunt's name as Miss Miller's protector. The same night he wrote an urgent note to Hunt warning him to expect a visit from the Superintendent.

Hunt wrote back but without due concern, 'The Peeler has not been. I want to write to the Inspector to ask what day I may expect him as I am going out of town. What is the Inspector's name and address?'[3] He invited Stephens to dine on Sunday night, by which time he would have returned to Tor Villa. Then they could talk the matter over.

Mrs Stratford and Miss Prout were not only dissatisfied with the delay in settling their accounts, but also disgruntled by the casual reaction of all concerned.

On June 18 they took a penny steamer to call on their friends the Bradshaws, at the Chelsea stationery shop. After all, it was they who had recommended Miss Miller as a respectable lodger.

Egged on by Mrs Bradshaw, fortified and self-righteous, Mrs Stratford marched round to Lindsey Row the same afternoon, and was admitted by the footman to the august presence of Mrs Bramah.

Mrs Stratford enjoyed telling tales.

As soon as she had finished, Mrs Bramah rang the bell to have

---

[3] I can find no trace of Annie Miller having been indicted for any crime between 1858 to 1859. The records have been searched at the General Middlesex Records Office.

this unwelcome caller shown out, and at the same time ordered her brougham and drove round to Sidney Street to see her nephew.

Tom Diplock, whose young wife had just had a son, was most anxious to placate his rich indulgent aunt, whose heir he was. He left the house at once in search of Stephens. It was all Fred's fault.

Stephens was just leaving to keep his appointment with Hunt at Tor Villa. Realising from Diplock's agitation that something was seriously wrong he went home with Tom to meet his aunt.

The same night, June 18, Stephens wrote to Hunt:

'I am sorry I did not see you this evening but I had gone to meet Mrs Bramah at Diplock's—when we were out of [each] other's hearing she introduced the subject of Mrs Stratford's confessions of the deceit practised upon all; saying that this confession was voluntary.

'Mrs Bramah said she herself was much shocked. It appears so much so that she then put the "question", to which Mrs S[tratford] replied satisfactorily. Mrs Bramah remarked that if she had known (or rather believed—for it seems her servants told her as much long ago, when she refused to hear or believe it) of such sustained duplicity on A[nnie] M[iller]'s part she could never have interested herself about her,—and putting it to me I could not but admit I would never have asked her assistance. . . .

'She seemed to be more than ever convinced that you were interested in a more serious way than she is aware (from either of us) and said A.M. understood so. On my question in what manner this was meant, she replied, "she says so herself."

'I dared not probe this part of the matter deeper less [sic] she [Mrs Bramah] should put a direct question to me, for really I feel ashamed to even tacitly leaving her so in error— based as that is upon my own former assertion, when less informed than I am now. This struck me the more deeply as she found as ready excuses for A.M. as ourselves could make, and was kind and indulgent as ever.

'I expressed my belief in the purity of the person of which she appeared satisfied from Mrs S's statement.'

The question that Mrs Bramah asked was whether she was to

infer from Mrs Stratford's garbled version of her lodger's conduct that in spite of Mrs Bramah's charitable efforts, her pupil had 'fallen to the lowest'.

Mrs Bramah was most reluctant to admit to herself or anyone else that she had been fooled by a designing whore. It was evident that Annie had behaved with the utmost indiscretion. This was shocking enough, but then Mr Stephens had never made clear the exact nature of Mr Hunt's interest. If he wished to marry the girl, he should do so at once. She was far too easy a prey to be left on her own.

Providing the rent was eventually paid, Mrs Stratford presumably did not want to lose a lodger with such grand friends, nor would she have wished her house to get a bad name. She replied to Mrs Bramah's *question* with calculated duplicity. She had received Miss Miller in good faith as a serious-minded lodger, knowing that Mrs Bramah was her sponsor. She now felt in duty bound to admit that not only had the young lady failed to honour her obligations, but seemed to be frivolous. Instead of applying herself with diligence to her studies with Miss Prout, she frequently absented herself with various escorts to attend disreputable places of entertainment in extravagant clothes. More disturbing still, Mrs Stratford strongly suspected that unbeknownst to Mr Hunt, his protégée was actually posing as a model.

Stephens ended this disturbing letter with yet another warning to Hunt:

'I am forced to say the more I think of what you told me the other day the more dissatisfied and uneasy I am about it. I cannot say despairing, but in much dubiety. For God's sake, my dear fellow think of what you do with all possible self-examination . . . it seems to me that these repeated discoveries may be taken for warnings as well as spurs. No one wishes you better than I do. Police officer's address is—Superintendent Gibbs, Police Station Rochester Row S. He does not know my name but you can mention it if you think proper. . . .'

Throughout this fiasco, Hunt seems to have been extremely

preoccupied with social life and business letters. He was also overtired from working long hours on the Temple picture. Anyway, he showed remarkable *sang-froid* in dealing with Annie's latest misdemeanours. He was determined not to lose her now, to fail in his plans for their future. It was not in his nature to admit or accept failure. Annie was certainly pleasure-loving, thoughtless and indolent, but she was irresistibly fascinating and beautiful, and he was obsessed by her still.

As long as she was not physically unfaithful, Hunt thought, he could remain, at least outwardly, calm. He strongly suspected that she had been seduced by Gabriel a few months ago, in spite of her insistence that the rumpus was due to Lizzie Siddal. Annie had simply confessed to high-spirited indiscretion.

He had only confided his former suspicions to Stephens; he told him now that he 'would like to find out the truth, and Mrs Bramah's reasons for *the question*'.

Knowing how desperately jealous Hunt was, Stephens replied that all concerned thought (he meant hoped) that Annie was *pure*. Hunt succeeded in convincing himself once more that this was so.

He did not however call on Mrs Bramah.

He instructed Stephens to tell Annie that in future she must keep detailed, business-like accounts. She was not to sit to anyone else. If she needed pin-money for fripperies and clothes, she must exert herself and prove to him and the world that she had finally acquired 'a smattering of education'. Some respectable employment would be found. For the moment, although they racked their brains, neither he nor Stephens could decide exactly what but through friends, no doubt, something would turn up.

Stephens was to tell Miss Prout to exercise stricter supervision, and to watch the post, and even intercept her pupil's letters. This lady became in fact so conscientious that she handed over Hunt's own latest homily to Stephens, doubtless hoping it was from Lord Ranelagh or one of Annie's other lovers!

When Stephens proceeded to read Hunt's letter to Annie aloud, 'it produced no impression whatever, but a steady and stern refusal to receive anything more from you . . . she declined to hear . . . refuted positively the proposition' that she should give up sitting for artists, and take some respectable job. She showed Stephens the door.

'[Twice he] returned to the frey [sic] and begged her to consider even to receive the £5 for Mrs Stratford's future account. This was refused. She did not know how long she might remain with this last person. She accused Miss P[rout] of all sorts of tale-bearing to you, and neglect of duty to her-self—when I asked why in that case she did not complain to you, said she had no opportunity—which I refuted by quotation of her having even recently written to you without Miss P's knowledge, such an act was therefore practible [sic] asserted you had neglected her that she firmly believed you sent her there to be rid of her. She threatened Miss P. with exposure of something she had learnt. She throws the whole blame on you, in shortness utterly intractable. Looked in excellent health.'

Poor Stephens found little time to concentrate on his work. Far from being embarrassed or subdued by the fuss, Annie was simply furious. On the defensive, she attacked as before. If she accepted another penny from Hunt, he would assume the right to restrict her every move. From what we know of her character she must have felt that he was too deadly earnest and that he could not really love her. Rather than condemn herself to a tedious life with that stuck-up lot of prigs on Campden Hill, she would carry on as before. Now that her debts were paid, she could manage very well. She had other friends, who appreciated her for what she was—an exclusive and popular model. They were far more amusing and richer too.

So for the time being Hunt had reached an *impasse* with Annie Miller. For three months, he did his best to ignore it as a temporary set-back.

In his circle, only Stephens and the inmates of Tor Villa, Emily, Halliday and Martineau, knew that something was wrong; as far as Boyce and others were aware he was engaged to marry Annie Miller.

After three months Hunt was unable to ignore her rejection. She refused to see him, to sit, to call, and in spite of Stephens' entreaties, the cheques, bouquets, presents, billets-doux were turned away at the door.

By the first week in September, he missed her so much he could not endure this state of affairs any longer and called at her lodgings himself. She was in. He found her more desirable than ever. She was blooming and prosperous, without his help. On returning home alone to Tor Villa, his mind was made up.

Although admittedly her education was lacking, her magnetic attraction and dazzling looks were compensation enough. He would forget their differences in the past, and as soon as his picture was finished and sold, he would marry her. He would work day and night for a year.

Having made this momentous decision, he longed to confide in someone: only Emily was at home. When she heard his intention, a stormy scene ensued. She had had enough. She packed her traps and took her easel to Ewell.

It was 8 September 1858. Left alone, Hunt felt an urgent need to talk to someone, anyone, who would appreciate his generous, well-considered decision. He walked round to King Street, Kensington, to call on Harriet, that 'dreadful slut of a sister'. In his excitement he knocked at the wrong house. A man squatting on the next doorstep grunted that 'Childs the gas-fitter lives 'ere'. Henry Childs had coarsened very much and Harriet had had four children in the last four years. Hunt wrote that night to Stephens: 'I came away, without exposing more of my design, telling her that Annie was quite well—for there were ears and eyes at every chink in the house not to say all the other houses in the street. . . .'

It was late, but he took a hansom cab to Mrs Stratford's. By happy chance Annie was at home. He would forgive her. He would marry her as soon as *Christ in the Temple* was sold.

For once amused rather than annoyed by his condescension, she turned the tables. She said she would let him know her decision in a week or so, but now he must go.

Exhausted and deflated, when he got home he wrote a vague, yet despairing, letter to Millais in Scotland.

Devoted as ever, Millais replied from Perth by return of post:

'My poor dear old boy, what is the matter with you? Come here by sea at once. You are actually inhuman to yourself. . . . It is a very good thing your sister is away, but a fourteen room house is now unnecessary unless you mean to put another lady in her stead.'

It was not good for Hunt to be alone. He hoped that Lear would stay with him for a few days at least, but what was needed was a change—a leisurely life, some rough shooting, pretty ladies: 'Kick art and pictures to the winds and enjoy yourself.'

Hunt chose to stay working in London, waiting for Annie's decision. She was having a very good time and in no hurry to decide. Even poor Stephens had some peace for a while.

When Hunt visited the Combes at Oxford to report his progress on the Temple picture, they were deeply concerned and agreed with Millais, who had written them reams on the subject, that Hunt was emotionally starved: leading 'a celibate life is entirely unnatural for such an energetic man'. If they discussed Hunt's problems with his other friends, they would have heard that the unfortunate and prolonged affair with a certain Annie Miller was over—or so it seemed. What a deliverance!

Mrs Combe promised to introduce him to a Miss Strong the next time he came to stay.

Having himself been called 'Strong' in the Calmuck story, he may have felt a twinge on learning their candidate's name. All the same, having heard nothing from Annie for weeks, he was keen to meet her.

He wrote the Combes a letter on 26 February 1859, in which he included his specifications for a desirable wife:

'As to Miss Strong—the more the merrier for I find myself very lonely and melancholy here at times . . . I feel inclined to rush out and beg for a companion to come and sit with me, I mean a female one. I really think that you ought to find me all the young ladies whose amiability you can speak of as highly as Miss Strong's to come and see me but in the event of your knowing one who is tall 5 feet 6 or 7 [sic] with rather aquiline nose, long round neck and very beautiful—complexion either fair or dark if good and not more than 24, you must first ascertain that she is not engaged, and that she could be content to live *on about* £500 a year as I might probably otherwise suffer unnecessary disappointment. Birth or money rather a disadvantage than otherwise—the former particularly as I'm a radical and don't appreciate nobility that is not gained by the man himself. On my word I see that I shall soon get shut up working and all the young ladies will be gone by the time I can take any rest and look about me unless you can send me one.'

He set about wooing Miss Strong that summer of 1859 with the same determination he had shown hunting a rare white goat in the wilderness. Perhaps Miss Strong was romantic, but alas she was also delicate. She refused his proposal politely, pleading that her health would preclude the life he described, involving such hazardous journeys and long sojourns in remote places.

Although he was not in love, Hunt resented a further rebuff: this fruitless pursuit had wasted valuable time.

He returned to London in mid-July. Had Annie come to her senses?

When he called at Bridge Row, Annie seemed delighted to see him. Mrs Stratford and Miss Prout were most welcoming. Annie was loath to eat humble pie, but once again she owed the Stratfords £10 for her board and lodgings.

The London season was over, and for the next couple of months the future looked drab. By August 12, Lord Ranelagh would have left to shoot grouse on the Yorkshire moors. His first cousin, Thomas Ranelagh Thomson, was preoccupied with family troubles—his parents were increasingly estranged. His father, old Lady Ranelagh's brother, was always a problem and a spendthrift: now he had taken to drink. His mother, on whom Thomas Ranelagh depended financially, needed her son by her side. She had told his father to leave, and was backed by her family.

For the past year Lord Ranelagh had been plagued by old Uncle Thomson arriving penniless and drunk at his bachelor rooms in New Burlington Street to spend the night. Like many women with dubious pasts, Lady Ranelagh had become censorious of others and in old age had turned against her disreputable brother and refused to receive him at Ranelagh House.

Most of Annie's artist friends would take advantage of the summer weather to paint backgrounds away in the country, against which they would later set their models for subject pictures in the comparative comfort of their studios in winter.

Hunt began painting Annie sitting on one of his new Egyptian-style chairs. He concentrated on her amazing hair and becoming clothes. A change was as good as a rest from the

Temple picture with its innumerable portraits of elderly Jews. He would leave her face until last.

He tried to be less severe, merely teasing her for her indolence by suggesting calling the picture *Dolce Far Niente*. Whereas he had left the fourth finger of her left hand conspicuously bare in *The Awakening Conscience*, now he provided it with an engagement ring.

This happy truce lasted until one Saturday night, when he was in her room at Mrs Stratford's. He noticed a letter, and picked it up. It was addressed to her elsewhere, presumably to frustrate nosey Miss Prout. It had a Belgian stamp, was from Brussels in fact, and the handwriting seemed familiar—whose? George Boyce? He was almost sure. Who was it from? Might he read it?

She snatched back the letter. It was none of his affair.

Tormented with suspicion, Hunt stormed out of the house. Quite recently George Boyce had been abroad. When the door slammed, Mrs Stratford and Miss Prout were all ears. He returned in a few minutes, his temper cooled, hoping to find Annie in a more co-operative mood. If they were ever to be man and wife, they must be able to trust one another.

Meanwhile she had burned the letter, which was only from a woman friend, she said.

As for marriage, she had stood on her own feet the whole summer, small thanks to him. As far as she could make out they were not engaged, so he had no right to be possessive. They continued shouting at each other. Whether they were to be married or not, he must know if she were a liar. He swore to find out who had written the letter.

To Mrs Stratford's dismay, they parted in anger. She must have been hoping that Hunt would pay the rent.

Hunt walked round to Lupus Street. For once Stephens was away. His landlady did not know when he would return, but invited Hunt into the parlour where he wrote: 'Go to the house of Boyce on receipt of this, quickly. . . .'

Stephens was to confide in Boyce that Hunt and Annie had quarrelled again and:

'. . . that another cause of disagreement is that she will not give up a certain letter which she received from Brussels

—or first perhaps—find out whether he passed through that city . . . say that I refused to read it because I preferred to prove my confidence in her statement about it . . . that I finally asked to see the letter and that she says that she has destroyed it. If he says it was not from him with appearance of sincerity, say that I merely judged from a resemblance in the handwriting and that she says it came from a lady. . . . This may enable me to judge of what value her word is now . . . the things to be mentioned are truth although not the whole truth.'

It was three days since the quarrel. Hunt expected Boyce to dine at Tor Villa the following night. No answer came from Stephens.

Although by now Hunt was inclined to think that marriage with Annie would be a mistake, he must know if George Boyce, as well as Gabriel Rossetti, had betrayed him with her.

Unable to work for miserable uncertainty, he called again at Lupus Street. No one was in. He left another note:

'I can't learn whether you have yet got my letter—if you have probably you are seeking B[oyce]. I came down to talk to you more in full about Annie's position and to suggest a more doubtful tone in talking to B and a good scrutiny of his letter table to see whether certain handwriting is there "a doubtful tone" I mean in referring to your knowledge of the matter anyway will do equally well however, of course I regard Annie's new feelings as the best chance for her yet, I am not sanguine—and as far as my own being connected with her salvation am altogether hopeless. I will do everything possible for her in the way of trouble or money but it seems that I am forbidden to entertain my first greatest hope . . . (I can scarcely think of anything she ever told me of her position that I have not discovered to be false—how can a person recover from such an awful habit as it is with her.)'

There is no record of the wretched Stephens complying with this latest and doubtless distasteful demand on his time. Nor is

204

there any proof that the Brussels letter was from Boyce. If indeed it was, presumably Annie warned him.

That Thursday night in August when Boyce came to dine, Hunt also invited other painters to enjoy a 'royal present of wine' recently sent him by Millais. If the weather was bad, perhaps Martineau and Halliday had returned for this party at Tor Villa.

None of those present knew that Hunt had recently enjoyed a reunion with Annie, however short-lived. As far as they were aware Hunt and Annie had parted months ago. They may even have had high hopes that this very night they would hear that he was actually engaged to marry that nice young girl produced by Mrs Combe.

Looking round his studio, apart from the faceless *Dolce Far Niente*, they were bound to see endless drawings of Annie—Annie as *Lady Godiva*[4] with her hair in a snood, Annie as the *Lady of Shalott* with her hair hanging down her back, or blowing about, Annie lying in bed for *Parting*[5] and Annie kneeling by the bed in Pimlico for *Morning Prayer*.[6]

On the same principle that induced Hunt to boil a horse to produce a skeleton on which to base an accurate portrayal of its outward appearance, he invariably painted his models in the nude before adding their clothes.

His friend G. S. Layard called when Hunt was painting the *Lady of Shalott* and wrote:[7]

'When I saw this canvas in April, the figure of the Lady was nude, and I could not but tell the artist that it seemed to me almost sacrilege to drape so fair and exquisite a conception, which taught the lesson at one flash that modesty has no need of a cloak. This lovely figure bore no evidence of having been servilely copied from a stripped model, who had been distorted by the *modiste's* art. It did not suggest unclothedness, for the simple reason that it gave no impression that it knew the meaning of clothes at all.'

[4] An illustration for Moxon's edition of Tennyson's poems, produced March 1857.
[5] An illustration based on *At Night in Once a Week* published 21 July 1860.
[6] An oil 9¼" x 7" signed and dated 1856.
[7] G. S. Layard, *Tennyson and his Pre-Raphaelite Illustrators: A Book about a Book*, Stock, April 1894. (Limited edition of 750 copies.)

That Thursday night with so many reminders of Annie about, it was scarcely surprising that one of the artists present, after drinking a few glasses of wine, should have referred to her. It may have been Boyce, wishing to throw Hunt off the scent, and unwilling perhaps to pay Annie's rent, who gave her away either inadvertently or intentionally.

Whoever it was said that everyone knew the girl was a 'hussy' and that Hunt was well rid of her, of course she was not to be thought of as a wife, nevertheless he felt rather sorry for her now. She would soon be thrown out of her lodgings. She had no money and nowhere to go. The inevitable result, he supposed, was that she would go on the streets. Lord Ranelagh had abandoned her.

This garrulous guest who let the cat out of the bag could not imagine that Hunt was still ignorant that Lord Ranelagh had been Annie's principal lover, since well before Hunt returned from the East.

Presumably, Hunt, with his iron control, said goodnight to his guests without betraying what a hideous shock he had suffered from these revelations.[8]

When Stephens returned to Lupus Street he found a third undated letter from Hunt awaiting him:

'I . . . must toil like fury despite the fact that I am sick to death of work. Bankruptcy otherwise impends. I learnt this creditable fact of the young lady who has caused me so many miseries that immediately before I sent her to school she was seen walking with a swell Regent Street whore—and also that she was met one day dressed in the extreme of fashion walking down St James' Street, with a live Lord Somebody—a great rake—a discovery which does not astonish me now, it disgusts me however to think that the person who saw her there who had met her with me only a few days before and who seems to have known what my feelings were for her then did not tell me at the time. . . .'

[8] A. C. Gissing in his biography of Hunt writes: 'W. B. Scott* in writing of him, says that his temperament was of the kind which as a rule showed no emotion, and that even when taken by surprise he gave no signs of being affected.'
* Autobiographical Notes of the Life of W. Bell Scott and Notices of His Artistic and Poetic Circle of Friends, 1830-82, edited by W. Minto, Osgood, London, 1892.

Martineau who still rented a studio in the house on and off, was always devoted to Hunt. He urged him now to leave Tor Villa for a while and join him at Fairlight, where Hunt had stayed a few years before, painting *The Strayed Sheep*.

All his close friends were agreed that the poor old Mad was in a bad way; his nerves were in shreds. His fever had returned, his hands trembled so that even if he remained with the picture in London, he was unfit to paint.

Hunt had suffered a long series of disasters since Halliday had fetched him home, ill, from Syria: the bad reception of his pictures, his father's death and financial worries, endless quarrels and complications with Annie, involving his friendship with Gabriel, the necessity of keeping in touch with patrons which demanded a strenuous social life, the rows with Uncle Hobman and Emily, the fuss and bother over the Calmuck story, Miss Strong's rejection and now total disillusion with his beloved, and indeed with most of his friends.

It was small wonder that he fell victim to a persecution mania. He had become so jittery and hypersensitive that he saw his problems reflected everywhere, and even imagined them mocking him in messages printed in the agony column of *The Times*.

In the 1850s and 1860s every day literally hundreds of lovers communicated by this means, no doubt to prevent parental or other supervision of their correspondence. To quote a few typical lines: 'Dove to Serpent do not wound me again: parcel will arrive Frederic Tuesday, ENOG. Read other way': 'Rosie to W.C. Father is annoyed write him at once. Do not forget camel and cat D.H.P. (initials reversed).'

The advertising rates must have been cheap, since clues to the codes employed were so often included.

Unfortunately the following letter is undated:

'Saturday. My dear Stephens, I wonder whether you have had *The Times* to look at this week.[9] I cannot understand the

---

[9] Much tedious research has convinced me that Hunt was suffering from paranoia and mistaken in believing these messages to be directed at him. The coincidence of initials, etc., is not surprising because of the vast mass of material involved. My secretary and I and two others covered *The Times* index from December 1856 to September 1865, but none of the 'A.Ms' and 'ENOGS' fit with other dated material.

advertizements as mere coincidences she does not write to me and day after day come these mysterious enigmas which can only be supposed *not* [?] to emanate from her. So exactly do they correspond with the state of the case from the consideration that she could never be so wicked and so barefaced as to be guilty of such monstrous and open disregard of honesty and faithfulness—one had her initials yesterday. I expect one soon to have my name written in full. They speak not only of her being away and unhappy but of some one being busy to get information about her which the person addressed is desired not to communicate. Some clue must turn up soon. One was headed with these capitals E.N.O.G. which inverted express her position in relation to her former residence . . . I have directed Miss Prout to keep an eye on all letters received and sent away by her and this may possibly unravel the mystery. Keep a look out on them if you get the paper. I am going out of town and may have difficulty in getting the papers each day. In haste.'

In the meantime Stephens replied to the last and most despairing of the three letters he found awaiting him at Lupus Street. Not knowing that Hunt had left London to stay with Martineau at Fairlight, he wrote to Tor Villa from the Hogarth Club, 6 Waterloo Place, on 19 August 1859:

'Your news about that miserable girl is indeed most miserable. . . . I met Mrs Stratford today and she told me her inmate still remained with her, that she was doing nothing to help herself, going out but little and then mostly with Mrs Bush[10] or herself, that she was out of health, her cough returned, her sister had been endeavouring to get money from her,—of course without success—that she unceasingly upbraided Miss Prout, and that her temper was become "Terrible bad". I, utterly heedless of your fearful impecunious state, repeated the assurance, that you disburse to the amount of £5. Mrs S[tratford] told me Annie did not seem to have any hope or idea that you would relent towards her,—and, as the

[10] Mrs Bush was a great friend of Mrs Stratford's and had once lodged with her at 16 Lawrence Street, Chelsea. She ran a millinery establishment, where the work was done by paying pupils.

conversation was entirely personal to ourselves I exposed my own belief that you had no such thought.

'I wish I could help you in the way of tin by paying over part of my debt to you but I'm fearfully hard up, in consequence of a run upon me by ancient creditors.'

When Hunt heard of Annie's plight it was with difficulty that Martineau restrained him from dashing up to London. Instead, Hunt wrote back to Stephens on 23 August 1859:

'Many thanks for your letter giving me partics gained from Mrs Stratford. . . . God knows how far such information as that I had maybe trusted, I am afraid however after considering the whole history that it is v. likely to be true in circs even if somewhat inaccurate as to time. The fact of her remaining at home now in poverty and difficulties certainly makes it seem that she dreads to fall to the lowest, if so she ought to be helped—perhaps she may be humbled enough to consider some plan of honest industry. . . . You might perhaps write one word to Mrs Stratford to say that *you* had sent it [the £5] and that you felt justified in saying that Mr H would be ready to do any friendly service for her in his power if she would consider what she might best be qualified for . . . and gives up her silly pride.'

As an afterthought he suggested that Stephens should buy a book called *Mary Barton* by Mrs Gaskell for two shillings and present it to Annie hoping that it might make a favourable impression.

In the event, this gift was not appreciated.

On 7 September Hunt, still at Fairlight, wrote to Stephens that on Martineau's advice he was purposely avoiding London and that now he had 'nothing more to propose to aid the poor devil but must thank you for your kindness and complete effort to save the silly fool'.

Hunt returned to Tor Villa at the end of September, determined to dismiss Annie from his mind and slog away at the Temple picture.

On 15 October 1859, George Boyce recorded in his diary: 'R[ossetti] had had a call from Annie Miller, who had left a card', and on December 22 Boyce wrote of her again:

> 'Miss Annie Miller called on me in the evening in an excited state to ask me to recommend her someone to sit to. She was determined on sitting again in preference to doing anything else. All was broken off between her and Hunt. I pitied the poor girl very much, by reason of the distraction of her mind and heart.
>
> 'Called on Hunt in the evening to tell him of her visit and that, finding she was resolved on sitting again, I should ask her to sit to me instead of to any stranger. He said it seemed now as if she could do nothing else for she rejected (naturally enough) all his efforts to find employment through friends. Finding he could not get her to do what he wanted to make her a desirable wife for him, nor wean herself from old objectionable habits, he had broken off the engagement; but the whole affair had preyed on his mind for years. The interview was friendly throughout.'

Hunt felt obliged to give Boyce the benefit of the doubt, but never really trusted him again, nor did he mention him in his memoirs.

Boyce wrote again on December 28: 'Annie Miller came and sat to me. Rossetti came in and made a pencil study of her. She looked more beautiful than ever.'

A month later Gabriel Rossetti gave Boyce this pencil drawing. It is inscribed on the back: 'D. G. Rossetti, the maker of this sketch to G. P. Boyce, January 26th, 1860'.

George Boyce and Gabriel Rossetti were once more rivals for her favours and both were delighted that Annie was free. Gabriel wrote to Boyce on 18 February 1860:[11]

> 'Dear Boyce, Blow you, Annie is coming to *me* tomorrow (wednesday). I'm sure you won't mind, like a good chap. Will you write to her for another day? She would hardly consent to ill-using you in this style, but I bored her till she did.'[12]

[11] Collection of University College, London.
[12] Annie was sitting to Rossetti for *Cassandra*.

CHAPTER XVII

Oh yet we trust that somehow good
Will be the final goal of ill.
TENNYSON

AT THE end of March 1860 Annie's father, the old soldier, died, aged seventy-four, at the Royal Hospital, Chelsea.

There was a military feeling in the air; men in uniform were everywhere. Since the outbreak of war between France, Piedmont and Austria, an invasion of England was feared. In April, Hunt and many painter friends joined the Artists' Rifle Corps, part of the Volunteer movement (which was ironically largely promoted by Lord Ranelagh).

In between rifle-drill, at which he was more expert than most, Hunt finished *Christ in the Temple*. It had taken him six years, on and off, to paint.

A letter dated 20 April 1860, to Palgrave, who shared Woolner's crib, shows that the completion of this picture, while suffering such emotional stress, had drained Hunt's mental and physical resources to the dregs. He was not only broke, but utterly exhausted, and excused his delay in replying to Palgrave (who was contemplating suicide at the time):

'. . . burdens of a miscellaneous nature . . . burning out one's senses and their organs are so tortured as to be almost too sore to rest even in sleep. . . . I know you would think that I could not sympathise with you in your feeling of indifference to life, you would assume . . . that I was a happy man—with active ambitions that made me look forward to the future with interest . . . it is not so—all men of sensitive natures suffer by my age. I am essentially a miserable man with a great sore, which cannot be cured. Thorns and Thistles grow out of my breast, as I once saw in a dream . . . they will not cease to pain until I lay [sic] in dead earth . . . first

I would not fight against it . . . the eternal gods however would not have it so . . . my choice was not between death and life but between a feeble diseased life and strong life—and I felt that I must do violence to my misery, wrestle with the devil and beat it to that degree in which it became subject to me . . . —all this means simply what a nicely married man does who commends matrimony, that you should follow my plan—and live at any cost defiant to melancholy and disease. I want you very much—you are the only fellow who can impart to me the learning which it was impossible for me to acquire when I was a boy—and which now I feel the want of more and more every day.

'I will see you soon . . . —in the meantime take my best thanks for your offer of tin which I will not scruple to ask for when the butcher bothers. I cannot go out of England yet—could not for my work and would not because if I were alone I should go mad—'

Within hours of writing this letter to Palgrave—which may have saved the latter's life as he was evidently so desperately depressed—Hunt was writing in his journal in a very different vein a more positive character, Wilkie Collins:

'No one could be more jolly than he as lord of the feast in his own house, where the dinner was prepared by a chef, and the wines select, and the cigars of the choicest brand. The talk was rollicking . . .'

In spite of, or perhaps because of, Millais' disapproval of both Hunt's and Wilkie Collins' irregular domestic lives, the two had become much closer friends over the last four years.

The Collins family, having always been on the best of terms with Dickens, were aware that the latter was anxious to make amends for publishing the Calmuck story. Now Wilkie recommended that Hunt should seek Dickens' advice on what 'thundering price' he should ask for the picture. Dickens, without seeing it, told him not to take less than 5,500 guineas including the copyright!

Gambart had first refusal. He invited Hunt to dinner: 'When I came up to the fire after the ladies had gone, pouring out another glass of wine, he said, "Now then . . . what is the price?" I stated it. "Oh, but that is impossible—no one ever heard of such a sum!"'

Within four days, Gambart agreed to pay.

There was enormous publicity. *The Times* carried daily advertisements in prominent type. Eight hundred to a thousand visitors crammed the Bond Street gallery every day. The crowds were such that when the Prince Consort called, he failed to get near the masterpiece. It was removed by Royal Command for inspection by the Queen.[1]

Hunt was acclaimed as the 'Plebeian Lion of the Season', in the gossip columns, pursued by hostesses and matchmaking mamas and pestered for autographs, while commissions and money rolled in.

This worldly and social success does not seem to have gone to his head, as, shortly after private view day, which he attended with Millais, he wrote to Stephens on 25 May 1860:

'I shall settle down and avoid every fashionable of any description whatever but until I meet a tradesman's daughter with some sort of pretension to the healthiness and beauty of the nob's daughter, and who will be content to take her portion in life with me, I shall give the nob's daughters the gratification of thinking they have found a victim of hopeless love, to laugh at, in the plebeian lion of the season.'

At the Cosmopolitan Club, when Thackeray congratulated him, he added how lucky Hunt was not to be married—single men had so many invitations and so few expenses.

'Meeting Dickens at a party in the full swing of the season, I was greeted by him with, "You have caused my hatter to be madder than ever. He declares that you have choked up Bond Street with the carriages for your exhibition so that none of his established customers can get to his shop."'

[1] One dark freezing day, the row of gas lights illuminating the picture set fire to the canopy which had been erected to prevent the dresses of the spectators from being reflected in the glass. The one pail of water on the premises for such emergencies being frozen solid, Lady Trevelyan sacrificed her valuable Indian shawl to extinguish the flames.

On receiving Gambart's first instalment of £1,500, Hunt went down to Oxford at once to repay Thomas Combe the £300 which had enabled him to finish the picture. Hearing that Hunt's old friend, Tommy Woolner, the sculptor, was in financial difficulties, Combe asked Hunt to pass on the money to him. Hunt also introduced Woolner to various patrons, famous or rich, who gave him commissions.

By the end of the summer of 1860 Hunt and Woolner were almost the only bachelors left of the original Brothers and their circle. They were both hunting for wives. Hunt longed to return to the East, but could not face a celibate life there. Having been engaged on and off for nine years, Gabriel Rossetti had married Lizzie Siddal in May. They curtailed their honeymoon on hearing that Robert Brough, the man who had written the story of Hunt and his shepherdess for *Household Words*, had suddenly died in poverty. They returned at once and pawned the souvenirs they had bought in Paris to raise money for his destitute family. There is no record that Hunt sent a cheque. In June, Charley Collins married Dickens' daughter, Kate.

Reading of all the jollifications in London, visits to country houses, walking tours and sketching parties, hobnobbing with the great, the impression is that Hunt thoroughly enjoyed himself and was a success wherever he went. He was thirty-three.

Caroline Fox[2] wrote in her diary:

'Holman Hunt is a very genial, young-looking creature with a large, square beard, clear blue laughing eyes . . . dimples, a sunny expression and full of simple boyish happiness. His voice is *most* musical and there is nothing in his look or bearing, in spite of the strongly-marked forehead, to suggest the High Priest of Pre-Raphaelitism . . . [he] is so frank and open, and so unspoiled by the admiration he had excited.'

Janet Ross[3] also referred to him in her journal:

[2] Caroline Fox, *Memories of Old Friends*, Smith and Elder, London, 1881-83. She lived at Little Holland House before Mrs Prinsep. She was much admired by William IV but died a maiden aunt.
[3] Janet Ross, *The Fourth Generation*.

'At a ball . . . I was amused by Holman Hunt asking me whether he had not improved in his dancing. I complimented him on it, but told him he must still practise hard before he could rival Leighton or Millais.'

Millais graced every assembly, and the two men were still the closest of friends. Hunt stayed with the Monckton Milnes's at Fryston[4] in the same house party as the Richard Burtons and an Anglo-French lady called Madame Mohl. She 'particularly liked Holman Hunt in spite of his unpunctuality'.

Monckton Milnes kept most of his famous collection of French and Italian erotica in the library at Fryston, where privileged guests were invited to browse before setting off for church on Sunday mornings.

Edward Lear was delighted to hear that Hunt and Woolner, his 'dear pa and deeruncle', were in good spirits, 'yourself particularly [sic]: and that both of you danced, which pa, though I called you both little asses I did, pa, I didn't mean nothink: but on the contrary it was a pleasure to hear. . . .'

But unfortunately by the autumn Hunt's complicated past was once more catching up with him.

Annie was now twenty-six. Gabriel and most of his friends were married, or about to be. Her reputation was distasteful to their wives. She was still very lovely, and the younger up and coming set were keen to use her of course, but they treated her without respect—she was Hunt's cast off, a 'has been', but still good for a tumble and needed the odd half crown.

Annie must have been sick to death of the criticisms made by Mrs Stratford, her aunt, Bess Miller, her sister, Harriet Childs, and all the Chelsea and Pimlico crowd. Mrs Stratford might not have backed a winner, but was not prepared to cut her losses now. She moved Annie into a small back room.

It is clear from the many letters concerning this affair that now all those who were financially interested in Annie must have met in parlours and pubs to discuss how her future affected theirs.

The most obvious solution would have seemed to be for her to sue Hunt for breach of promise. After all, Annie had received

[4] Fryston Hall, Wakefield.

a written proposal of marriage from Syria and that most respected lady Mrs Bramah, her nephew, Dr Diplock, and Dr Sanneman —surely the best part of Chelsea—would be able to bear witness in Court. However, probably those who were literate, such as Mr Stratford, his friend, Superintendent Gibbs, and Hughes the clerk, were afraid—being aware of her indiscretions—that Mr Hunt would be able to plead justification for breaking off his engagement.

Mrs Stratford was a woman of action and wearied of such speculation. She called at Lupus Street and found Mr Stephens at home. A born strategist, she played the innocent, as she had once before with Mrs Bramah. After polite exchanges, she said that as far as she knew Mr Hunt was still Miss Miller's protector, and responsible for the debts which she incurred. Mr Stephens never told her anything to the contrary. She probably added that she was the first to understand that artistic folk had their ups and downs, she had heard about that from Chelsea land-ladies, such as her friend Mrs Bradshaw, but then she kept a shop. It is not difficult to imagine the interview.

Stephens was no match for Mrs Stratford. He caught the next steamer and then, by way of a hansom, hurried to Tor Villa. Breathless, he reported to Hunt what trouble was brewing.

Whatever Hunt's feelings were, as usual he showed no panic whatsoever; but to Stephens' amazement, calmly instructed him how to deal with the situation.

Firstly, he was prepared to examine Mrs Stratford's accounts, up to date only. As for the future, he was neither morally nor legally responsible for Annie. Stephens must make this absolutely clear to Mrs Stratford.

To provide for her, he would either pay for Annie's training for some respectable career, or would assist her, through the good offices of Mrs Herbert.[5] This lady interested herself altruistically in plans for emigration to Australia—a promising future might await Annie there. Stephens must explain all the advantages to be gained by such a move.

Hunt thought it best not to negotiate directly with her. Stephens must cope: he was after all even more beholden to Hunt for numerous introductions and recommendations as an

[5] Wife of the Hon. Sidney Herbert, Secretary for War, and lifelong friend of Florence Nightingale.

art critic to various periodicals. Also, it seems that Stephens' conscience never slept, regarding Annie Miller. How dearly he was paying for that loan of long ago, and perhaps one kiss stolen in a punt.

As Stephens was about to leave, Hunt gave him an envelope for Annie, enclosing some money, but no letter.

Annie had been prepared for marriage at Hunt's expense with valued guidance from Mrs Bramah. But what was she to do now? Mrs Stratford and Miss Prout must have been bewildered on receiving Hunt's ultimatum. What career was open to Annie apart from marriage?

No solution was found.

Hunt wrote a letter to Stephens, simply headed *Thursday night*, which I think should be placed here.

'. . . Could you oblige me by writing a line to A.M. to remind her to come to you prepared with Mrs S's account and her own ideas as to what she is ready to do to [avoid?] the danger of her taking it as an assurance that she will be enabled to do what she pleases, add that these will be necessary . . . it may be possible to assist her.

'. . . Refer to the instance she gave of her intemperate decision—and urge upon her the necessity of considering in after life whether for the sake of a momentary gratification of ill humour and pride, it is worth while to sacrifice an opportunity that can never occur again, and the loss of more than a year of life from the chance of establishing herself.

'Remind her of the importance of making a decision in her affairs—on this occasion as well as others, that may be judicious not merely for the day but for the future.

'Instance her choice of sitting against our urgent advice as an instance of her light-hearted judgment, and if she says anything about Rossetti's assurance that she would have a great deal of employment point out how nearly all people talk just to appear pleasant at the moment. . . .

'If she cannot be preached to from the texts of her own bitter experience then she cannot be awakened at all.

'Do not omit to say that in rejecting my advice to avoid going to Rossetti and Boyce to sit she sacrificed my interest in her welfare to a very great extent. That her refusal to take my assistance over and over again at last induced me to employ my money in another way and that what I can do now at the most is only a very little in proportion to what I could have done then.'

As instructed both verbally and by letter, Stephens told Annie to bring him Mrs Stratford's itemised accounts.

At this stage of the negotiations, which Mrs Stratford knew were only preliminary, she was not sure how high a price she dared ask.

The following correspondence shows how the situation developed. On 12 November 1860, Stephens wrote to Hunt:

'. . . She came accordingly [to Lupus Street] but did not bring the accounts, saying from Mrs S that she would be content with *what you thought proper to give*—this seemed nonsense to me, so I urged A.M. to get Mrs S to *send* the accounts—saying that you could not have any idea what you could do, or were even required to do, till seeing these.

'A.M.'s ruling idea, for her own future was to become a pupil of Mrs Bush, and enter upon a course of millinery. I said that in England this was very unpromising the market being dreadfully overstrained Mrs B[ush] might keep herself from starvation, but that was due to the number of years she had had to form a connection. I then suggested the emigration in the Terms you propose.

'At first this was evidently taken as a most suspicious move —in effect that you wanted to get rid of her. This was hinted at so broadly that I felt bound to be sharp with her, saying you did not care a button if she *remarried* etc. [Italics are mine.]

'Your wish being for her good I then put forward the advantages of the adventure, laying some stress on probable matrimony (which was evidently not looked for as a probable suggestion on part of *your* agent) the getting rid of all old associates and painful memories, starting a new life, etc and better promise in a new country.

'The whole thing was preemptorily [*sic*] rejected "Let him only pay Mrs S[tratford] this once more and I will never Trouble him anymore. I'll go and be a lady's maid".

'Pointing out the utter absurdity of any human woman with a *husband* [employing?] such a person as herself (it was curious how this told) I showed her a long string of advertisements for situations of that sort and the consequent over-crowding of such damzels, and that knowledge of trends was almost *sine qua non*. This abandoned, she came down a peg, and appeared to think. She would need she said, to learn something even if she did go, [emigrate] why not in the Bushian Academy?

'Seeing her so strongly bent on this idea I hesitated to break it sadly, and said that if she determined *not* to emigrate something of that sort might be *thought* of at least. But that if she agreed with our opinion that emigration was her best recourse and would promise to abide by such advice, you would enquire of Mrs Sidney Herbert as to the best means of discipline and preparation. Without some such promise you would not move in *that* direction.

'Strategic enquiries were then made of me as to what *charge* she would go out under, and the plain inference given that any control of the "matron" order would be unacceptable. Shewing [*sic*] her that no captain of a ship would even take a young woman, except under such control, and that she could not shoot herself out in Melbourne city except under some decent auspices, she began to see the true state of the circumstances, and to think greatly about it.

'I ought to tell you that all this time her eye (it was almost azure) has been wandering towards the note you gave me, which in order that it might not be overlooked I had placed on my mantelpiece. Unable to bear the suspense of what it might contain she broke out sharply at this point, in the imperative mood: "Is not that a letter for me?"

'On handing it to her I studied her face and fingers— resolution was gallantly maintained until the ignominy-bringing moment of the gold falling out and opening the paper, finding it was written upon [the envelope] but not a letter. . . .

'The Devil would have laughed at the presumptuous question "Is this for me? I'm afraid there is some mistake" etc.— Putting this down rather disdainfully she hedged about in a new bitter way about the emigration project and evidently was inclined to fence for the Bush pupilship––with Melbourne as a vanishing point a good way in the picture. I did not contend against this except by repeating as above.

'The upshot after 2 hours talking on many subjects, was that she must see her friends, sister etc., and think seriously over the matter. This seemed not unreasonable, so after trying to get a decision made by an earlier day . . . I agreed to see her again *next* Sunday at 11 for her decision. She took your envelope and cash and went.

'I must Tell you, I hope without passion or prejudice, that the young lady seems by no means to have got rid of her haughty pretensions, and if it were not for the risk of utter ruin I honestly believe a good deal of serious suffering would be much for her benefit. But however this was more on the surface than in act, for she evidently felt strong compulsion was upon her, and seemed to enter into the emigration idea with less reluctance than at first. Fearing to dictate to her pride I made this not at all an ultimatum on your part, but earnestly urged its reasonableness for her own sake.

'As I am not without fancies that she may attempt to [feint?] about going, and never intend to carry it out, it will be well for you to decide upon a positive line of conduct. If you will, or not, assent to, and assist her in studying under Mrs Bush, or if you refuse any other form of help than Towards emigration. I did not commit you to anything more than a general promise of assistance and shall be glad to know your determination.

'Your note of morning just arrived 9 p.m. Ever Yours. . . .'

On discovering this letter, with its reference to *re*marriage, I strongly suspected that Annie Miller had secretly married while Hunt was in Syria, and that this was 'the deceit practised on all' discovered by Mrs Stratford and which had so shocked Mrs Bramah.

I then read, or rather deciphered many other letters, including those from Stephens to Hunt, and set to work placing them as best I could in chronological order.

I was bewildered. Could Annie already have a secret husband? Madox Brown, Stephens and others had concealed their marriages for years. It was even possible that her secret husband was Hunt. After meticulous research, I can state as a fact that no marriage of the Ann[i]e Miller of our story was registered between 1850 and 1863.

I therefore came to the conclusion that what Stephens meant in his rather incoherent letter was if Annie were to marry someone else, i.e. other than Hunt.

Within three days, 15 November 1860, Hunt replied:

'I cannot say that I have very much hope in the steadfastness—if even in the immediate earnestness of A.M.'s profession of desire to exert herself to gain an industrious livelihood.

'If I found reasons for thinking that she had entirely changed since she wasted the opportunities I purchased for her before, it would seem to me a duty to make the greatest possible sacrifice to help her once more.

'I have been made a fool of too often tho' not to require some better evidence than anything in word or manner of hers in her interview with you on Sunday when you kindly laid before her my views as to her proper course—and better than any I can find in the note from the Stratfords—the tone of which she is doubtless responsible for, really putting all the little incidents together—the ridiculous suspicion that in my suggestions (which, as they involved the sacrifice of no little money—time and trouble and what is more the exercise of some gratuitous christian forgiveness—might have been taken with at least an appearance of thankfulness) nothing was to be seen but a selfish desire of mine—and that this was to get her out of *my* way.

'The notion she expressed that *I* had taken her out of her original position and the inference that her present one was that of a person of the higher classes—in spite of the too obvious fact that she can't write two lines of English as well as the youngest tutor in a charity school . . . the fact that the bill is made out to me—and the application for payment is made not as a favor, but in a tone of command, make it appear as if she considered that the world ought to consider it very kind of her that she allowed it to labour for her—and that at this particular time I was to serve as the patient ass who was to carry her through the mud, and to have for reward a few more blows than I had had already.

'The suggestion of hers that I should place her with Mrs Bush does not I confess tend to give me more confidence in her sincerity. I am not quite certain indeed that it is not made to annoy me for she knows clearly enough that I have no great reason to repose trust in that lady and she does not give me any reason for changing my opinion.

'She is I suspect a hopelessly proud—improvident girl who does not know the value of money because she has never worked for it—and if she at this moment had a hundred pounds in her hands the probability is that it would still more encourage her in the ridiculous idea that she was much too great a person to work—or to spend it for any but her immediate pleasure. . . .

'I must require to be very strongly convinced that she has undergone a great change in mind and feeling before I can feel warranted in spending another pound upon her. You must not understand that I withdraw my offer to her—I still wait to hear what she decides upon—and if she appears really in earnest I will do what I can—even altho' she wishes to remain in England against my advice—but I write now I confess while I am still angry at the tone she adopts in making the application that you may clearly make her understand that I am not going to throw away my money without the chance of its being of some *permanent* good.'

During the next few days Hunt was preoccupied by his grandmother's death and funeral. She was eighty-eight and had had twenty-one children.

He wrote again to Stephens on 22 November 1860:

'I am in all of your opinion as to the best thing to do in re A.M. and I shall now only fork out £5 to Mrs Stratford.

'One may be certain from the rejection of the proposal for AM to try her fortunes in a new country that she had no idea of really conquering the difficulties of her position and I am convinced that the giving [of] a large sum of money to any of them would be an effectual means of making her put off any troubles that afflict her for another term.

'I send you a check payable to yourself. If you could see

222

Mrs Stratford and give it to her in gold or a bank note I should be more obliged if you could ask her how it is that she has charged her lodger at the same rate while nothing but the most indispensable accommodation has been afforded, as when she had the best room in the house and the best prospects of paying for it. This surely requires some explanation for if it goes on of course AM will never have the slightest chance of recovering herself by a career of simple industry.

'The sum total of the bill would, with the money which she herself has paid, make the rate of expenditure something like £1 per week—wh. no girl of her ignorance could be likely to earn. Perhaps at a later time I may be able to reduce Mrs Stratford's account against her lodger by another payment—but this must depend upon circumstances.

'The project of A.M.'s to be apprenticed to Mrs Bush I shall not assist at present—if at all. In the event of her success proving it a judicious and steady resolution I may be induced to assist in paying Mrs B for the time and trouble she has spent upon her pupil—'

The immediate reaction to these letters of Hunt's, when they were read aloud and expounded by Stephens to Annie, the Stratfords, Miss Prout and other interested parties, was vociferous indignation and disgust.

However, over Christmas there was a temporary lull, while all ordered their dispositions for the battle to come.

In the New Year Annie must have called at New Burlington Street, found Lord Ranelagh at home and announced that her engagement to Hunt was broken off. It was impossible for her to sue for breach of promise because Hunt would at once introduce Lord Ranelagh's name.

Lord Ranelagh told her not to worry on his account. Surely she must have received countless passionate letters from Hunt: they would be worth a fortune now to a newspaper. Hunt would be anxious to buy them himself.

His first cousin, Thomas Ranelagh Thomson, also present, thought this a capital idea. Ranelagh had to go out.

It was the first time that Annie and Thomas had been alone together. Thomas told her that he had hoped for this all along. Alas, he was a bit hard up himself: his mother was splendid, but his father was such a drain on her. She paid him to stay away, and he squandered the money on low living and was scarcely ever sober now.

Perhaps for the first time in her life, Annie fell in love. She returned to Bridge Row in fine fettle and told the Stratfords that she had gained a beau, a gentleman too, Lord Ranelagh's first cousin; but Lord Ranelagh himself had produced a most sensible idea. All those letters from Hunt were worth a fortune. Probably she could scarcely bear to think of the number she had crumpled up and tossed in the fire, but she still had plenty, and some drawings of herself too . . .

Elated with her success, she handed over five guineas—a gift from Thomas or Lord Ranelagh?

Mrs Stratford wasted no time. On 24 January 1861 she reappeared at Lupus Street. She had no wish to bother Mr Stephens, but since Mr Hunt was unable or unwilling to deal with his own affairs, she was calling on behalf of Miss Miller. She, her husband and Miss Prout were all very fond of their lodger; otherwise they would not have stood by her when they were all so let down by that hard-hearted Mr Hunt. It was surprising that a Christian, religious gentleman should turn against humble folk. She added darkly that Miss Miller had other friends, without meaning no offence to Mr Stephens, perhaps aristocrats were more reliable than artists after all. Annie had a trunk full of letters from Mr Hunt and drawings of her—Mrs Stratford sniffed—*studies* she believed they were called. That very morning the poor girl had paid over her savings.

After Mrs Stratford left, Stephens mulled over this sinister conversation and became increasingly alarmed. Later that night he dashed off an agitated report to Hunt.

Scenting blackmail, Hunt was at last sufficiently perturbed to take direct action. On 25 January, instead of sending his deputy, he actually called on Lord Ranelagh.

Far from denying the affair, Lord Ranelagh freely admitted that Annie had been his mistress for years. Why not? He had had many others, of course: Hunt was completely baffled.

Lord Ranelagh protested that it was not his fault that Hunt had been such a fool as to write compromising letters and propose marriage to a tart. This scrape in which Hunt found himself now was not his concern. He was quite understanding.

It is most unlikely that cousin Thomas was present at this interview.

Hunt took a cab to Bridge Row. When Mrs Stratford admitted him, he ignored her and strode up the stairs.

Completely under control, though probably smoking and gripping the arm of his chair, he casually asked Annie if she knew a Lord Ranelagh?

She replied with a shrug: 'No, the name meant nothing to her!'

Hunt calmly proceeded to refresh her memory by describing Lord Ranelagh in detail. There was a long silence, after which 'she protested . . . that she didn't know his name and had not seen him but within the fortnight—as an unknown fellow who followed her home against her will'.

Hunt got up and left without a word. Mr Stratford met him in the hall and handed him an envelope. He and Mrs Stratford would like a few words. They had talked matters over, and now felt it was their duty—Mr Hunt ought to know. Curtly, he replied that communications would be through Mr Stephens as before. He would call at Lupus Street on his way home.

Stephens was out. The Stratfords' envelope contained an account made out to Mr Hunt for Miss Miller: board and lodgings and *extras*, for some months.

When Hunt arrived at Tor Villa he found yet another letter from Stephens written the night before. So much had happened in the last twenty-four hours.

Hunt wrote Stephens two letters before the last post, both dated 25 January 1861:

'I wonder what Mrs Stratford has now in her treasury of secrets? we must wait and see. of course till we find out it will be impossible to decide the proper way of handling the young vixen who can only be managed in any state by very delicate advances, and, even at times, show of cross-purposes. You must see how she takes the announcement of Lord Rs name—if she is proud of his noble friendship—of course it would be unwise to threaten her with exposure of his connection with her in court. If you find he is instigating her to make use of the letters to annoy me—do not hesitate—because black as he is he would rather dread having an account of his

225

behaviour come out—as I should, he would know rather damage him in the eyes of those who hold him in honor, as well as those with whom he is trying to get on with now by virtue of the Volunteer movement.

'I will let Mrs Stratford have some tin when I see you again —I am afraid I am giving you a good deal of trouble.'

The second letter:

'If A.M. has not been to you it may be worth while to suggest—in the event of her declaring that she will annoy me by the publication of the letters a statement by you of the fact that I am prepared with very good information to explain my course in case of need—and by way of convincing her that I have something more than the suspicion, strong as it was, on which I acted you had better say that Lord Ranelagh's name in connexion with her conduct will be enough to stamp the character of it as infamous particularly when I prove the length of time for which the intimacy went on and the manner in which he spoke of her. . . .

'Say that the papers she holds are not worth talking about for immediate purposes, and that my only desire to get them comes from a knowledge that after her lifetime and mine they might get into someone's hand who would print them when there was less chance of the secrets in them being explained but that I shall be prepared for that emergency by leaving the evidence which I have on the subject ready to be produced to prove how far from cruel or inconsiderate my conduct towards her—and end by showing how the principal advantage in having them to me would be that in that case I need not any longer lumber my drawers with papers which show how I was once fool enough to believe in her honesty and goodness.'

Clearly, during the following month, Hunt cannot have taken Dickens into his confidence.

Instead of fulfilling promising commissions, and enjoying a 'plebeian lion's' share of the world, Hunt sacrificed many precious hours trying to discover everything disagreeable or disreputable about Annie's past and to discredit Lord Ranelagh.

Hunt seriously intended to defend himself and to deter her from selling his letters by grubbing up and publishing matter already stale to many, which he nosed out at last from old scoundrels like Hill, for the price of a few drinks at the Chelsea pubs.

Of course, she was both untruthful and promiscuous. Surely, the fact of her having been born a victim of social injustice and having grown up 'illiterate, infested with vermin, living in the foulest of yards, using filthy language, in a state of absolute neglect and Degradation', until Hunt was sufficiently attracted to come to her rescue, would only have added interest and gained her a sneaking regard from the most prudish and smug. Such an article might have awakened more consciences than his famous picture.

Even in those days, it seems incredible that Hunt, a self-made man himself, did not realise that all good people would marvel at the way she had not only survived, but progressed despite her deplorable background.

As a result of this concentrated sleuthing, Hunt wrote Stephens a letter of about two thousand words, instructing him in 'THE PLOT'—how to trick Annie into parting with the letters, drawings and books, which he had lovingly dedicated to her, for 'a paltry £7'.

This letter, dated 15 February 1861, was full of such sanctimonious statements as: 'Mr Hunt gets his money by hard work and he is not foolish enough to throw away what can only be got again by a great deal of self-denial—and sacrifice of healthful relaxation,' and threats: 'whatever unpleasantness for the moment might be caused by him by this getting *known* (not published) it would be very quickly destroyed by the information which he would then be obliged to furnish about yourself.'

Stephens was instructed to write out a separate document as a receipt for Annie to sign:

'Received of W. Holman Hunt seven pounds in consideration for which I return to him the books and all the letters sent from him to me at different times excepting no one . . . and I hereby declare that [here and elsewhere there are many deletions and excisions] I retain no right or claim of any kind against him. (When you are writing it and have got to here say

227

"shall I add an acknowledgement of his past friendly attention to you"—, if she says "just as you like" write) and I express my sense of the unselfish kindness ['attention' crossed out] and liberality with which he always treated me" . . . if she says in the course of conversation "will he give me back my letters" say "will you give him any money for them". This may possibly end the bother and the necessity of my troubling you any more in this disagreeable business.'

As a postscript he added : 'Begin the conversation immediately she comes into the room if she has waited anytime . . . she will bolt without hearing the whole. I have put the shock early and the soothing parts at the end you will see'.

It is not surprising that Stephens did not succeed in persuading Annie to part with these souvenirs for seven pounds, or that Hunt was obliged to settle the Stratfords' account. To the latter's disgust, they lost their profitable 'goose': Annie left Chelsea and Pimlico for ever, to live with her new lover in Mayfair: Thomas Ranelagh Thomson.

Although he was not well off they were both confident that, if they chose the right moment, Hunt would pay a reasonable price for the letters. Thomas was in love with Annie by now, and probably reluctant for her to sell them to a newspaper, as such publicity would prejudice his mother against her.

On August 25 the following notice appeared under *Deaths* in *Gentleman's Magazine*: 'Suddenly in London Thomas James Thomson Esq., formerly of H.M.'s 34th Rgt. and uncle of the present Lord Ranelagh.'

To everybody's relief Thomas' drunken father had died of a heart attack at the Brown Bear, Bridge Street, St Saviour—at that period a district famous for the cheapest and sleaziest of brothels.

He left twenty pounds. His widow was able to increase Thomas' allowance, but died within three months at her house in Richmond.

Thomas was her executor and principal heir, but because of complicated family trusts, it took nearly two years to settle her affairs. On 23 July 1863, Thomas Ranelagh Thomson (gentleman) married Annie Miller (spinster), at St Pancras Church. Thanks to Hunt, instead of making her mark, she was able to sign the Parish Register.

She and Thomas moved into his mother's comfortable house in Richmond.

For a while they kept the marriage dark. Annie had lately heard some Kensington gossip from her sister, Harriet Childs, who still lived near Tor Villa: Hunt was in love, and planning to take a most respectable bride out to Syria. The engagement was not yet announced, but the moment was approaching when he would become increasingly anxious to buy the letters.

CHAPTER XVIII

Thy soul I know not from the body, nor
Thee from myself, neither our love from God.
D. G. ROSSETTI

DURING THE period when Hunt was suffering tortures of jealousy, and intriguing over Annie Miller, his friend Tommy Woolner was, as usual, leading an energetic social life and pursuing stunners.

Just as Hunt confided some of his hopes and fears to Mrs Combe, so Woolner wrote to Mrs Tennyson from 27 Rutland Street, Hampstead Rd, N.W., on 16 January 1859:

'On Thursday evening I went to *Letherhead* [sic] in Surrey to see a great beauty whom I have long been promised a sight of—my friend who mentioned her having thought she would do for my Trevelyan Lady. Altho' it certainly was an awful bore leaving my work yet I was munificently repaid for the lady, Miss Waugh was one of the grandest creatures I ever saw and her face is not far from what I want for my Lady: I hope to get her to sit—I stayed all the next day at Letherhead to try and make friends with her and I am rather in hopes that I succeeded; but whether I did or not, I did her a great deal of good, for I converted her to Browning and almost—of course not quite—but almost made her look with suspicion upon that schoolgirl poet Longfellow; Tennyson was her established poet, but she looked with a gentle eye upon the Yankee and could make neither head nor tail of the great Robert: but by taking a good deal of pains I made the Yankee sink into comparative insignificance with the subtle, sturdy and craggy Englishman overloaded with Italian tendencies. I should not have taken so much trouble with her mental development had she not been so majestically beautiful, for my sense of fitness was violated in knowing that such an imperial-looking creature should have anything like serious admiration for Longfellow, and yet turn from Robert Browning as from a thing of not much importance. I will tell you more of her if I manage to get her head to do, but now I cannot write you a long letter.'

My grandmother often described the evening that Woolner first brought Hunt to dine with the Waughs in their Bayswater home in Queensborough Terrace.

It was in the spring of 1861. Alice and Edith, the two youngest of the eight beautiful daughters, had been banished to school-room supper and bed. Their turn would come one day.

Alice was sixteen and very pretty. She was most envious of her elder sister, Fanny, whose admirer Mr Woolner was her ideal. He was not only good-looking and a gifted sculptor, for whom fame and fortune lay ahead, but such a fluent and witty conversationalist. He was on intimate terms with all the most brilliant men—how all the girls longed to meet them—Darwins, Carlyles, Tennysons and the most interesting set, but only Fanny was so privileged. She was escorted to marvellous dances and parties.

It was incomprehensible to Alice that darling Fanny seemed so unappreciative. After all, she was now twenty-eight, and when all the sisters were discussing their romantic futures the other night over their embroidery, Fanny had announced that although of course Mr Woolner was charming, she would be quite content to remain an old maid! Papa had been delighted: how he adored Fanny. Mr Woolner had told them how possessive Mr Barrett had been with his daughter Elizabeth before she married Mr Browning—Mr Woolner knew everyone and everything—all the girls were agreed that Papa's feelings for Fanny were similar to Mr Barrett's, to say the least.

This particular evening Alice crouched by the banisters beside Edith on the first landing to catch a glimpse of her hero when he arrived. It was exciting to see the top of his head.

Edith was only fifteen and worshipped Fanny whom she resembled. She modelled herself on her, although about twelve years younger. 'We become what we admire', they said.

Lately Edith had felt rather 'out of it', and bored by her seven sisters' confidences, especially Alice's infatuation for Mr

Woolner. As yet, Edith had never found a man attractive.

That night, when Mr Woolner brought his friend Hunt to dinner, peeping down from the second floor, watching the men and hearing them talk to each other, as the footman escorted them up to the drawing room, she fell in love at first sight.

What a wonderful man! All men had beards nowadays, and Mr Woolner, jokingly, had admitted that his made him look as if he had tied a hearth-rug under his chin, but his friend's beard —she could not see his face very clearly—was magnificent, red-gold and silky. He was so well-groomed and fashionably dressed. What a musical voice he had. She turned to Alice: they would sit up for Fanny and find out more of this marvellous man.

By May 1861, Woolner had been courting Fanny for two years. He had succeeded at last, over the port, using all his eloquence, in persuading her father to allow him to propose. Mr Waugh was confident that Mr Woolner would be refused.

For once left alone together in the drawing-room, Fanny rejected Woolner 'in the gentlest manner', adding that by now her parents and the girls were all so fond of him that he should continue to call at Queensborough Terrace and Leatherhead, as he was now a family friend.

Later that night she confided in her mother that Alice was already in love with him, and suggested that although Alice was not quite seventeen, she might be allowed to join the grown-ups in the dining-room on informal evenings.

Only Edith remained upstairs. How melancholy it would be for her to sit alone with supper on a tray! Fanny pleaded that she should be equally privileged. Edith's manners were impeccable.

Mrs Waugh eventually agreed. She still had several unmarried daughters. She would get rid of the schoolroom maid and order some new dresses for Alice and Edith. She had observed that on first meeting, Fanny and Mr Hunt had been mutually attracted. Mr Woolner might do very well for Alice in spite of the difference in age.

Now Fanny was free to accept Hunt's invitations. Together they went to private views such as one described by Mary Howitt on 20 June 1861.[1]

[1] Mary Howitt, 'The Pre-Raphaelites', *An Autobiography*, edited by her daughter Margaret, 2 vols. Isbister, London, 1889.

'On Friday evening we went to a great Pre-Raphaelite crush. Their pictures covered the walls and their sketch books the tables. The uncrinolined women with their wild hair which was very beautiful, their picturesque dresses and rich colourings, looked like figures out of some Pre-Raphaelite picture. It was very curious. I think of it now like some hot struggling dream in which the gorgeous and fantastic forms moved slowly about. They seemed all so young and kindred to each other that I felt out of place, though I admired them . . .'

There was no mistaking Fanny for a model. She never wore crinolines or stays, but dressed in the Pre-Raphaelite fashion which was all the rage amongst the *avant garde*. Hunt enjoyed designing women's clothes and designed Ellen Terry's wedding dress when she married Watts in 1864.

Hunt wrote to Stephens that it was 'curious that no rumour ever got about of my devotion to Fanny, she always looked so awful[2]—that although I went with her to every picture gallery' there was no gossip for a change.

However in September 1862, there began a prolonged row which inevitably widened the breach between Hunt and Gabriel Rossetti. William Rossetti and others referred appropriately to this unfortunate and hitherto inexplicable confusion involving many famous people as 'the Imbroglio'.[3]

The more Hunt saw of Fanny during the summer of 1862, the more anxious he was to get rid of Annie. I think that this scrap of a letter, probably to Mrs Combe, must have been written about this time:

'I wish more than ever that I could be married, but then I am in greater difficulty than ever because I know that most women would be crushed at the idea of the sort of life I should have to offer them. I never care one farthing for any women but highly bred ladies whose grace and refinement sit naturally upon them without any affectations or otherwise—'

[2] Evelyn Waugh was convinced that in this letter the word 'awful' was used in the eighteenth century sense, and meant awe-inspiring, formidable-looking.

[3] See Appendix.

If only Stephens could succeed in persuading Annie to emigrate! Many potential brides and cast-off mistresses were shipped off to Australia at that date, to save embarrassment to their former lovers.

Before Woolner proposed to Alice, Hunt wrote to Stephens on 27 October 1862: 'I have made arrangements for sending a poor girl to Australia. . . . She is in great want of money—give her a sovereign. If you have not got it send her to Woolner. Her address is Amelia Henderson . . . off Regent St. Her writing is so bad I cannot tell which is the right name of the street.' She had appealed to Hunt as Woolner's friend. As usual Stephens obliged, and wrote back that he had 'handed the sovereign to an aunt of "Miss H" who was escorting her to the ship last night'.

I read this letter first, and wondered if the 'H' could be an 'M', but alas for Hunt, Woolner's past sailed away, and his own sword of Damocles was still to descend.

Each time Hunt came to dinner poor Edith, watching him and Fanny, fell more and more in love with him, but she never gave away her feelings by so much as a glance. Mrs Waugh was delighted to see how easily Woolner transferred his attentions and affections from Fanny to Alice. Mr Waugh approved and by the summer of 1864, to Alice's joy, Woolner had proposed.

All his women confidantes wrote ecstatic letters about his choice. Mrs Carlyle referred to 'her graceful gracious figure . . . and if she makes you as happy as I want you to be, I shall love her with all my heart'.

In a letter to Hunt Stephens admitted to

'. . . being (between ourselves) rather disappointed with her looks, having taken into account what they seemed by candlelight at Palgraves and Tommy's own account of them. The nervous sort of reserve she exhibited when I saw her before has gone off and she is much improved in manner and really a pleasant little party to look at and talk to Woolner was quaintly husbandlike.'

Stephens went on to comment that hitherto Woolner had a 'sort of dog-like suspicion of outsiders which probably grew strong in Troublesome Times. I have great hopes of the effect of matrimony upon Tommy. . . .'

All concerned hoped that Woolner's example would encourage Hunt to propose to Fanny. Edward Lear was relieved to hear in letters from Hunt and others that at last the affair with Annie Miller was over. In a heavily censored letter written on 2 August 1864, he wrote: 'I hope all this matter has ceased to make you vexed, and (as an obstinate optimist as I always am) I believe we shall see "it is all for the best" someday.'

Although so much in love with Fanny, Hunt could not make up his mind.

On 20 July 1864 he wrote to Stephens for once beginning:

'Dear Fred, I am afraid I was not very sincere in the way in which I talked of the lady you write of when we were coming home the other night. I had no real question in my mind as to whether to make up to her. I have in fact no intention of matrimony at all now. Two mistakes in a life do not leave a man of my slow nature in that state of faith which is essential to serious love making—with conditions of cold blooded strategy fixed as they are by fathers and mothers in this day. If you brought the lady to my study and left her with me alone for a day the chances are that I should end by declaring myself in love and be either rejected or accepted— but as it is I have to make my calculations cooly [sic] and these do not encourage me to take any such step. I have not made a reasonable sort of income for the last 4 years. I have been drawing for the whole of that time upon my capital not of course for a large proportion of my expenditure but for enough to make it clear that I ought rather to diminish than increase my outlay . . . my spirits are not up the old mark— and so I look forward to the quiet sleep with a feeling of something nearer to contentment than I have for any other prospect in the world. The only thing that disturbs me in this outlook is the evidence that sometimes . . . my passions still burn within me and the fear that these—having no lawful hope—should burst out by contact with unlawful tinder into an unholy flame. When I have to reflect on some danger of this only just escaped I would do much to encourage a legitimate passion but not anything like the sort of thing that Woolner is going thro' now. I have no patience . . . to be hampered with the arrangements of the family in all my movements for three—four or six months before I married would be just impossible to me. You may say that had I been successful in my suit I should have to be doing this now. Very true! But two or three months experience of a disappointment of such importance makes a difference in one and I am another person now to what I should have been had I met with another fate.'

When the wedding took place on 6 September 1864, Woolner's father, the letter sorter, signed the register describing himself as a civil servant and George Waugh as 'Chymist'.

Hunt was best man and made an 'interminable speech'. Fanny was maid of honour. Edith's feelings as bridesmaid were 'dreadfully confusing'. In fact she felt sick and noticed that the little bouquet of roses she clutched became limp while Fanny's stayed fresh. Although she knew that their father's permission had not been sought by Hunt—as yet—she expected his engagement to Fanny to be announced by Woolner any minute.

If Fanny was disappointed she did not show it. In spite of encouragement from all his friends the following extract from a letter written by Hunt to Palgrave from Burton Park, Petworth, soon after the wedding, on 27 September 1864, implies that he feared a refusal:

'My idea of remaining an old bachelor is now so many months old that I had almost forgotten it as a new intention, it has the advantage in practice of saving me many fruitless disappointments of future happiness which for so many years I had cherished as a friendly dream. Your notion about my finding all things practicable when the *real charmer appears* would be convincing were it not that as an argument it has served too many of my predecessors who have all the same tracked their solitary way to the peaceful grave.

'I almost wish I were in town now that there seems to be one of my friends there to speak with—in fact I do quite wish it for I have not the love of the country general amongst artists, not enough to make me quite happy in it after the first two weeks of rusticating—however I shall have to stay another two—or, perhaps, three weeks.'

The following month Woolner wrote to Mrs Tennyson, from 29 Welbeck Street (where he and Alice lived all their lives):

'I am sorry to tell you that Hunt has made up his mind he says to go to the East for 2 or 3 years, and means to start in about 2 months. It seems a pity he should go to stay so long in that dangerous climate, but he has got the notion of painting religious pictures and it is of no use trying to dissuade him.'

By the spring of 1865, in spite of Woolner's prophecies, Hunt had still not left for the East.

He fulfilled various commissions and, as usual, Mr Combe invested the income wisely. Hunt's and his pupil Martineau's exhibition at the Hanover Galleries was a success, notably Hunt's picture *London Bridge on the Night of the Marriage of the Prince and Princess of Wales*. He had painted himself together with many portraits of his friends amongst the crowd. He also included Mr Combe, whom the Prince, when talking to Hunt, recognised as, '. . . an Oxford man whom he had seen out hunting with his beard flowing over his shoulders'.

Hunt and Fanny were meeting frequently with and without her parents' knowledge. Mrs Waugh seems to have allowed her daughters more liberty after Alice became engaged. The sketch by Hunt, so artfully entitled by my grandmother *After the Ball* years after the event, shows Fanny in the centre with Edith and Alice each side. They are unchaperoned and informally dressed after some party at 7 a.m. They would never have attended a *ball* wearing dresses with long sleeves.

In my opinion, it was during this period that Fanny secretly visited Hunt in the mornings and that he completed *Il Dolce Far Niente*, the picture he had begun in 1860 with Annie as his model but to which he now added Fanny's face for which Annie's reddish gold wavy hair made a most unsuitable frame.

The relaxed pose of a professional and the clothes are typical of Annie. Fanny's strong yet sensuous features, without the long straight hair she had, make the total effect so incongruous that the model looks like a female impersonator in a wig.

It would have been quite impossible for them, the Waughs, or anyone else to admit that Fanny had actually *sat* for a picture, as opposed to a portrait.

By June 1865 Hunt was confident that Fanny loved him enough to follow him to the end of the world, let alone the East.

Although she did not say so, Fanny had heard plenty of gossip about him relayed by Woolner to his bride, who in turn told her mother and sisters, including Fanny and Edith.

Hunt had quite a past it would seem. Mrs Waugh had liked him from their first meeting and was anxious to see Fanny married, but knew that Mr Waugh was most possessive regarding his daughter.

Even if Tommy Woolner, garrulous over the port, had been indiscreet to Fanny's father, all were agreed that it was unlikely that he would consent to the marriage—however famous and prosperous Hunt was or might become.

On 27 June 1865 Hunt wrote to Stephens:

'I am at home here every morning but not V. often in the evenings cos vy it's a great secret yet so don't let anyone see this note. I am making assiduous court to Miss W[augh] and I am encouraged by the darling to persevere altho' she has not yet pronounced definitely in my favour . . . the lady herself is most shy about it and if I mention the name of any friend she straightway asks me whether I have told the awful fact of my profane worship to him—and if I have to say yes! I lose ground considerably. She thought of taking her beautiful self unembraced to Heaven and she cannot really reconcile herself to the great change of life I propose and I believe she wld adhere to her first resolve and never see me again if her tender heart did not dread causing me real pain. . . . I had no choice —by a curious chance, but to tell Mrs W[augh] all the history of the A.M. affair—she was shocked beyond measure at it and at my part in it really regarding it as incredibly perverse and shameful. Mr W[augh] is now ill in bed—he is a good old fellow but awfully jealous of me with his daughter—moreover he has had a v. quiet and essentially respectable life himself so when he gets better I expect him to come down upon me rather desperately and insist upon the opportunity for the fullest investigation of the facts—He may therefore have to see Mrs Bramah—if so I will let you know, in the meantime I shld like to be told whether she is still at her old house in Chelsea. Fanny doesn't yet know of this dreadful history!'

Stephens replied the same day:

'Mrs B[ramah] still resides in Lindsey Houses and is not likely to leave town this year.

'As to the other matter you may rely on my secrecy, partly because I shall not believe the tale until you tell me it is all settled. If I could believe that it is really in a safe way you know that no one would be so eager to wish you joy as myself. I anticipate probabilities in saying that you deserve more than you are likely to get in any such directions as those which the thing in view proposes. Is not this a diplomatic sentence?

'What sort of idea can be entertained of the A.M. affair which is not to your eternal honour I cannot conceive.

'God bless you old boy. . . .'

Probably, Mrs Waugh called on Mrs Bramah and did all she could during the next two weeks to find excuses for Hunt's bad reputation with women.

His strange conduct with Annie Miller and Emma Watkins had to be explained to Mr Waugh as inspired by lofty motives—he was a victim of circumstances.

Hunt became impatient and wrote complaining to Stephens on 11 July 1865 that, 'at the present rate of action . . . no chance of getting the young lady to settle the day in this century. Tommy cooly [sic] proposes that I should have patience—not attempt to urge her too much now but go away to the East. Keep up a steady correspondence'.

Within another two weeks, although Mr Waugh had not given official consent, it seems to have been generally accepted among the family and their closest friends that all would be well for Hunt and Fanny.

On 24 July, Mrs Tennyson wrote from Faringford to Woolner:

'Many thanks for your kind letter and our best wishes for the beautiful Fanny and Mr Hunt. I trust that the marriage will not only make them happy but add, if possible, to your own happiness and Mrs Woolner's.'

While this uneasy courtship of Hunt and Fanny was taking place, Stephens was preoccupied. At long last he had secretly married his widow Mrs Clara Charles. She was presentable now and could even read and write.[4]

By August 18 Mr Waugh had reluctantly given them his blessing and Hunt and Fanny were officially engaged. Hunt wrote to Stephens, addressing him for the first (and last) time as,

'My dear Stivvy,

'You will be glad I know to hear that all is concluded now in my favour and my engagement to Fanny Waugh may be spoken of publicly. It makes me more truly happy than I have been for many years. Everyday I see the darling I discover some new merit in her or find one I knew before stronger and more important. The marriage cannot take place it seems until about the end of November so there is some exercise for my patience yet. Here endeth the first Chapter.

'I have at last finished the Temple sketch and got some tin —so I am in a position now to fulfil the promise you accepted to help you in investing—I can let you have whatever is necessary. Now is a very good time for buying—this and perhaps about month later. Here endeth 2nd Ch.

'People have the astounding effrontery to say you are married. If it is not so tell me and I will contradict it. On the other hand if it is so it must at any penalty be made public. . . .

'In my courting lately I have seen more of a good English family and learnt more of the homely prejudices of ladies than in all my past life and on the strength of this I assure you that no difficulty—however great it may be—should prevent a man from declaring his marriage from the first. So if you are really a husband choose between two things—either retrace your steps—of course I mean only in appearance—profess to be no further advanced than I am and fix a time for your second marriage and then with one or two friends go thro the ceremony to the satisfaction of everybody. Otherwise state to some of your old friend[s] the fact of your marriage—the date

---

[4] Her exercise books are preserved at the Bodleian Library.

of it and all the circumstances which concern the world and leave us to overrule all objections. . . .

'In any case the matter will not be so serious because everyone who knows the lady likes her—and appreciates her too highly not to be certain of her unimpeachableness. Here endeth Ch 3.'

He added a postscript:

'Whether Mrs Charles or Mrs Stephens pray tell her of my good fortune and say that I desire her congratulations—and that I feel it will be a great loss to the School of Design now the students cannot without decided impropriety speak of my being in love with some fresh lady once every six months. . . .'

On August 26 Stephens replied admitting that he was no longer a bachelor and regretted therefore that he would not be Hunt's 'best man'. He was annoyed that anyone had heard rumours of this secret marriage.

'When we meet I will Tell you all there is to Tell but I shall Tell it to you, and to *you only*, making *no* exceptions. As you have been so much annoyed by the discussion of your own affairs among strangers you will guess why I am reticent and determined not to gratify impertinent persons.

'As "society" and I have been strangers to each other for some six or seven years I may leave you to guess how much surprised I am at this sudden display of interest in my affairs. For the sake of the lady I *should like to learn from you who are the persons thus concerned for her.*

'What can you do, *pray do not make excuses for me.* I do not wish to have any "objections overuled" [sic], and to be excused is to be accused.'

In the same long letter he congratulated Hunt on his engagement, and gave him some sound advice on his reformed opinion of women since meeting Fanny and his recent idea that women were superior to men:

'My dear fellow you undoubtedly are able to discover new excellencies exalted in the lady. . . . These are not to be judged by the standards you have been applying to your own sex. . . . I believe the idea that a woman is but a variety of man, to be the cause of a great deal of unhappiness, you will not need to be warned of this error, the Truth may be novel to you, nevertheless [accept it]. . . . Two Thirds of my life has been gladdened by our affections and that if you make as good a husband as you have been loving a True friend the lady will not, as Time passes fail to become more and more happy in her position as your wife.'

The rest of Stephens' letter is pathetic, and shows how much he longed for release from the demanding rôle in Hunt's life that he had hitherto played out of what he refers to as 'a sense of indebtedness'.

More and more I feel that Stephens' devotion and subservience were motivated by guilt because of the relatively unimportant but regrettable incident with Annie Miller already described, as well as his gratitude for financial assistance and endless introductions and recommendations as an art critic. He longed for Hunt to be 'off his hands' and happily married, and confessed:

'I have been for several years, and "at every sacrifice" endeavouring to deliver myself. I shall be wholly free in a short Time from those shackles which were—altho' be [sic] no means unfairly—left to me, and also from such as were properly my own. Altho' those good people who waited any Time for delivering myself, made the said shackles nominal yet they were really most painful to me, and I Thirst for the day when I shall owe you nothing but thanks.'

Alas for Stephens, it was not for another few months that he was released.

A month later on September 28, Hunt wrote to him complaining:

'My own affair does not I am sorry to say give me anything [but] unmixed satisfaction—the conventionalities of the world have much too great a power in my case to make my position a delight—there are reasons for delay—accouche-ments of sisters, illnesses of father and uncle etc. etc., each in themselves of importance and of a kind that individually one cld not but be patient towards but which collectively are most intolerable and most ruinous to my wordly position— say that they will occasion me a year of the most infurious slavery when I am in the East and perhaps with all the loss of the season and consequent bankruptcy of all my Hanover St. schemes—I try to forget all this as much as poss but I can't help acknowledging to myself that if I had only foreseen these difficulties I shd have regarded it as nothing less than madness to take the step which has led me captive—You dis-pute what I say about the superiority of women to men . . . all I wld say is that women are better in being more innocent and . . . unfortunately however we have yet for a span to remain on earth and during this period a certain amt of mundane wisdom is required which I see not much form of in them.'

During the next two months Hunt and Stephens exchanged various letters concerning the presents they would eventually give each other's wives. Hunt explained that Fanny already had 'a good share of trinkets', but 'no great taste for Jewelery—Ear-rings she has never worn.'

Stephens was 'glad the lady does not mutilate her ears with holes for earrings, I do not permit my wife to do so, altho' of course, like all women, she longs to do that which she ought not—only "oppossition" [sic] moves her fancy'.

Hunt wondered whether to give Stephens a wheelbarrow, and weather glass . . . or a coal scuttle and preferred to leave the 'selection of bijoux' for Stephens' bride until he should arrive in the East and find something of more interest than 'anything I could find in Bond Street. . . . Unless my journey to the East be prevented by the wretched news of the Cholera in Jerusalem published by the infamous *Times* yesterday (which frightened Mr Waugh out of his scarcely established composure at our bedouin intention).'

After Christmas 1865, Hunt's wedding to Fanny took place at Christ Church, Paddington on December 28. She was thirty-two and he thirty-eight.

By now Mr Waugh was so rich (he owned blocks of property, not only in, but around Regent Street) that when signing the register, he felt justified in promoting himself from 'chymist' to 'gentleman'. He made generous settlements on all his daughters and Fanny was his favourite.

According to Stephens, William Rossetti had 'for some reason been against everyone and everything lately', but now he had recovered his humour, it seems, as he and Mr Combe, amongst others, were witnesses. My grandmother said: 'Everyone who was anyone, old and new friends, attended.' There was a splendid reception at Queensborough Terrace.

Edith was nineteen and a bridesmaid again; she was kissed warmly by Hunt for the first time. At Alice's wedding his beard had brushed her cheek. This time he put a hand on each of her shoulders and held her closely to him. The effect of this brotherly kiss and the scent of sandalwood oil were so overpowering that had she not been 'so well brought up, she would have fainted'.

CHAPTER XIX

O Sorrow, wilt thou live with me
No casual mistress, but a wife?
TENNYSON

AFTER THE wedding various threats, apart from cholera, delayed Hunt's and Fanny's departure for the East.

Annie was determined not to let him get away. The time was ripe to negotiate. There is no evidence of whom she used as a go-between. Certainly, in the early spring of 1866 neither Hunt nor his close friends had any idea that Annie was married—and had been—since 1863. The thought of her publishing the letters immediately after his marriage to Fanny must have been not only repugnant but terrifying.

The Waughs were not amused by the skits and caricatures involving the Pre-Raphaelites and Hunt that appeared in *Punch* two weeks running: March 3 and March 10.[1]

Mrs Waugh had already been at pains to explain away Hunt's dubious past (the Calmuck story amongst other things). Mr Waugh had demanded detailed accounts of his prospective son-in-law's finances. Hunt had precipitated the wedding at a most inconvenient date; pleading how urgent his departure for the East, he now made every excuse for delay to Fanny and her family. *Dolce Far Niente* must be finished, even Emily's picture of the dovecote, *The Festival of St Swithin*, must not be left uncompleted. Emily had long ago abandoned it.

Stephens was amazed to receive a letter from Hunt on 13 February 1866, thinking that by now he and Fanny must have reached 'Italy or Jerusalem'. Loyal as ever, he answered Hunt's appeal yet again:

'I will, if you wish it, take charge of the papers and portrait

[1] For detailed analysis see Leonée Ormond's "A Legend of Camelot", *Apollo*, January, 1967.

in question, that is if you would not rather destroy them, or, for the former at least, place them for security with your banker or lawyer. I will gladly come and Talk the matter over with you when you like and receive the Trust, if that is the safest way. As soon as I heard your marriage was settled I placed some boxes of old letters, among which are many of yours, some of which refer to this matter, in extra security, with the intention of selecting and destroying those which Treat of it, as soon as I could spare Time to do so I am glad this has not been done, as you do not seem to share my belief in the harmlessness, if not the gratitude of that unhappy person. It is possible, though I cannot now say so much, that those I have already may be useful on your side in the event of any develry [sic] being attempted. I pray you will not, my dear Trouble your mind about that affair, either for the past or the future. I am a witness and can be an advocate to declare the Truth of it. To compass all chances, however, it will certainly be better to retain the documents, the only object of destroying them would be to get rid yourself of all remaining Traces of an experiment which cost you so much. All mine wish you and your wife a happy life.'

There is an undated scrap of blue paper amongst the Hunt-Stephens letters referring to 'the loss and signing away of £1000'. Perhaps this was the sum which Hunt had to pay in the end for his love-letters to Annie.

In Hunt's memoirs and in A. C. Gissing's biography, there are references at this date to some financial catastrophe, which my half-uncle Cyril, for one, found unconvincing as accounting for so large a sum as supposed by the Waughs.

However Hunt and Annie settled the business, there were repercussions. Two weeks after Stephens's last letter, he wrote to Hunt again on 28 February 1866:

'Ecce Sathanus! I am sorry to bother you with this filth, but cannot help it, because it may concern you.

'Of course I can answer for my own acts at this house—of all places under Heaven—and likewise for my belief in those which connected you with it.

'Can you come and talk the thing over here on Friday

evening, so that one may answer Rossetti? I am very hard at work or would come to you. I shan't be in Tomorrow, Thursday Saturday at all.

'There may be some portion of Truth in this woman Moody's assertions, apart from either of us; this is not the first time I heard such a thing of Mrs S[tratford]'s establishment, but I have no authority beyond gossip at Mrs Bramah's, an *exaggerated receipt* of which might well bear the preposterous questions. Who the Devil was Moody?—Isn't the whole thing a dodge to get cash?'

It is possible that others who had known of Hunt's affair with Annie and the true facts of Mrs Stratford's establishment were also anxious to cash in by writing sensational stories for the newspapers and magazines about this newly-wed famous man.

Francis Moody was the Pimlico artist who painted Annie's father as the red-coated pensioner in the Royal Hospital Gardens, Chelsea. The 'woman Moody' referred to in the letter was the daughter of Francis Moody and still lived at 34 Lupus Street. She was an animal painter and it is more than likely that she knew Gabriel Rossetti, who lived quite near with his private zoo.

The only explanation that I can find for this mysterious letter is that Miss Moody gossiped with Gabriel one day saying that she and everyone in Lupus Street knew only too well what kind of life Hunt and Stephens led while Annie was one of Mrs Stratford's inmates. It is possible that Gabriel wrote a vaguely or even wholly jocular note to Stephens—also newly married— warning him that some fresh scandal was brewing. Gabriel, to me, never seems to have been spiteful. Perhaps Hunt paid up again to protect his bride and her family's feelings.

It is curious that this last letter of Stephens mentioning Gabriel Rossetti, dated 28 February, was followed so closely by a letter from Gabriel to Stephens on March 12, mentioning in a postscript:

'P.S. I remember your expressing a doubt as to Annie Miller being really married. I should mention in justice to her, that Mrs Stratford, though not now on good terms with her asserts that she is. I have met the husband who seems a very good gentlemanly fellow.'[2]

[2] Iggulden collection of letters at the Bodleian Library, Oxford.

This shows at least that Gabriel had been in touch with the Pimlico crowd, the Stratfords and Annie, quite recently.

About the same time, Millais wrote to Hunt that he too had met Annie, and found her husband 'a decent fellow', much to his taste.

Perhaps Thomas Ranelagh Thomson was innocent of the game Annie played. Having won hands down, the Thomson estate being at last satisfactorily settled, how natural that she should wish to show off her husband, respectability and prosperity to people like Mrs Stratford. Equally, she was perhaps anxious to impress Thomas with her friendships with famous men like Millais and Rossetti. It would seem that she and her husband paid quite a few calls in the course of that week. Annie had just become aware that she was expecting a baby; but she and Thomas kept this a secret from their old friends.

There are but a few more references to Annie in this story. The first I quote from Professor Doughty's book A Victorian Romantic. Unfortunately I have failed to find the original source. After a short spell at Richmond, Annie and Thomas lived in Hampstead until 1867 at least. The following encounter rings true, although it must have taken place after Hunt's second marriage:

> 'In later years Hunt, accidentally meeting Annie, "a buxom matron with a carriage full of children, on Richmond Hill," and learning that she, like himself, was now happily married, forgave "the offence, which in fact," he said, "worked me good rather than harm." In real life, Annie was obviously no apt example of the moral she had illustrated in Hunt's painting, The Awakened Conscience.'

Last year Virginia Surtees[3] told me that sometime before 1939 Mrs Janet Troxell[4] received a letter from a Miss

[3] Her book, Dante Gabriel Rossetti—A catalogue Raisonné, is to be published by the Clarendon Press, Oxford, early in 1970.
[4] Mrs Troxell owns an outstanding Pre-Raphaelite collection in the United States, which includes water-colours, drawings, first editions of their published writings, twenty volumes of manuscripts and autograph letters. She is well known as the author of Three Rossettis: Unpublished Letters to and from Dante Gabriel, Christina, William. Harvard University Press, Cambridge, Mass., 1937.

Thomson, addressed from an English seaside resort, written in a quavering hand implying great age, asking if Mrs Troxell would like to buy some drawings of 'her lovely mother Annie Miller, by Dante Gabriel Rossetti'.[5]

Mrs Troxell bought the drawings and kept Miss Thomson's letter among other papers for a long time, but now it seems to be lost, at least temporarily.

If Hunt's departure for the East was in fact delayed by Annie, she thus proved herself his femme fatale and was to prove the cause of Fanny's death.

Annie, as well as Fanny, was already seven months pregnant by the time Hunt had settled all his troublesome affairs and it was not until August 1866, instead of early spring as originally planned, that Hunt and Fanny were able to leave.

Her parents were distracted at the thought of the perilous journey ahead. How could Fanny and their future grandchild survive the heat, the rocking boats and the filthy trains? Although it was clear that Hunt worshipped her more each day, he seemed to expect women to have the same mental attitude and physical strength as men. He had already taught her to shoot and boasted that she was by now as good a shot as he.

When they reached Egypt on the final stage she would be expected to ride a mule up and down dangerous mountain tracks. Everyone knew that the country 'seethed with brigands and was riddled with disease'. Small wonder they all wept when they said goodbye. Mr Waugh raved about 'the Cursed Promised Land'. Tommy Woolner was to blame for ever bringing Hunt to Queensborough Terrace. He had even confessed to Alice, who of course repeated it, that Hunt had always been known as 'the Maniac'.

Edith was torn between guilt and grief. Her illicit passion for

[5] In fact this Miss Thomson, who was called Annie after her mother, died 'a spinster of no occupation' aged seventy-nine from cancer of the liver in 1946 at Shoreham-by-Sea. She had been present at her father's death from chronic bronchitis when he was eighty-seven at 6 Western Road, Shoreham-by-Sea in 1916. (He outlived Hunt by six years. They were both born the same year and both died of the same disease.)

Miss Thomson was also with her mother Annie née Miller at the same address when she died aged ninety in 1925. As far as I can discover she had only one other child besides this unmarried daughter, a son Thomas James born in Hampstead in 1867. The family probably moved to Shoreham-by-Sea to be near the Thomson aunt, a Miss Sturges.

Hunt preyed on her mind. There was no one in whom she could possibly confide.

Because she looked like Fanny, Mrs Waugh implored her to spend hours at her father's side comforting him, in the hope that she would eventually replace the favourite. Mr Waugh had once more taken to his bed and was convinced that he would never see Fanny again.

When Hunt and Fanny reached Marseilles, cholera had broken out and no ship was permitted to leave. They decided therefore to cross the Alps and approach Egypt from Italy. The heat was intolerable. The same ban existed at all the Italian ports. They decided to settle temporarily in Florence and rented a studio at 32 Via Montebello. Here she posed for Hunt day after day. She stood, rather than sat, behind an armchair to conceal her eight months' pregnancy, a little black bonnet dangling from her hand. She looked very ill with rings of fatigue under her eyes—her hair was lank with sweat.[6]

When too exhausted even for this, she lay on the bed without a mosquito net, her dark hair spread on the pillow and her huge eyes staring ahead.

Hunt wrote that Florence was 'stinking and pestilent'. They rarely went out until the merciless sun had set and when they did, what they most enjoyed was buying beautiful things, furniture, glass and ornaments to decorate the studio. Hunt said that these purchases would prove a sound investment. They did.

News reached them from home. Clara Stephens was pregnant, but so far marriage had brought no happiness to Fred. In order to accommodate his mother and his wife, he had moved out of the old lodgings and taken a whole house in Lupus Street.

He confided to Hunt that he was not only still in debt, but,

'like a rat in a trap shop, and Clara Turns pale now at the least sign of a row. Strange as it seems I have found the most effectually [sic] defence weapon to be the legally drawn up promise of a separate maintenance for her, this was prepared

[6] Years later my half-uncle Cyril tortured himself and horrified me with the ordeals she must have suffered for this portrait, which descended to him and then to me. When it was too hot for her to pose fully dressed, she leaned against the chimney piece wearing only a nightdress. The tiles were cool to her bare feet.

at her demand, but when it came to making it [the] tide changed and we got a sort of armed peace, so we go on and this is better than perpetual quarrels or the alternation [sic] of Throwing one's mother out of doors or seeing one's wife worried as if by a wild beast; as to the "why" of which one knows no more than the Man in the Moon and yet is able to understand the infernal ingenuity and cruelty of the process.'

Hunt's description to Stephens of his own marriage, in an extract from a very long letter, was an extreme contrast:

'. . . sometimes without premeditation I know misunderstandings and temporary crosses come into even early married life . . . [Fanny] frequently reminded me we had never had any word between us but those of unbroken love and happiness. the difficulties of our life had been certainly very vexing but they had only made us cling to one another the more. we had been in spite of everything supremely happy. . . .'

On 11 October, Annie gave birth to a daughter, Annie Helen, at Montrose House, Lower Heath, Hampstead. Two weeks later, on October 26 my half-uncle Cyril Benone[7] was born and on 10 November 1866 Hunt wrote to Stephens:

'Poor Fanny suffered most cruelly at the confinement her preliminary pains were so extreme and the danger was so great that it was resolved upon as the only means of saving her life that instruments shld be used to extract the child by force—by some chance little short of a miracle—as it seemed with a knowledge of the violence employed—the poor little child was born alive altho so badly injured about the head as to leave great doubts whether he wld live a day. . . . the poor mother however was injured much more seriously—(for 9 days the baby is not getting proper food) poor Fanny has had to lie at the very gates of death many and many an hour. Now I bless God it is thought she is out of imminent danger altho she is sadly wasted and v. feeble.'

[7] Hebrew for 'child of distress or sorrow'.

Six weeks later, on December 20, Fanny died but as if by a miracle the baby survived.

As soon as the news reached England, the Waughs' first thought was to send one of their daughters to Florence immediately to rescue the baby. Hunt wrote to Stephens: 'Poor old Mrs Waugh is waiting to take care of him, longs to find him in her arms as the only consolation she can receive in this world for the dearest and sweetest of daughters.'

Edith was only twenty, far too young to travel unchaperoned to Italy. One of her elder sisters was sent to fetch the baby. Mrs Waugh agreed that once their grandson arrived, Edith, with the aid of a nurse, should take charge of him: there was plenty of room at Queensborough Terrace. Hearing of this, Emily wrote indignantly to Hunt insisting on her priority. The boy was a Hunt, she was his aunt, she proposed to claim him. But Hunt could not bear to part with this last link with his beloved Fanny. Some English friends, the Spencer Stanhopes, who lived in Florence, had already engaged a Tuscan foster-mother and taken him in. So both aunts were frustrated.

Hunt wrote to Stephens on 5 April 1867:

'. . . my sister Emily . . . will never forgive me. the many unkindnesses she has had to bear from me are more than the most Christian flesh and blood can stand . . . when I politely expressed myself pledged to other plans in answer to overtures from her to take my baby and bring him up for me . . . she for once and all determined to wash her hands of all further responsibility for me. I believe she is engaged to a silly [illeg.] young city man who has about £75 per annum . . . and when she is married and has a large family of half stupid and the other half pig headed children with a violent determination to adventure I may do her and the state some service—at a comparatively cheap rate—by sending them to Australia.'[8]

Hunt wrote to Stephens on January 19 that Woolner went out to Florence separately from his sister-in-law to help him

[8] Emily Hunt married a Mr Wyman and died at Bedford Row, in 1920. She was a rich widow and having no children left everything to her Peagrim nephews in Australia. Some years previously her elder sister Maria had married the upholsterer's shop assistant, Thomas Peagrim. After this quarrel, she was estranged permanently from Hunt and the Waughs.

'with all the disturbance of a material kind connected with the death and burial of my wife—and I am alone now—more tragically solitary than ever I knew a man in this world could be.'

He could no longer bear the studio where he and Fanny had lived and moved to 14 Lungarno Acciajoli—a studio recently vacated by his friend Simeon Solomon.[9]

In an earlier letter, written on 19 January, 1867, he wrote to Stephens of his loss of faith: 'I cannot say "thy will be done" and bless God for this affliction from anything but my lips.' In the same letter he wrote:

'It is the one comfort to me now that she loved me beyond all measure. that she valued this affection for me so highly that I was her first thought in the hope that her life might yet be spared to her. with so short a term of married life it would have been melancholy if there had been any but a continually growing admiration of her—an increasing desire to exhibit affection for her on my part. . . .

'How long now must I be in doubt whether she still loves me? the still silence makes me dread that she knows all my unworthiness and despises me. I will however gather all my strength to be worthy of her—she shall not see me worse than she knew me if the God in whom I trust will not humiliate me. Give my kindest regards to your wife. I have put aside some little thing of the few trinkets and such like that my wife had with her as a present—a keepsake—for your wife. The Waughs will let you know when it arrives.'

It was during the next few months in Florence that Hunt became interested in spiritualism. He longed to communicate with Fanny, to feel and enjoy her physical presence.

---

[9] It is interesting that neither Hunt nor his wife Edith deleted Simeon Solomon's name from the memoirs as 'after the disgrace of his legal conviction for pederasty in 1873, Simeon Solomon was sent to Coventry by the Pre-Raphaelites who henceforth agreed to pretend . . . that he had simply never existed. Swinburne, at whose doorstep the degradation of Solomon has frequently been laid . . . later referred to Solomon as "a thing unmentionable alike by men and women, as equally abhorrent to either—nay, to the very beasts . . ."' William E. Fredeman, *Pre-Raphaelitism, A bibliocritical study*, Harvard University Press, Cambridge, Mass., 1965.

Not only in Florence, but in London and Paris too, spiritualism was all the rage. After Lizzie's death, Gabriel Rossetti also became increasingly interested in seances.

According to Hunt, if swirling masses of gas in the cosmos could solidify into thunderbolts and land on the earth, so the spirits of the dead could return in their natural bodies. He longed to hold Fanny in his arms again.

All Hunt's friends wrote each other horrified letters about the tragedy. Condolences poured in. Millais' letter of 6 January 1867 was one of the first to arrive:

> 'My wife has nearly died more than once in childbirth and I know the Terrible nature of the Trial . . . seen that one evening that you dined with us quite enough to show that you had chosen wisely and that she [Fanny] possessed all the grace and nobility of character which you speak of and which shone unmistakably [sic] in her beautiful face.'

On his arrival in England Woolner reported to William Allingham that 'Hunt was plunging deep down into work hoping to keep the hard fixed sorrow at a kind of bay. . . .'

He began designing a monument to Fanny and combined the two pictures he had painted of her, the one barefoot in her nightdress and the other lying in bed, into one composition *Isabella and the Pot of Basil*. The pot was substituted for the pillow and placed on an inlaid prie-dieu which I remember very well as a child. He and Fanny had bought it just before she died. The combination of these two pictures of Fanny into one accounts for the awkward pose. The face was a little changed. The Waughs were affronted by his using of these last tragic records of Fanny, in such 'a cold-blooded, commercial way'.

On 5 April 1867 he wrote to Stephens that all his leisure time had been occupied in:

> 'attending to my baby's wants which have been many and serious on account of the villainy of a wet nurse who was attending him and who nearly starved him. . . . When Stanhope's poor little child was ill of scarlet fever it was necessary for me to find a new home for him . . . many chances I tried turned out to be hopeless but a certain Mr

Dunn, an English dentist here was good enough to take them.'

The unsatisfactory wet-nurse was dismissed and took with her Fanny's 'portmanteau—a silk shawl, and several things belonging to the baby'. The police discovered that she had stolen an even greater number of Fanny's personal possessions—clothes and trinkets—from the studio while she lay dying. Endless complications ensued as the nurse's family bribed various witnesses to swear that Fanny had given her all these things before she died and Hunt was threatened with 'an action for false imprisonment, and also assassination by a private messenger to be executed by himself and his wife's brother . . . people say I am certain . . . to meet with a verdict against me with very heavy damages'. There are no further references to these problems so presumably they were resolved satisfactorily.

By late spring, he was thoroughly disgusted with Florence and the Florentines. He longed to get away, but dared not risk leaving his delicate baby.

He wrote to Millais on 26 May 1867 showing that he was extremely interested in the French Impressionists:

'I still wish you were going to the Paris Exhibition. Of late I have been feeling very strongly indeed the responsibility which every man, and especially remarkable and successful men are under pressure to do the utmost that is possible with their talents and I believe that for these it is essential that they should know of everything, as far as possible, that others are doing in the same branch of work.'[10]

In a letter to Stephens which is written almost like a journal over a period of several days, he refers to a pamphlet[11] which Stephens wrote about Hunt's early life:

'[The Hunts and Hobmans] . . . all my relatives . . . have

[10] J. G. Millais, *Millais: The Life and Letters of Sir John Everett Millais*, Methuen, London, 1899.
[11] F. G. Stephens, *William Holman Hunt and His Works: A Memoir of the Artist's Life, with Descriptions of His Pictures*, Nisbet, London, 1860.

been in a state of feverish indignation at the references therein to my state of poverty during student and other early days. they declare that it is all untrue that I was provided for most liberally, if not extravagantly, and that my allowing such statements to remain as those w[hich] convey the idea that I was in some difficulty for want of proper patronage is an unpardonable wickedness: about once every six months or so their wrath boils up and I make up my mind to ask you to look over it and see where there are any passages on the subject of early difficulties which could be cut out should G ever be printing further copies. I of course have forgotten the intention to speak on the subject ten minutes after leaving my wealthy and ever thoughtful and indulgent friends, but now comes a fresh explosion from my uncle and aunt and also my Mother and sister. It is I fear much too late for me ever to get into their good graces again enough to hope to become their heir but as you know to me it is a perfect matter of indifference whether people think me to have been a shoeblack or a prince I will be moved by their desires enough to leave the subject in your hands. If you could describe how a carriage and a pair on wet days and a blood horse and a mounted groom on fine days always took me and sometimes a lucky friend round to the restaurant in Lisle St for our petit diner you might perhaps increase my income a few hundred pounds in my old age. I give the last fact as an argument if any be necessary to persuade G to allow alterations. For my uncle I can see some excuse for the silly pride. he didn't know much of the sterness [sic] of Fortune to me at from 17 to 23 or 24 and he thinks now it is a reflection upon him to have it known that he didn't help me. God knows, I would not insinuate any blame on him. He had too many hopeless nephews and nieces too—and it would be rather ridiculous to say that he should have picked me out of the batch and supported me in defiance of the opinion of nearly everyone who opened his mouth on the subject that I was a miserable ne'er-do-well. On this account I would try and humour him so I leave you to do the best you can.'

By September of the same year (1867) Hunt felt an urge for adventure again and confided in an undated unaddressed scrap of a letter that he longed to 'escape from Florence and the sad associations and the restricted atmosphere of the English community however forebearing and kind my friends have [been].' He resolved to 'break my journey in Paris which should prove a desirable change'.

He engaged a new *balia*, a wet nurse, for the journey. Her impoverished family assured him, in typical Italian superlatives, that she had enough milk for twins. Full-breasted and smiling, she looked promising.

By the time Hunt reached Paris, Cyril Benone looked very ill, but Hunt blamed this on the change of nurse and the tiring journey. He left them both at an hotel and went out alone to enjoy himself in search of old haunts and friends.

Since his last visit Paris was much changed. Thanks to Worth, the English couturier, French women had finally abandoned their crinolines and stays. Hunt had always detested this distortion of women's bodies.

There was a spirit of licensed revelry in the air. He too felt elated and thought that the stimulating atmosphere was largely due to the Great Exhibition[12] which had attracted so many artistic and uninhibited visitors.

Established French painters, such as Corot and Ingres, were well represented at the Exhibition, but the hanging committee had rejected works by Pisarro, Cézanne, Courbet, Manet, Monet and their followers. However, these 'rebels' had been allowed to produce a *salon des refusés* at their own expense, where the public could scoff or leer at *Déjeuner sur l'herbe* for fifty centimes a head.

There were magnificent balls night after night. The latest Strauss waltz the *Blue Danube* was probably played, whistled or sung everywhere Hunt went.

Returning to his hotel in the small hours, he was relieved to find that the exhausted baby had fallen asleep.

The following day Hunt had an appointment to lunch with Gambart's engraver, Auguste Blanchard, who lived about twenty miles outside Paris. Seeing a copy of Feuillet's *Monsieur de Camors* on the station bookstall, Hunt bought it to read in the train. A lady in Florence had already strongly recommended this book to him.

[12] Which opened on 1 April, 1867.

When he arrived at Blanchard's house, he left the book in the hall while his host showed him round the studio and also showed him an engraving of one of Hunt's pictures on which he was working.

At luncheon Hunt found the family and all the friends who had been invited to meet the English religious painter were 'models of mutual reverence and politeness'. Even Hunt's memoirs make the party sound deadly dull.[13] Later, when Blanchard spotted Hunt's copy of *Monsieur de Camors* in the hall, 'horrified he exclaimed, "Whoever has brought that abominable book into the house?"' On learning it was Hunt's, he begged him to hide it from his respectable guests and went on to regale him out of the others' hearing with the 'perilous decadence and revolting immorality' of the contemporary literary and artistic *monde* in Paris. Venereal disease was rampant. Baudelaire had been paralysed with syphilis. He had died on August 31 in a clinic at Chaillot, aged forty-six, only the other day. De Maupassant, Dumas fils and Manet also suffered from syphilis. (Renoir once remarked that he could not be considered a true genius as he alone amongst contemporary painters had not caught this particular disease.)

As for so-called High Society! Auguste Blanchard went on that although the Empress Eugénie had been perhaps in some way maligned, she had certainly had a regrettable influence on ladies' fashions. Surely Hunt must have noticed and been incensed by the immodest gowns worn in the cafés and streets? This Second Empire was notorious for extravagance! The much discussed Tuileries Ball had cost the equivalent of £160,000. They rejoined the other guests, who echoed all he said. What remained of the old aristocracy kept aloof nowadays. It was the year of *les grandes horizontales* and *les grisettes*, famous courtesans such as Cora Pearl and the English demi-mondaines were thriving. Even newspapers, full of scandal, were made of rubber so that the idle rich could luxuriate in their baths reading pornography. The latest disgusting and favourite spectacle, found hilarious by these sybarites, was watching fat turkeys dance in

[13] My grandmother was a great admirer of Auguste Blanchard and the effort he made to reform 'undesirable elements' in the Parisian art world. The contemporary scene is well described by Alistair Horne in *The Fall of Paris*: Macmillan, London, 1965.

agony with their feet on red-hot metal plates.

By the time Hunt left the house, his mood had changed completely: he felt disillusioned and depressed.

Auguste Blanchard's luncheon party certainly prejudiced him against the French; he complained to Stephens of their 'getting the pox, writing filthy sentimental novels, not putting Nap. in quod, keeping lorettes and drinking absinthe. . . .'

Hunt returned to his hotel to find Cyril in a frightening state. The nurse shrugged and grinned. He decided to leave Paris for London by the next train.

CHAPTER XX

Amid the bitterness of things occult.
D. G. ROSSETTI

BY THE time Hunt arrived at Queensborough Terrace on October 9, it was obvious to Mrs Waugh, with ten children of her own, that her grandson Cyril was dying. She postponed dinner and summoned a doctor. Edith was horrified and hovered about wearing her prettiest dress, feeling helpless. She had looked forward so long to this reunion, however tragic the circumstances.

She had imagined the welcoming embrace that she would give, how she would take the cherubic baby in her arms. She had even studied Italian recently in order to communicate with the *balia*. But the whole evening was chaotic.

The doctor examined the nurse. She was a fraud. She had not a drop of milk in her breasts and probably never had had. She was also diseased; the child had been starved for days and was moreover covered with sores.

George Waugh, who was, after all, druggist to the Queen, dispatched messengers to his Regent Street shop for bottles, teats and some of the recently patented infant foods. These remedies only made the baby sick. Finally doctor and chemist agreed with Mrs Waugh that although the child was eleven months old human milk was all he could digest. Members of the family went at top speed in hansom cabs to various addresses. Edith was sent upstairs to explain to the terrified *balia* that she would be sent back to Italy as soon as this could be arranged.

Before midnight an English girl, whose child had died that day, was brought to the house, just in time, and put to bed with the famished baby. Cyril Benone's life was saved.

The household settled down to a new routine. Hunt was free to visit old friends and went away for days on end. He was elected a member of the Athenaeum. Gambart bought *The Pot of Basil*. When the Waughs actually saw this composite picture of Fanny, their comments were restrained: the situation was delicate. George Waugh pointed out that, after all, Hunt was a professional painter and needed the money. He followed the example of other patrons and commissioned various portraits of his family. When those of Mrs Waugh and Edith were exhibited the following year at the Royal Academy as *Portrait of a Lady* and *The Birthday*, Tom Taylor,[1] the critic, described the sitters as 'repulsively ugly'. Hunt wrote indignantly to Stephens that no critic had the right to say this unless he added that the originals had been done an injustice.

Edith was painted with the presents she received on her twenty-first birthday. Hunt had given her the cameo brooch belonging to Fanny—one of the few trinkets that survived. The painting was to be a companion portrait to the one of Fanny. He designed a pair of identical heavy gold frames decorated with bone inlay.

It was while Edith was sitting for this portrait that he realised that she had always been in love with him. She was now a younger, more beautiful edition of Fanny, as well as Cyril's devoted aunt, with whom the child was so well and happy.

It was in the conservatory, presumably at Leatherhead, that they first spoke of their predicament. The same day he painted on her fan, another birthday present, a little fly—the fly in the ointment was, of course, the cursed Table of Affinities.[2] After this he had the frame of Edith's portrait inscribed with a quotation from *Romeo and Juliet*:

'My true love is grown to such excess,
I cannot sum up half my sum of wealth.'

They decided to part, never to speak of their love for each other again.

Pleading ill-health to the Waughs and his dread of the English winter, Hunt left for Florence almost immediately. Every week he posted long, beautifully illustrated letters addressed to *Cyril*, but obviously written for Edith. Cyril was barely two and a half. One letter reproduced in his memoirs enclosed a detailed drawing of himself in a crowded restaurant. The other customers were

[1] Tom Taylor 1817-1880. He was closely connected with the Pre-Raphaelites, a Fellow of Trinity, Cambridge, barrister of Inner Temple and a professor of English literature at London University. He became the editor of *Punch* and drama critic of *The Times* and wrote many plays himself.

[2] The Deceased Wife's Sister's Marriage Act was not given Royal Assent until 1907.

enjoying themselves. He was sitting all alone with a glass of wine in his hand and a bottle of chianti on the table. This drawing is inscribed *The Sunday Toast* March 1869. He was obviously drinking Edith's health as well as Cyril's.

The marble carver he had engaged to work on Fanny's tomb was so idle and slow that Hunt 'took up his tools and finished the work' which was eventually placed in the English cemetery.

As a widower Hunt was much in demand at parties in Florence. John Bradley, who was a professor at the local Royal Academy of Fine Arts, became his closest friend. Various people, including the Combes, visited Florence. Rumours as well as reliable news reached the Waughs.

They heard that Hunt was painting 'fancy-heads' and very 'saleable work'. He was investing in 'old Masters' and antiquities. He had spent 'a good deal of money' on a Giovanni Bellini, a Velasquez and two Tintorettos, bidding against the Uffizi he had bought various pictures from 'impoverished nobles'. Mr Combe seemed to approve and Stephens was put in charge of insurance.

The memory of Fanny was fading now, as was the image of Edith. Once more he became susceptible to girls. These included a beauty from Rome and a certain Miss Lydiard, also, as he confided in Stephens, 'a very beautiful fair American girl'. She had not needed any persuasion to sit for *Bianca*.

He admitted that, whereas 'here all amateur models gave a tremendous lot of trouble not turning up for the last sitting' this one being of 'good class American family' was reliable.

When the picture arrived in London and Edith saw it, she must have been dismayed by the inscription on the frame: Bianca, 'The Patroness of Heavenly Harmony'.

Among themselves, the Waughs discussed the gossip. The letters Edith read to Cyril Benone no longer held any secret messages between the lines. Mrs Waugh said gloomily that she would not be at all surprised if Cyril were sent for and removed to the other side of the world by Hunt and his American bride.

Edith felt that she must have someone in whom she could confide. Frederic Stephens was Hunt's privileged friend. Perhaps she could discover the truth from him. Although he and all Hunt's circle, including Edward Lear and William Rossetti, came to call at Queensborough to see Cyril Benone, and took him out for *treats* and then wrote glowing reports of him to Italy, Mr Stephens had never introduced his wife. She was not of 'the same set'. She had been a widow and the child by her first marriage had died.

When Edith decided to call on her at Lupus Street, Clara Stephens was delighted. She explained that since her remarriage, Mr Stephens' and her social life had been very restricted. She had been 'expecting Christophers' so much of the time.[3]

The first year she had suffered a miscarriage; but last year (15 November 1868) she had had a son to whom she now referred as 'Holly'. (Hunt was his godfather and he had been christened Holman after him.) Edith said how charming it would be for Holly and Cyril to become friends one day.

Stephens was gratified when he heard that Edith had called on his wife—they were about the same age. When he and Clara discussed the Waughs' apprehension over Hunt's possible marriage to this American girl he wrote the following letter to discourage him:

'Cyril goes out with me in the boat, sits carefully still, according to promise, and evidently enjoys the water rarely. Now, although you pretend to disdain my opinion of the beauty of the Yankee females and because I have *"not, like yourself, seen American families of a good class"* etc . . . (as to which, by the way, I don't know why that ecstatic priveledge [sic] has been denied to me; but so, it seems, it has and you have ruthlessly roused me to knowledge of the sad fact); now, I say again, although you disdain my opinions of "Yankee girls" I am still brutal enough to recognise something not finer than the British barmaid in your beauty, and should not believe in her breeding, be she British, Yank, or anything else, altho' she Told me of her supreme descent . . . that, not withstanding my beastly ignorance of Yankee angels of noble blood and exquisite breeding, Providence has thrown away on me certain opportunities of seeing British beauties such as are mercifully left here to leaven the darkness of the [illeg]isle. Yea! . . . I have raised mine eyes to gaze on creatures in whom my caliban-like instincts recognised something glorious;

[3] The Pre-Raphaelites always referred to their wives' pregnancies as this.

upon my word I did once shake hands with a lady, decidedly not a Yank; whom you described as lovely and I rejoice to say I believed you. What am I going to say, did you ask? Well this and I Tell it to you as a secret—I whisper to few, that I am satisfied Cyril has one of the most beautiful faces I ever saw. Those to whom I have confided reply "Oh! he's so like his father", and thus protest, not ineffectually, I must admit; do they thus protest, but I still declare that (despite ignorance of Americans of good descent) Cyril has, especially in certain points of view, one of the most beautiful faces I ever saw or shall hope to see: I heartily wish I admired your "American Virgin". . . . I disdain to reply, thinking that the man who painted . . . "Isabella" need not bemoan himself over that poor creature. Cyril weighs 2 stone, 9 lbs, 8 oz.'

During August and September 1868, one of Hunt's correspondents—Stephens presumably—enclosed newspaper cuttings concerning a scandal involving Lord Ranelagh. Hunt must have read these reports avidly.

A 'Madame Rachel' who kept a house of assignation in Bond Street and was also a 'vendor of cosmetics' succeeded in persuading a Mrs Borradaile that Lord Ranelagh was in love with her. '. . . in order to become the wife of a nobleman, she Mrs Borradaile must be enamelled and "made beautiful for ever" at a cost of £1,000'. In court, Lord Ranelagh admitted to patronising Madame Rachel's establishment occasionally, but 'swore he knew nothing of the matter ("and his testimony was clear and conclusive"). . . . Madame Rachel was sentenced to five years penal servitude'.[4]

It is most unlikely that Clara Stephens, who must have heard plenty about Lord Ranelagh from her husband, discussed this affair with Edith, but it was during the trial of Madame Rachel that she enclosed a carefully written letter to Hunt, in one of Fred's, saying that she had 'called at Tor Villa with Mr Stephens and that Cyril grows more like his beautiful mother everyday and young Miss Waugh is now the spit and image of your dear wife everybody says'.

Edith had found two valuable allies, but at present this was of

[4] For a concise account of this affair refer The Complete Peerage, St Catherine's Press, 1959, p. 736.

no avail as although Hunt longed to see Cyril Benone, he was still anxious to avoid meeting Edith for fear that his feelings for her might be revived and that hers were unchanged.

In June 1869, he decided to leave Florence for the East: perhaps the various feminine distractions had made his life too complicated.

Before leaving for Jerusalem he determined to visit Venice which he had never seen. On June 30, in the Piazza San Marco, he suddenly found himself face to face with Ruskin who had just arrived. It was about fifteen years since they had met informally.

Ruskin 'was faultlessly groomed, and despite his soft felt hat,' to Hunt's relief did not look in the least like an art critic. He hated men to dress unconventionally.

The two men were delighted to see each other again and, accompanied by Ruskin's valet, hailed a gondola immediately and spent the day visiting the Chiesa and the Scuola di San Rocco.

Hunt's account of this outing conjures up a comical image. While they stood together before Tintoretto's *Annunciation* Ruskin said: 'Now, my dear Holman, we will see what I wrote about twenty or more years ago: I have not read a word of it since.' (Hunt had first conceived a passion for Venetian pictures when he was twenty, after reading Ruskin's book *Modern Painters*.)

The valet was waiting conveniently 'at the door with a volume of the original edition . . . Ruskin beckoned him and opening the book at the required passage—he began deliberately . . . to read. . . .'

At the end of a lengthy extract 'he handed the volume back to his man' expressing his favourable opinion of it: 'I am well content.'

The same evening the two of them wined and dined well at Danieli's. They were able to discuss 'unreservedly' their estrangement since Millais' marriage to Effie. Hunt confided the true reason for his quarrel with Gabriel Rossetti, which led no doubt to an account of his entanglement with Annie and on to the tragedy of his wife's death. It was this which impelled Hunt to talk of his hope and faith in the after life. Ruskin declared that personally he was an atheist and denounced the whole story of divine revelation as 'a mere wilderness of poetic dreaming: Tintoretto did not believe any more than I do in the fables he was treating; no artist in illustrating fairy stories troubles himself about the substantiality of the fiction'.

Ruskin's lack of religious faith does not seem to have worried Hunt particularly.

Ruskin wrote to his mother the next day 1 July 1869:

'The painter, Holman Hunt, is here, and yesterday I showed him the Scuola di San Rocco, and I thought again if there could have been got two photographs—one of the piazza at Verona, with Longfellow and me, and another of Tintoret's *Annunciation*, with Holman Hunt and me examining it—both of them would find some sale with the British public.'[5]

From Venice, Hunt travelled to Rome where with a friend, Captain Luard, he 'swam daily in the Tiber, glad to find that the strong current could not prevent us from covering about a hundred yards ere our strength was spent in the struggle'.

After a short stay he left for Naples where he embarked for Palestine at last. He reached Jerusalem on 31 August 1869, having hoped to arrive there with Fanny almost exactly three years before. He missed her and Cyril Benone more than ever and was miserably lonely. Seddon, Graham, Sim—so many old friends—were dead or had left.

He had largely forgotten his Arabic, but he negotiated successfully for a large, dilapidated house in the Moslem quarter (which had belonged to the consul of Maximilian, the short-lived Emperor of Mexico).

It was cheap, but it took so long to repair that for some months he was obliged to live in a tent in Bethlehem. He decided that his next painting should be of Christ actually working as a Jewish carpenter and that he would call the picture *The Shadow of the Cross*, or *The Shadow of Death*.

He set out in search of authentic backgrounds. As usual he

[5] Cook's *Life of Ruskin*, Allen, London, 1911. Vol. II, Ch. IX. Hitherto unpublished correspondence between Hunt and Ruskin in the '70s and '80s shows that their relationship grew increasingly intimate after this meeting. Ruskin's letters to Hunt are more affectionately demonstrative than any he ever received from other men, with the exception of Millais. (Ruskin conceived a passion for my Aunt Gladys when she was a little girl in the 1880s.)

was determined that all costumes and props should be traditionally correct. Happily, the tools had not changed for about two
thousand years.

When his house was habitable at last and he moved in he
became painfully aware why it was cheap and why it had proved
so difficult to persuade the builders to work there.

It had a 'weird reputation and was regarded by all as being
cursed and under an evil spell'. He was approached by a group
of Moslem necromancers who suggested holding an incantation
ceremony in the house with the object of producing 'a *revenant*
from the other world'. This spirit would be invited to occupy a
vacant chair. Hunt asked for more details: 'The Arch-magician,
would begin by burning aromatic herbs . . . he would then
call upon "Shaitan". . . .' In gratitude to the Evil One for grant-
ing the desired favour all would swear to be his devoted servants
for ever.

He had no need to *summon* the devil. That hairy beast had
haunted and tormented him uninvited for years. He refused to
entertain the necromancers.

The descriptions of his life in this house in letters to Stephens,
Bradley, W. B. Scott and others read like a nightmare. 'At night
the windows rattled as though beset with angry spirits.' The
casements burst open, the lamps blew out. One night he distinctly heard a noise of someone or something coming up the
stairs. He knew that the servants would not dare leave their own
quarters in the dark. He lit a candle and went to meet whatever
it was. Halfway down the stairs he was confronted by an army
of rats advancing towards him. They scattered when he charged,
but the house was infested. 'Among (other) intruders there were
serpents.' He often shot them from his bed. The crackling of
scorpions and centipedes crawling over drawing paper in his
bedroom woke him up at night.

As before, his chief problem was to find suitable models. On
the roof he had designed and constructed mobile shelters for
his use. These enabled him to get the right light on Christ's figure
at all hours of the day in good weather. After only a week 'the
model's bronze skin became red and then chocolate brown and
he had to be kept indoors for a month by which time he was too
thin and looked sickly.'

The Shadow of the Cross and another picture he conceived

during this visit to Syria, *The Triumph of the Innocents*, seem to have been doomed to cause the maximum of trouble.

He relied on Bradley to send him painting materials from Florence and wrote to him frequently:

> 'Your letter and packet of colours came today . . . the postal people extracted the vermilion and perhaps some other things from the parcel—yet I hope to be able to manage. . . .'
>
> 'I have to use certain tubes as tho' they were diamonds or rubies. . . .'
>
> 'I think I have now enough colours for my work and with your 7 brushes . . . I may make my present v small stock of Poppy Oil eke out for this picture.
>
> 'I wanted it to dilute some copal with—for a long time since I have been painting on my picture with copal thinned with this oil, and now I am afraid of using any other lest it should be stronger and cause the picture to crack. I have Nut Oil and Linseed Oil which would do equally well for another painting —at a pinch I think I may use Nut Oil now and without serious misgivings but I like to be puritanic in such affairs. . . . Olive Oil I once tried by mistake in a sky and after a month's patient and fruitless hope I wiped it off as wet as at first. Castor Oil ought to produce a wonderful effect but I would rather try it on an independent picture as I should not like to have the bowels of this picture opened at this point.'

Captain Luard came to stay with Hunt for a while but otherwise his constant companion and friend was a man called Ezaak, or Isaac, a Jew whom he had picked up in Bethlehem as a potentially useful male model. He used him and others for the figure of Christ. Ezaak turned out to have been 'a notorious highway robber'.

In a letter to W. B. Scott (30 September 1871) Hunt wrote:

> 'He has become very much attached to me, and when I want to find out-of-the-way places I take him with me on excursions at times. He rides like a Centaur, but with his knees up to the horse's shoulders, as all Arabs do; and as his old character is still accredited to him, we strike a wholesome dread into all the country wherever we go.'

The model for the Virgin was also a native of Bethlehem called Miriam. She moved into his house and acted as cook, housekeeper and model. Although this domestic arrangement lasted a long time it was not ideal as a letter written to Bradley on 25 August 1871 makes abundantly clear:

'One of the things that keeps me hot is the stupidity of the servant Miriam called "that madwoman" whom at last I am just getting rid of. I have had her the whole time I have been here—her recommendation was that she was scrupulously honest and that she was handy for sitting to me the more because she had a great assortment of drapes. She had a most persevering propensity for sweeping which was no little torment to me, if she found me out of my studio for a few minutes she would enter with her broom and sweep everything clean. When I bullied her for this she would in spite of all my declaration stick to the idea that I admired her for her tidiness and repeat to the last that so far from making a dust it was taking it away and as for the draperies she had disturbed, why she had put them back again exactly as she had found them. How I hated her as she stood proudly justifying herself.

'One day when I had just gone to the W.C. I heard a knock at the street door and the stranger admitted. In a minute she was in my painting room—talking to herself—and calling for me. In my ridiculous western fastidiousness I refrained from answering until thinking the coast clear she brought her broom and was beginning to sweep at which I screamed out to her. In a minute she had gone downstairs and brought the messenger saying, "there he is in the W.C.—sit you there with your back against the door and then you will see him the first thing as he comes out" then addressing me with a loud knocking she said "Oh my Lord! I have brought the boy up he has a letter for you." And then if I had not emerged immediately I should have heard the sweeping up of my studio proceeded with. Several times I threatened to dismiss her but as I did not do so at last she began to think and to say that I could not do without her, and she screamed and quarrelled to such an extent and she intruded upon me to justify her against the man so unreasonably that my life became unbearable. Last week because I told her that I would not have the water for the washing taken from the drinking well she declined to wash altogether and I had to send for a washer-woman to do her work.

'On Monday last she had a quarrel with the man early in the morning and she put on all her costume and told [me] she was going to Bethlehem to stay with her friends, a day or two. As for my dinners, I was to do what I could for them and as she went and stayed till Wednesday by which [time] I was out of patience and I had got another woman in her place. At first on her return she was just as independent as ever, told me if not satisfied I was to pay her and she would go. She never would stop with an Abyssinian to dictate to her but when she found I had at last made up my mind to have no more of her nonsense she became very contrite and went about the town to friends of mine to ask them to intercede with me for her—it is quite a comfort now to pass the day without hearing the old woman's shrill voice ringing thro' the house. The creature has been too great a pest to me to allow me to write of her in any way that would be amusing to you but it may help to give you some idea of the kind of life if it can be called this—that one leads here.'

Throughout this visit to Syria he wrote regular and minutely illustrated letters to Cyril. It became increasingly clear to Edith that Hunt was not pining for her but for the child. I think it was then that she began to resent Cyril and gradually became more and more jealous of him. She suffered deeply. Her parents and sisters found her lack of interest in parties and eligible men quite inexplicable.

When her brother George was drowned within sight of a house that Fred and Clare[6] Stephens had taken seven miles from Dartmouth, Edith seemed scarcely affected whereas her sister, Alice, was much distressed. Stephens wrote to Hunt on 3 October 1869 that:

'The Woolners sent their children to stay with us for six weeks and got much benefit from the change out of that dismal

[6] After her second marriage Clara changed her name to Clare.

Welbeck St. We wish you could Trust Cyril with us, so that he might have the benefit of masculine associates for a while. Try and persuade Mrs W[augh] to spare him.'

As usual Stephens included his family news and the latest London gossip. He insisted that although he 'adored' his mother, 'her charges against my miserable wife were intolerable . . . I knew were untrue and infast [sic—infaust?]'. After a final rumpus old Mrs Stephens was turned out of the Lupus Street house and went to live with her two daughters. She died shortly afterwards. Stephens blamed himself and Clare 'miscarried again and was v. ill thro' distress and shock'.

Everyone was 'disgusted by the scandalous indeed libellous book by Mrs Beecher Stow[e] with infamous allegations of Byron's incestuous relationship with his sister Augusta'.

Gabriel Rossetti and Whistler were still in ecstasies over the two Spartali girls. They were of 'extraordinary loveliness', according to Graham Robertson, and the daughters of the Greek consul-general in London. Marie, who had been christened Mary, served as Gabriel's model for many pictures including *Dante's Dream* and *A Vision of Fiametta*.

Hunt had already met Marie Spartali at parties in London. She was a pupil of Madox Brown's, whose style she imitated. Hunt agreed with Stephens that 'she really was a very beautiful girl'. Lord Ranelagh was madly in love with her and had actually proposed. It would seem that at least for a time she was equally attracted, for when she did marry someone else, Hunt wrote to Stephens on 24 July 1871:

'The marriage of the Tall Miss Spartali with Stilman [sic][7] one of the amusing things of the world I dont pity her father much for he must be of a discontented disposition for they say he actually broke off an intended marriage with Lord Ranelagh which the beauty had set her heart upon and which

[7] William James Stillman, 1828-1901, American journalist and painter. Co-editor with John Durand of the first Pre-Raphaelite periodical in America, *The Crayon*, January 1855-July 1861, and author of several works on the Pre-Raphaelites, in particular Rossetti for whom he modelled and of whom he became a close friend. He was blamed for Rossetti's addiction to chloral and denied responsibility in an article entitled 'Rossetti and Chloral', *Academy*, LIII, no. 1350 (19 March 1898).

his Lordship too had condecended [sic] to agree to . . . I only wonder that all the young men with roman noses did not fight about her that is before the Ranelagh infatuation wich wld naturally take the presumption out of any fellow of ordinary degree.'[8]

More news in Stephens' letters referred to Woolner's latest craze for collecting pictures including ' "old Masters", obvious forgeries'. It was embarrassing for Stephens, the art critic, to be asked his opinion of these and in a letter dated 24 November 1869 he complained: 'Tommy goes on collecting Turners in a way which staggers belief and will not hear a word against them.'

In another letter Stephens confessed that he feared for Cyril's 'exciteability of Temperament'. He and Clare both felt that the child was 'molly-coddled by his Granny' and that his normal instincts for healthy exercise were being frustrated.

Hunt wrote to Millais:

'Life here wants something to make it bearable, having no sort of counter interest my work becomes the most frightful anxiety to me. . . . I am like you in loving my Art very intensely now, the more it seems that I am denied all other love, but I am reminded of the remark of a child who talking about love . . . said it *pained* so. . . .'

On 9 October 1870 he wrote to William Rossetti, 'Go and have a look at my little boy and Tell me how he seems. I am wondering whether I shall ever get hold of him. I want him so much *here*. I must have someone to love near me.'

Although Stephens pleaded with the Waughs to let Cyril come to stay with them so that he could play with Holly, it was usually to no avail.

At last Hunt wrote to old Mrs Waugh (not to Edith) saying he wished Cyril not only to learn to ride and swim but also to be then sent out to join him in Syria.

[8] Lord Ranelagh died unmarried in 1885 and had no legitimate heirs. He did not mention his cousin Thomas, or Annie or their children in his will, but left everything to Arthur Clarence (sole executor), illegitimate son of a Miss Mary Edwards.

Although Edith offered to accompany Cyril and 'an English nurse with pioneering instincts' Mrs Waugh expressed her horror. The boy was far too young.

Edith consoled herself that at least her mother's attitude made Cyril a hostage. From then onwards Edith's letters to Hunt, answering his to Cyril, made the boy sound more and more attractive. She hoped that Hunt would be persuaded to return from Syria sooner than intended, but Mrs Waugh's refusal to send Cyril to the East made Hunt more and more determined. He wrote to Stephens:

'. . . some good people here suggest of taking him into their house near at hand with their [grand?] children. I object [illeg.] because I recognise in it a plan for inducing me to marry their daughter [an old maid in her forties] which for many reasons I can never think of doing. . . . Sometimes the thought of his [Cyril] good makes me think I shld marry again but I am rather frightened at this idea for to marry a woman near my own age wld be impossible. The Waughs I am sure wld be much distressed by the thought. . . in some extraordinary way the Waughs got it into their heads that I was in love with the [American] girl and going to marry her—of this I never took any notice it was too absurd. . . . whatever the picture [Bianca] may have been the girl was one of the most beautiful I ever saw altho' to me personally . . . of no more personal interest than a flower wld be.'

Nevertheless he seriously considered returning to Florence with his unfinished canvasses in search of a woman beautiful and young enough to marry. In a letter to Bradley he expressed one fear that might prevent his carrying out this proposition:

'[Those who] call themselves models in Florence and who if most enterprising and punctual would scarecly [sic] be dark enough for any pictures I may bring unfinished from here. . . .

'If my good wife had lived my stay here while times were quiet would not be at all unpleasant—house things might be kept in order without my being disturbed. Letters might be attended [to] callers staved off and in the evening and at meals there would be the babies and a chat about home friends to divert one instead of being a "brother to owls and a companion to dragons" as I am now. I sometimes find this reflection as well as the difficulty of getting possession of my little boy with any reasonable chance of being able to take care of him suggests to me the ideas of marrying again. I say this in confidence and principally as an introduction to the question of what has become of Miss Lydiard? Who by this time if unmarried might not be so girl-like as she was two years ago. I mean in mind for in appearance she always looked wonderfully established. I am obliged to revert to the very small circle of unmarried ladies I knew before for here there are none. Miss Roberts at Bellosguardo you did not I think know. She was a good sensible girl that I shall go and see if there be time when I am in Florence perhaps, she was delicate in health. I write all this however, fully recognising that the chances are I shall never now get married again—this I feel to be most probably fate from the fact that tho' I dearly admire particular women it is only with the staid and unjealous feeling of a painter not with the fervour that at a particular moment makes one ready to leave every place and prospect for the sake of paying one's court to someone. At forty-three the "blood is cold and waits upon the judgment." This with me only because I have got so into the habit of working ferociously and *grilling* over my labor that I have no leisure to get wanton in my fancies and I see that after so many years of this habit of living and thinking only for my art it may be too late now to adapt myself to the duties of a husband with the danger of being thought neglectful. Five years and a half ago and with my wife who was so exceptionally wise and interested in art I did not despair but a few years make all the difference after the middle of life and when one has had a great defeat of all one's most cherished hopes.

'My little boy I thank God is always reported to be well and strong and growing tall—and to be retaining and developing his love of fun which was certainly remarkable in him even when he was almost starved by Florentine *balias*. It will certainly be a tremendous pleasure to me to see him again. I am so fond of children that even were he not my nearest in blood I should having the knowledge I have of his earliest days be very anxious to see how he gets on.'

274

He became so ill from overwork, malaria and jaundice that this 'wife-hunt' did not materialise. In a letter to Thomas Combe he wrote:

'In my sadly exhausted state I have scarcely any faith left. I have laboured and hoped and prayed so long to gain power to surmount the prodigious difficulties of this picture that I am now well if not quite broken spirited—no words that I could use would give any idea of the utter depth of misery that I have suffered and still suffer in the prosecution of this task.'

He wrote to W. B. Scott on 30 September 1871:

'I have no loving eyes to cheer me such as I hoped to have ever with me when I left England. . . . I thought in the middle of the summer it would be the death of me. I got but four hours' sleep each day, and these were scarcely rest, for my feverish anxiety went on through the night, and I dreamed of nothing but newly-discovered faults—of paint drying before it could be blended, of wind blowing down my picture and breaking it, etc.—until my eyes sank so deep into my head, and my body seemed such a heavy, stiff and unelastic corpse that I thought the next stage must be coffinward. And now that it is past, people tell me they thought me a doomed man.'

By the following spring Millais had persuaded him to return to England. He and Effie now had a London establishment where Hunt could send his unfinished pictures ahead of him. While Millais was fishing in Scotland Hunt could continue to work there in peace. It would be a joy to meet again. Hunt would be surrounded by friends, see his little boy and get the best medical attention of which he obviously was now so in need.

He followed Millais' advice. About three weeks later he arrived to stay with the Waughs at 15 Queensborough Terrace.

CHAPTER XXI

Oh, sacred be the flesh and blood
To which she links a truth divine!
TENNYSON

MRS WAUGH took Cyril and his nurse to meet Hunt at the railway station. Edith stayed behind with her bedridden father to welcome them home.

Hunt described his reunion with Cyril to Bradley, who was still in Florence, without mentioning Edith, but enquiring 'is my Roman heroine there?'

'The first interest I had in returning home was to see my little boy, he had been brought to the station not knowing the object of visit. I looked round at first without seeing him and so concluded that my letter had not reached in time. When attending to a trunk passing the customs house people I heard a girl saying "you must not go there Cyril"—the name was too uncommon not to make me turn—there was a tall, straight, delicate looking boy, with long uncurled hair, very yellow—making him look girlish—he was dancing and twirling about as tho' for the life of him he could not keep his feet flat on the ground for a single minute.

'I could not see his face but it seemed to me that it did not matter because he could not be my boy for a friend had written that his hair had become dark as mine—as I was turning away a sudden jump of his brought his face round and I could see the blue veins which became so conspicuous when he was being starved by the *balias*—I stooped down and said "Can you tell me what is your name?" "Yes, Cyril Benone Hunt." "Do you know who I am?" "No! never!" "Are you sure?" "Yes I am quite sure." A servant guessed the truth and said, "Why, he is your father Cyril." He grinned as tho' amused by a joke and when I repeated, "Yes, Cyril, I am your father," he ran away to his Granny and said, "that

276

man says he's my father"—seeing them saluting me after-wards he concluded that after all I was not an imposter [sic] and he rode home on my knee quite reconciled—he is a merry little cricket—full of life and fun without an atom of shyness and quite determined to come back with me to Syria.

'My next concern was about my picture it arrived home in little more than a week after myself and Millais gave me his studio to receive it in—as I had never had a chance of shewing it to any artist of any kind and had never throughout its progress had the opportunity of putting it by rather shud-dered at [illeg.] it when it was unpacked, three or four weeks rest of my eyes had given me the power of seeing some defects but after a consultation with Millais whose opinion I could trust as that of a well qualified artist and true old friend I was relieved of my anxiety so far as to conclude that there was nothing wrong that could not be put right with a little work. . . .'

Hunt did not stay with the Waughs for long, but moved nearby to 2 Wilton Terrace, Campden Hill and worked at *The Shadow of Death* in Millais' studio. Every morning he took Cyril to the swimming baths, or a riding school.

Edith had now been in love with Hunt for ten years. Although he was friendly and polite, showing his appreciation of all she did to ingratiate herself with him and his child, he seemed de-liberately impersonal.

At first, she attributed this to his self-discipline and self-denial, his noble character and high principles. But by the end of the summer she could not endure the situation any longer. She wrote to him declaring her constant love and confessing what agonies of loneliness and longing she had suffered all the time he was in Syria. Since their parting three years ago she had been miserable. She no longer cared for man-made laws. She and Hunt were made for each other. Cyril was devoted to her. It was fate, pre-ordained, God's will. . . . She would never love anyone else and was prepared to follow him and Cyril to the ends of the earth.

He was touched and flattered by this unsolicited letter. Such a union would certainly prove the best possible solution for Cyril. But he was world-famous as a religious painter now, his patrons included such people as the Combes, the Queen herself. How far could he afford to flaunt the conventions of the established Church? His answer to Edith's letter showed concern for her and appreciation for her constancy of affection, but he was non-committal. For the past three years he had accustomed himself to the idea that where Edith was concerned marriage was taboo. He regarded her as a sister now. Although she strongly resembled Fanny in looks, he was already aware that in temperament they were very different. Although living and working so close to each other, they began writing frequent letters.

On 14 October 1872 he confided in Stephens his 'idea to marry her', saying that both she and he were aware that they would have to face violent opposition from the world in general and especially from the Waughs:

'It saddens me to think how much pain I have cost her, her mother, and her sister, and still more to consider how much more she will have to bear which ever way the thing will end cld it be undone by going back I wld willingly do so, altho I see more than ever what a good and affectionate creature she is.

'I am unfortunate in having to go to many dinner parties now. I can scarcely bear them but the numbers of guests force one to put on a show of bravery. Altho' as I emerge into the street I weep . . . I have not slept 2 hours since I last saw you last night I did not fall asleep a single minute. Oh the misery of life like this in the night!'

In the meantime Edith had broken down and told her mother and her sister, Alice, how things stood. Both were horrified.

From Hunt's letter to Stephens it would seem that he was not in the least in love and regretted the situation in which he found himself. He complained to Bradley that he was 'so badgered by dentists, by business of all kinds, and more especially by bores of supreme quality for which this metropolis seems pre-eminently remarkable'.

He still suffered frequent attacks of malaria. When he attended 'a very swell affair' as it was described by Madox Brown (a party given by the Burne-Jones's to show off their house decorated by 'The Firm'), Hunt was 'worn out and ill suffering from ague'.

On hearing of Hunt's decision Stephens wrote him an encouraging letter enclosing 'phamplets [sic] for Edith which will at best compose her spirits (many important and Christian people marry even if only abroad)'.

When Hunt and Edith faced the Waughs together and formally announced their decision the most frightful family scenes ensued. Tommy and Alice Woolner were much involved. Old Mr Waugh died over Christmas. Edith's mother blamed her: she said his death was precipitated by the shocking news. Mrs Waugh could not bear the sight of Hunt and avoided him when he called for her grandson.

Edith continued to write her beloved Holman daily letters until the end of April the following year. She was by then at the end of her tether because of her mother's tantrums and the rows with the Woolners. Tommy called on all members of the family to oppose the project of the so-called 'marriage'. If Edith persisted in this wicked idea she must consider herself an outcast. For the rest of her life, none of her family would speak to her. She would be the death of her dear mother.

On 2 May 1873, Hunt wrote to Stephens:

'I have just got an answer from Edith and it is to say, what do you think? that she cannot be my wife since the law would not recognise the marriage as tho she had not been writing to me all this while, and had not called me back from wooing elsewhere with the repeated declaration that she did not care for the law when opposed to God's written will. I have replied of course kindly and considerately saying that I felt that the decision was the wisest for her but pointing out that there must be no more letters pass between us.

'I must now try and get interested in some other woman for the disquiet and untrusted longings of this last mistake of mine must go on no longer.'

Two days later on May 4, he wrote to Bradley a letter which seemed to emphasise the fact that he was not in love:

'I wish I had a chance of finding the right young lady to make my life a little less cheerless than it is—what with painting and the hideous worries of attending to the business

279

side of my profession and my own family matters etc. I really
scarcely ever get a moment to spend on my own personal
prospects in life and so I go on from day to day wondering
often what there is to make life bearable, my little boy is a
great comfort to me but I often have reason to regret that there
is no one to take the place mother to him. Sometimes I pass a
girl in the street with the thought that if she would tell me
she were unmarried that she were free and would take her
fortunes with me and would be married the next morning—
or the next week without the bother of consulting relations and
friends I would take her at once I need someone with whom
I can share my joys and worries. I should be only too happy
if I could profit by the opportunity in Florence of finding a
wife. I am still prejudiced in favour of Miss Lydiard I love her
nose and fine chin and good eyes and hair—but I am afraid
of sending a letter to her friends lest she should have changed
or already got married. I think she would not object to a year
or two in Syria now—Perhaps however among your lot there
are some other aquiline nosed ladies and when I see you I will
ask about them but they are almost certain to come here just
as I go there for Fate does not favour industrious people like
me in matrimony.'

Ten days later, he received an answer from Bradley saying that
he was shortly leaving for England and much looked forward to
seeing Hunt.

In the meantime Hunt was very preoccupied negotiating the
sale of *The Shadow of Death*, with copyright for engraving, to
Agnew for £11,000.

Hunt wrote to Bradley by return on 14 May 1873:

'I am afraid I am rather too late with a brilliant idea that
has come to me but it [is] worth trying even for chance of
success: It is to ask you to bring with you cartes des visites
of the young ladies who are likely to suit me so that if I
found good reason for thinking it not a wild errand I might
put aside my work for a fortnight and go over to Florence
without waiting for my Eastern journey and do my best to
capture her and bring her back to delight my eyes while I

am making my arrangements for my start—A portrait together with a verbal description ought to enable me to know
pretty accurately what the young lady were before I saw her
—You may already have left Florence when this arrives or it
may be too late for you to attend to such a delicate matter—
but this will be my fault for not having thought of it before.
In any case I know I can trust you to have friendly patience
with me for asking you this, altho' it may be difficult for you
to realise how great a service you would be doing me by helping me find a good wife.

'I was at a swell party for a quarter of an hour this afternoon—but *my work* had detained me till all were on the
move—even had I been earlier however I should have found
that the maidens were too tender too idle and blooming for
me the widows and old maids too serious an undertaking. One
must think only of women who know something of the
seriousness of life and work. I had some talk with Princess
Louise, who was exceptionally courteous and declared that
her mother [Queen Victoria] had continually talked on my
picture since she had seen it. . . .'

During the last fortnight, Stephens had been in Paris. Since
Edith's letter of April 30 refusing to marry Hunt after she had
proposed to him, she was beset with doubts. The fear of being
condemned to the life of a martyred old maid, looking after
her querulous mother and losing the man she loved, overcame all
her scruples at last.

On 19 May, Hunt wrote to Stephens:

'I did not get done with the anxious question immediately
when I had written to you. further correspondence kept me
uncertain whether E. had not after all the courage to take the
step but in the end it has been permanently settled in the
negative.

'The correspondence kept me from writing to Paris when
you come back let me know. Love to your wife and Holly.'

However this confusion changed within a month and on
June 20 he wrote to Clare Stephens:

'Fred has doubtless told you that Edith Waugh is to be my wife spite of the Lords and the High Church parsons. I have seen her twice and I feel certain that she will adhere to her resolution now. there will however be a frightful explosion when she communicates her intention to her Mother. I must not however leave her at home with the family if they cannot recognise her right to do what she in her own conscience sees to be right and so I have told her that she must at once come to you if they make it uncomfortable at home. I know I can rely upon your goodness to befriend her. I only explain the need there may be for your hospitality because I can imagine that after she had exercised her courage enough to stop on knocking at the door for it to be opened she might not be able to unfold to you the need she was under to stay. This may or may not be before Sunday but in any case I have arranged to meet her at Hammersmith Station at 10½ on that morning to go to morning service and afterwards to come on to you to lunch at 1 or so. Should this be impracticable from any engagement you have please let me know.

'Cyril stays at Margate another week.'

Hunt's family all turned against him and Edith now. His own mother struck him out of her will—all she left him was his father's scrapbook. Uncle Hobman threatened to disinherit him too. In September 1873 Hunt wrote to Stephens: 'I have done with Ewell.'

Years ago his younger sister, Emily, had cut him out of her life because he would not relinquish Cyril; by now, Sarah his favourite sister was estranged. Her husband, the upholsterer, Wilson, had gone bankrupt and Hunt had recently written to Millais complaining of 'his stupidity and indifference: the father of little Teddy, has too many children for me to think of supporting'.

Mrs Waugh pointed out to Edith that under the terms of her father's will, she would not be eligible for a marriage settlement if her 'association' were illegal.

The more opposition they met and the more Edith depended on Hunt, the more protective he felt towards her. It was during the following months that they became so close and once more he fell in love with her.

Friends old and new among the famous and rich, rallied round, but during this difficult time Hunt and Edith became very socially sensitive and imagined slights where none were intended. This is made clear in Hunt's letters. He even suspected, for a while, such loyal friends as the Richmonds and Edward Lear of siding with the Waughs. Happily, the latter wrote from Geneva on 18 October 1873, 'I am glad you *are suited as you say:*— . . . The conduct of the W[aughs] and W[oolners] is very vexatious and Trying, because it seems to me that you have given them no reason for it, except to take little Cyril away. . . .'

Madox Brown wrote to congratulate Hunt 'on the good looks of the young lady you have selected—I mean good-looks in the largest sense of the term—something more than mere beauty— I formed my conclusions in these matters at first sight and am decidedly of the opinion that she is well worth losing two fortunes for—'

Life at Queensborough Terrace became so impossible for Edith that for weeks on end she and Cyril stayed with the Stephens's, whose house in Lupus Street was largely furnished with the beautiful things on loan from Hunt which he had collected in Florence and the East.

When Edith sat to Hunt he complained to Stephens in a letter dated 26 August 1874, 'no effort of mine is capable of making her smile from morning till night—except when we are eating lunch —she says philosophically "Well, give it up!"' Stephens replied, 'I don't see how you could expect the sitter to smile under the operation. She has borne up gallantly so far. I congratulate you both.'

On 20 January 1875, Hunt wrote that he 'could not get a gleam of a smile all day. Tomorrow I shall follow up my work to finish the face and I shall take Cyril to the studios to keep the young lady alive.'

When I first read the seemingly endless and tedious letters concerning the Waughs' and Woolners' efforts to destroy and prevent Hunt's and Edith's marriage and happiness, I was tempted to quote various petty examples of bitterness. But finally I decided that my second cousin Amy Woolner was right: in her book she dismissed the whole affair in a couple of lines: 'About this time [1875] owing to distressing family reasons, which do not concern the general public, a complete break between

283

Woolner and Hunt took place.' (As a result of this absurd family feud, the descendants of Hunt and Woolner have never met.)

But before Hunt and Edith could leave for the East they had to deal with many practical problems. *The Shadow of Death* was such a success that the Queen commissioned a small replica of Christ's head. For Edith's sake, he postponed painting this. In November Edith left London with Dinah Craik[1] for Neufchâtel in Switzerland. Hunt travelled separately.

Edith was married in church, 'a radiant bride in white', and at last (under Swiss law at least) she and Hunt were man and wife. Cyril and a splendid English nurse[2] whom they had recently engaged, joined them, probably in Venice.

Many problems lay ahead, not only in Syria.

Clare Stephens wrote 'a gently chiding letter' which welcomed them in Jerusalem. In the last confusion of their leaving they were 'a happy pair who seemed to have wandered off like Babes in the Wood', leaving behind 'boots, ice-machines, ground glass bottle-stoppers, baby clothes, bolts of flannel from the Army and Navy and endless other essentials. . . .'

None of this forgetfulness mattered very much. He loved her and she worshipped him for the rest of his life and after his death in 1910 for another twenty years.

I still own her carefully written instructions: 'The dedication of Holman's memoirs is to be copied and put in my hand when my body is burnt:[3]

"TO

MY WIFE

as one of my insufficient tributes to her whose constant virtues ever exalt my understanding of the nature and influence of womanhood."'

---

[1] Dinah Craik 1826-1887, authoress of *John Halifax, Gentleman*, London, 1857. She was the sister of Tom Muloch, an old friend of Hunt's from Academy School days.

[2] She is portrayed as the good-looking young English nurse with my aunt Gladys and my father in the right-hand lower corner of *The Miracle of Holy Fire*. I remember her well fifty to sixty years later as a fat bundle of grey shawls with thin grey hair parted in the middle. I always shook hands and made my bob, while my grandmother shouted in her ear: 'Master Hilary's child, Miss Diana.' She became a devoted 'family retainer' and died at 18 Melbury Road in her nineties.

She called this piece of paper 'my passport to *Heaven*' and often admitted to me how disturbing she found the idea that not only her beloved Holman, but Fanny too, would be waiting to greet her.

[3] Her ashes were interred next to his in Painters' Corner in the crypt of St Paul's Cathedral in 1931.

APPENDIX I

The Imbroglio.

M Y GRANDMOTHER laboriously copied Madox
Brown's clearly written letters to Hunt in her own
hand, and attached them to the originals: if she added
any whitewashing explanation it has not survived.

The first Madox Brown letter was written on 7 September
1862:

'I find myself under the necessity of writing to you about
what you told *me* Swinburne had said of [Gabriel] Rossetti
at Monckton Milnes'. On thinking it over, I resolved it would
be necessary to warn Rossetti against what naturally seemed
to me Swinburne's excessively exaggerated [*sic*] and inconsiderate way of talking of his friends.

'However before doing so I consulted [Burne] Jones who
agreed with me that it was absolutely necessary that something should be said to make Swinburne more cautious in
future. So Jones told Rossetti that I had something to say to
him about Swinburne, and Rossetti asking me what it was, I
told him you had heard Swinburne say at Monckton Milnes',
that *procuring abortions was an every day amusement*, to him,
Rossetti.

'To make a short story of it, Rossetti, like myself, fully impressed with the fact that Swinburne must have said so, in his
random way of talking to astonish people, went to him and
expostulated with him (though mildly). This must be now
10 or 12 days since—Rossetti afterwards told me that Swinburne on hearing it became so painfully excited that he could
not press the point, but that he felt that it must be *Swinburne*
who had forgotten what he had said—so the matter seemed
dropped, and is, as far as Rossetti is concerned.

'But 2 nights since Jones called on me about Swinburne,
who it appears is still in a most excited and disturbed state
denying that he ever said so and wishing for an interview with
you at my house.

'Jones and I thought this if possible to be avoided owing to S[winburne]'s excitability of temperament, and so it was agreed that I should call on Swinburne and then write to you.

'I accordingly called on him and prevailed on him to leave the matter in my hands—the result is that I promised to convey to you this message from him "That you must have been mistaken in your impression that he Swinburne had spoken to you about Rossetti as he distinctly remembers that he never said anything about him to you or in your presence" —of course if there be any mistakes about the matter, I shall be rejoicing if I can be of use to clear it up; for though in doing so, as I did in deliberate consideration, I never thought the matter would come to this, but considered it entirely Swinburne's own concern now, however, the earnest way he takes the matter to heart, makes me hope that it may yet turn out to have come to you through some *other* channel; no one cares which, it being only Swinburne's desire that he may be cleared of it—you see I am in my new house, can you come and dine here Sunday or any other day or shall I come to you. Yrs. ever Madox Brown.'

Hunt must have been dismayed that such mischief had been made. Had he imagined that Madox Brown would be so indiscreet as to relay this sordid gossip to Burne-Jones and Gabriel in the first place, he would not have repeated it.

Probably that night at a typical Monckton Milnes party they all had plenty to drink. Swinburne had always been an exhibitionist. He had first attracted Gabriel's attention five years before, when an Oxford undergraduate, not only by his flaming red hair, for which Gabriel had a weakness amounting to a fetish, but by his determination to shock. It was he who had lent Gabriel such books as *Les Liaisons Dangereuses*, and various works by the Marquis de Sade. Gabriel was relatively innocent and referred to this amazing author as 'du Sude'. Monckton Milnes encouraged Swinburne's aberrations. Swinburne was a regular client of an establishment in 'St John's Wood, where, in luxuriously furnished rooms, two fair-haired rouged ladies whipped gentlemen who came to them for this service'.[1] When

[1] Jean Overton Fuller, *Swinburne: A critical Biography*, Chatto and Windus, London, 1968.

the latter had had too much to drink, his 'frantic delight, was apt to be too much for the disciple of the Marquis'[2]—more than once, Hunt saw him have a self-induced fit in public.

When Swinburne and Gabriel entertained the company at Monckton Milnes', they did so by taking it in turns to read out loud particularly lurid passages from *Justine*. Their dramatic rendering of 'the dissection of the interesting Rosalie and her infant, and the rest of that refreshing episode',[2] was so relished by their audience, that Swinburne later wrote that he and Gabriel 'rolled and roared . . . and I wonder to this minute that we did not raise the whole house by our screams of laughter'.

In such company, the subject of abortion was quite likely to crop up. Probably Swinburne, hoping to shock Hunt, was hoist with his own petard.

It would have been characteristic of Hunt, just as he calmly continued to paint even under fire, to observe casually that he was well aware that procuring abortions was an everyday amusement for Gabriel. Swinburne would then have sobered up, suspecting a sinister though inadvertent implication.

His beloved Lizzie had given birth to a stillborn child and died from an overdose of drugs, only a few months before—not quite a year after her marriage to Gabriel.

Swinburne had adored her. Like many men with deviations, he worshipped beautiful women as sweet indulgent mother-figures. If they treated him fondly as a spoiled, naughty boy, they were no sexual challenge. Exquisite creatures like Lizzie are usually narcissistic and often frigid. Ruskin, impotent with mature women, exalted her in the same way.

When Swinburne was drunk, Lizzie would hand him over to a 'cabbie', with a label attached to his collar: 'Algernon Swinburne Esq., to . . . From Mrs Rossetti.' Her recent death had greatly affected him.

On this particular night at Monckton Milnes' in the autumn of 1862, Swinburne was suddenly struck by the possibility that Lizzie's death could have been the indirect result of a bungled abortion some years before.

This theory would explain Hunt's reply to Madox Brown on

[2] Rosalie Gryn Grylls' *Portrait of Rossetti*, Macdonald, London, 1964.

October 12 in which he stated: 'Swinburne is perfectly correct in saying that *he never spoke to me of Rossetti at Monckton Milnes*' . . . and I am quite perplexed to find how it would have got into your head that I mentioned *him* as my authority. . . .' [The italics are mine.] Hunt added that he 'had heard such stories from *other* sources'. He meant Annie Miller, but of course did not name her.

It was not Swinburne who had told him the story, but *vice versa*; however Hunt did not wish to add to 'the Imbroglio' by explaining more details now: this letter to Madox Brown was the simple truth.

Although in his book, when recording events and dictating from memory or scrappy old diaries, assisted by his second wife —my grandmother—he is sometimes inaccurate or confused, in his letters his version of events is reliable.

The next day, October 13, Madox Brown wrote in reply:

'I am glad that the matter as far as Swinburne is concerned can be cleared up so easily—I have composed a note for him, which I believe will perfectly answer the purpose, I enclose it —if you are content to abide by it, post it and nothing more need be said on the subject.

'However as between ourselves though, as you see, I am willing to put the matter in an ambiguous light to smooth it over, yet you cannot expect me to take the whole blame of the incorrectness on myself, as yours to me would seem to suggest—seeing that I remember distinctly that you told me 1st that you heard the report at Monckton Milnes'—2nd that it was Swinburne's statements on matters of this nature must be received with extreme caution owing to his habit of reclessly exaggerating [sic] in order to astonish people.

'Surely you will remember this—I did not repeat any other word of our conversation . . . that you either believed the report or not, no one doubts that you heard it from some one, I for one don't care from whom, and I never should have wispered [sic] a syllable of it had I dreamed there was any doubt about it having been Swinburne who said it at Monckton Milnes'—which would indeed have been a grave indiscretion on the part of so intimate a friend.

'There is something inexplicable about the misunderstanding—you appear to have forgotten all about it, and I think it had better be forgotten by all parties—only if you are not satisfied with my explanation to Swinburne and fresh discussion of the matter be occasioned I shall have no recourse but to adhere to my original recollection of it I must now protest that I had not the faintest intention of making mischief between you and Rossetti—neither Jones nor myself ever considered it in any other light than an instance of extreme indiscretion and exaggeration of Swinburne's, which naturally provoked remarks, and required setting down—for while admiring his great genius and regarding him with affection his extraordinary way of talking does at times dismay one and it is gratifying that it turns out not to be his blame this time—I hope you are enjoying yourself, I am. Oakham Park is a lovely spot—Sincerely yours Ford Madox Brown.'

A note, with no date or address, from Madox Brown to Hunt, would seem correctly placed here:

'. . . .The scrimmage has been settled on easy terms by an apology which I never should have dreamt of offering as of being accepted—I am glad to be out of it because though of course I was not the aggressor, and morally in the right, yet all the lawyers seemed to look with doubt to the issue—and consider it a serious matter—Yours ever Ford Madox Brown.'

Clearly in the meantime, most of those involved had consulted their lawyers.

The one who comes best out of this strange affair is Gabriel himself who in the 'midden' of it, and in deep mourning for Lizzie, wrote to Madox Brown on paper with a wide black border:

'My dear Brown, I meant to come but being prevented I write. I suppose it is better you should write to Hunt (though I am sorry for your trouble) as Swinburne wishes it and lest I should seem to want the matter suppressed. But as for doing any material good in making me less the subject for foolish scandal and tattle, that I perceive would be vain to attempt.'

It would seem that Hunt intended to write to Swinburne himself, and wrote of this intention to Madox Brown on October 15, although the letter has not come to light. Madox Brown replied at once:

'My dear Hunt. I don't clearly understand whether you have dispatched the note to Swinburne or are waiting to hear from me—if you have not done so already I think from the contents of yours of yesterday's date, I should prefer its not going. Should you have posted it however it is no matter, because I have my note in which it was sent to you to refer to should anything further be said about it. Should the note come back to me I shall understand that you will take what course you prefer under the circumstances. Should it have gone on the other hand I shall hear of it from Swinburne— Between ourselves it is now impossible to say a word further on the subject—as should you wish to pursue it, it can only be carried on through third parties—I for one shall take no pleasure in recurring to the subject and indeed unless I hear more of it, shall not, except as to the necessary winding up of the matter with Swinburne in the event of the note returning to me. Sincerely yrs. F. Madox Brown.'

The Only Pre-Raphaelite
—EVELYN WAUGH

MRS CUTHBERT—Diana Holman-Hunt—is much younger than I but genealogically we are of the same generation, having a great-great-grandfather in common. By the circumstances of her upbringing she might belong to an earlier generation, for her childhood was spent almost alone with her two grandmothers. With one she made her home, at the other's she made occasional visits. The first was conventional, frivolous, self-indulgent and, it appears, rather cold-hearted. The other (*née* Waugh), the widow of the painter, was emotional, pious, stout-hearted, well-read and reckless of personal appearance. I knew her, but not well. I had tea with her in her sparsely inhabited, richly furnished house in Melbury Road and listened eagerly to her reminiscences of the Pre-Raphaelites, delighting in her strong intellect and sharp expressions, but I was totally ignorant, as I suppose were most of her guests, of the extraordinary features of the ménage which her granddaughter here delightfully reveals. It is 'Grand,' Mrs Holman Hunt, who dominates the book. Mrs Freeman, the maternal grandmother, might be any well-to-do woman of the period. Mrs Holman Hunt would have been extravagantly original in any age.

The book, *My Grandmothers and I*, has already been noticed in the *Spectator*, where it provided the theme for an essay on domestic servants. If it is now treated as an excuse to write about Holman Hunt, homage must first be paid to the great skill of the author. In her preface she describes her work as 'true in essence, but not in detail' and there are a number of obscurities and discrepancies that will puzzle a reader who treats it as a source of biography. Dates and ages are usually left vague. Impressive characters such as 'Big Aunt' loom into the story as they must have done in the child's life without introduction or full identification. It is the secret of the book's charm that the author has not sought to elaborate her memories with research. Adult curiosity remains unsatisfied. How much money, one would like to be told, did 'Grand' leave? Her extreme parsimony was clearly due to choice rather than to necessity. But were the gold coins in the drawer real sovereigns? Was the father, who makes a brief and endearing appearance, running through the modest but far from negligible family fortune? When and where did 'Grand' adopt ritualistic practices so alien to her presbyterian origins? Simeon Solomon died before Diana Holman-Hunt was born. His name had been expunged from the memoirs of the period. Can 'Grand' really have hoped to encounter him and relieve his destitution during the period of the First World War? Can she really have been ignorant of the causes of his downfall? How old was the Duke of Gloucester and how old the author when she invited him to go fishing in Kensington Gardens? But these problems cease to tease when the book is accepted for what it is—a triumphant re-creation of a child's memories.

Mrs Holman Hunt had long been widowed when the grand-daughter became aware of her and, no doubt, had developed her peculiarities in loneliness. Not that she was a recluse. Her social life was vigorous and varied but in her later years it seems to have been confined to the hours of daylight. Once the burglar traps had been set the little household retired hungry to their comfortless rooms and the old woman was left with her memories. What reverence the English painters and writers of the nineteenth century excited and perpetuated among their womenfolk! 'Grand' copiously and regularly weeping over the slab in St Paul's Cathedral which covered her husband's ashes; 'Grand' tenaciously defending, and training a third generation to defend, his just claims to have been the originator of Pre-Raphaelitism; 'Grand' literally labelling the tea cups out of which eminent Victorians had drunk; can we hope to see such *pietas* among the relics of our modern painters? Nor was she, singular in so much else, unique in this. The great men of the mid-Victorian era imposed themselves on their immediate posterity when no apparatus existed to record their spoken words. They imposed not only their achievements but their reticence. Whatever their weaknesses and doubts they did, almost all of them, regard themselves as the custodians of morality. We know very little of their private lives, particularly of their pleasures. Some traces have been left of their early manhood—of smoking-parties, boating-parties, an easy cameraderie in lending and borrowing money, but from the moment they marry we are given only a record of professional triumphs and official honours. Rossetti was a man of flagrantly Bohemian habits but his brother William succeeded in obliterating almost every trace. Of Holman Hunt we know less than of any of them. We have his own fascinating autobiography (the second, two-volume, fully illustrated edition of which, incidentally, was paid for by 'Grand') but apart from that almost nothing. His works, he believed, ensured his immortality. Perhaps it is prurient to ask for more. Perhaps in this prurient age more attention would be paid to his works if we knew more of his life than he was prepared to disclose.

'Grand' was in a somewhat ambiguous position. She was the sister of his first wife at the time when such marriages were illegal in England. Ten years elapsed between the two marriages during much of which time Hunt was abroad and alone. One is reminded of Augustus Egg who ended his days in Algiers with a wife whom, the official biographer states, he was, to his regret, unable to present to his friends. Did Hunt have any escapades in his young manhood in Palestine? We know nothing of his courtship. Had he taken the younger sister's fancy at his first wedding? Her descriptions of his full scented beard are distinctly amorous—as indeed they should be. But one wonders what went on in the years of his widowhood and how he finally settled for 'Grand'. Not, apparently, as I had always supposed, partly to provide a second mother for Cyril. He, according to 'Big Aunt', was soon sent packing by 'Grand'.

There can be no one alive today who can claim Hunt's friendship. There were few at the time of his death, and there are not many anecdotes of him in the reminiscences of the period. He does not seem to have been a likeable man. My father, who got on with most people, stayed with him as a young man when Hunt was at the height of his fame and found him impenetrably aloof. Mrs Plunket-Greene, who knew him in her childhood, reported him as cruel and pompous. The charge of cruelty was based on the story that he had starved an animal to death in his garden to paint the *Scapegoat*—a less hilarious incident than

Diana Holman-Hunt's description of his boiling a horse. Max Beerbohm represents him as plebeian in appearance and patronising in manner. After the age of thirty he seems to have made or kept no close friends. But 'Grand' certainly doted on him, and his son Hilary unexpectedly remembers him as an indulgent father who was constantly getting him out of scrapes. His portrait of himself suggests the saint and the sage.

His character will, presumably, remain enigmatic. His works remain and they are, I suppose, the least appreciated of any comparable painter's. When I was last in Birmingham his superb *Shadow of Death* lay in the cellars of the city Art Gallery. He was, beyond question, the original Pre-Raphaelite and the only one to pursue throughout his whole life the principles of his adolescence. Pre-Raphaelitism in popular use has come to connote picturesque mediævalism of the kind exemplified in the water-colours of the 1860s which Rossetti painted under Ruskin's direction. Pre-Raphaelitism to Hunt meant the intense study of natural appearances devoted to the inculcation of a lofty theme. He was obsessed with the structure of objects (hence his attempts to reduce the horse to a skeleton) and with the exact tincture of shadows. While his contemporaries in France, whom he regarded with loathing and contempt, sought to record a glimpse, he sought to record months of intense scrutiny. Their works are eagerly sought by the modern *nouveaux riches*; Hunt's are probably of less value than when they were painted. It must be admitted that they are ugly, compared with the Italian and Flemish masters he professed to emulate. He was in his work, as apparently in his life, notably lacking in the wish to please. He rejoiced in defying contemporary standards of prettiness (except in a very few deplorable cases). Why does not the present age rejoice with him? A kind of cataract seems to seal the eyes of this half-century, which has accepted with relish monstrosities of every sort, to the invention, accomplishment, untiring vitality and dedicated purpose of these great and often hidden master-pieces.

BIBLIOGRAPHY

Acton, William, *Prostitution considered in its aspects*, etc., Churchill, London, 1869.

Agnew, Geoffrey, W. A., *Agnew's 1817–1967*, Bradbury Agnew Press, London, 1967.

Aitken, James, Ford Madox Brown (1821–1893), *English Diaries of the XIX Century*, Harmondsworth, Penguin Books, London, 1944.

Angeli, Helen Rossetti, *Dante Gabriel Rossetti: His Friends and Enemies*, Hamish Hamilton, London, 1949.

Baldwin, A. W., "The Burne-Joneses, 1860–1920", *The Macdonald Sisters*, Davies, London, 1960.

Bell Scott, W., *Autobiographical Notes of the Life of W. Bell Scott and Notices of His Artistic and Poetic Circle of Friends, 1830–82*, edited by W. Minto, Osgood, London, 1892.

Bickley, Francis Lawrence, *The Pre-Raphaelite Comedy*, Constable, London, 1932.

Blanch, Lesley, *The Wilder Shores of Love*, John Murray, London, 1954.

Chapman, Ronald, *The Laurel and the Thorn, study of G. F. Watts*, Faber and Faber, London, 1945.

Clodd, Edward, "William Holman Hunt (1827–1910)", *Memories*, Chapman and Hall, London, 1916.

Cook, E. T., *Life of Ruskin*, George Allen, London, 1911.

Davidson, Angus, "Holman Hunt and the Tennysons", *Edward Lear, Landscape Painter and Nonsense Poet, 1812–1888*, Harmondsworth, Penguin Books, London, 1950.

Doughty, Oswald, *A Victorian Romantic: Dante Gabriel Rossetti*, Muller, London, 1949; second edition, Oxford University Press, London, 1960.

Doughty, Oswald, and Wahl, John R., *Letters of Dante Gabriel Rossetti*, Clarendon Press, Oxford, 1965.

Dunn, Henry Treffry, *Recollections of Dante Gabriel Rossetti and His Circle (Cheyne Walk Life)*, Elkin Mathews, London, 1904.

Fox, Caroline, *Memories of Old Friends*, Smith and Elder, London, 1881-83.

Fredeman, William E., *Pre-Raphaelitism, A bibliocritical study*, Harvard University Press, Cambridge, Mass., 1965.

Gaunt, William, *The Pre-Raphaelite Tragedy*, Jonathan Cape, London, 1942.

Gaunt, Wlliam, *The Aesthetic Adventure*, Jonathan Cape, London, 1945.

Gissing, A. C., *William Holman Hunt: A Biography*, Duckworth, London, 1936.

Glynn Grylls, Rosalie, *Portrait of Rossetti*, Macdonald, London, 1964.

Hall Caine, T., *Recollections of Dante Gabriel Rossetti*, Stock, London, 1882.

Horne, Alistair, *The Fall of Paris*, Macmillan, London, 1965.

House, Graham, *Dickens' Letters*, Oxford University Press, London, 1965.

Howitt, Mary, *"The Pre-Raphaelites"*, *An Autobiography*, Isbister, London, 1889.

Hueffer, Ford Madox, *The Pre-Raphaelite Brotherhood: A Critical Monograph*, Duckworth, London, 1907.

Holman-Hunt, Diana, *My Grandfather and I*, Hamish Hamilton, London, 1960.

Holman Hunt, William, *Pre-Raphaelitism and the Pre-Raphaelite Brotherhood*, Macmillan, London, 1905; second edition, revised by Edith Holman-Hunt, Chapman and Hall, London, 1913.

Hunt, Violet, *The Wife of Rossetti: Her Life and Death*, John Lane, London, 1932.

Ironside, R., and Gere, J., *Pre-Raphaelite Painters*, Phaidon, London, 1948.

Laver, James, *Age of Optimism*, Weidenfeld and Nicolson, London, 1966.

Laver, James, *Whistler*, Faber and Faber, London, 1950.

Layard, G. S., *Tennyson and his Pre-Raphaelite Illustrators: A Book about a Book*, Stock, London, 1894.

Longford, Elizabeth, *Victoria R.I.*, Weidenfeld and Nicolson, London, 1966.

Lutyens, Mary, *Effie in Venice*, John Murray, London, 1965.

Lutyens, Mary, *Millais and the Ruskins*, John Murray, London, 1967.

Maas, Jeremy, *Victorian Painters*, Barrie and Rockliff, London, 1969.

Marcus, Steven, *The Other Victorians*, Weidenfeld and Nicolson, London, 1967.

Noakes, Vivien, *Edward Lear: The Life of a Wanderer*, Collins, London, 1968.

Overton Fuller, Jean, *Swinburne, A Critical Biography*, Chatto and Windus, London, 1968.

Pevsner, Nikolaus, *The Englishness of English Art*, Architectural Press, London, 1956.

Reitlinger, Gerald, *The Economics of Taste*, Barrie and Rockliff, London, 1961.

Reynolds, Graham, *Victorian Painting*, Studio Vista, London, 1966.

Ritchie, Hester, *Letters of Anne Thackeray Ritchie*, John Murray, London, 1924.

Robertson, W. Graham, "The Spell of Rossetti", *Time Was: Reminiscences*, Hamish Hamilton, London, 1931.

Rossetti, William M., *Dante Gabriel Rossetti: His Family Letters with a Memoir*, Ellis, London, 1895.

Rossetti, William M., *Pre-Raphaelite Diaries and Letters*, Hurst and Blackett, London, 1900.

Rossetti, William M., *The Works of Dante Gabriel Rossetti*, revised and enlarged edition, Ellis, London, 1911.

Rossetti, William M., *Ruskin: Rossetti: Pre-Raphaelitism: Papers 1854–1862*, Allen, London, 1899.

Rossetti, William M., *Rossetti Papers, 1862–1870*, Sands, London, 1903.

Rossetti, William M., *Some Reminiscences*, Scribner's Sons, New York, 1906.

Rossetti, William M., "Holman Hunt", *Fine Art Chiefly Contemporary: Notices Reprinted with Revisions*, Macmillan, London, 1867.

Rowley, Charles, "Holman Hunt", *Fifty Years Without Wages*, Hodder and Stoughton, London, 1911.

Ruskin, John, *The Works of John Ruskin*, edited by E. T. Cook and Alexander Wedderburn, George Allen, London, 1903–12.

Seddon, John P., *Memoir and Letters of the Late Thomas Seddon, Artist by His Brother*, Nisbet, London, 1858.

Slade, William, *A Centenary Appreciation of Holman Hunt*, privately published, Hastings, 1927.

Stephens, F. G., *William Holman Hunt and His Works: A Memoir of the Artist's Life, with Descriptions of His Pictures*, Nisbet, London, 1860.

Taine, Hippolyte, *Notes on England*, translated by Edward Hyams, Thames and Hudson, London, 1957.

Thirkell, Angela, *Three Houses*, Oxford University Press, London, 1930.

Troxell, Janet Camp, *Three Rossettis*, Harvard University Press, Cambridge, Mass., 1937.

Watts-Dunton, Theodore, *Old Familiar Faces*, Jenkins, London, 1916.

Waugh, Evelyn, *Rossetti: His Life and Works*, Duckworth, London, 1928.

Waugh, Evelyn, A *Little Learning*, Chapman and Hall, London,

Whitehouse, J. H., *Vindication of Ruskin*, Allen and Unwin, London, 1950.

Williamson, George C., *Holman Hunt*, Bell (miniature series of painters), London, 1902.

Woolner, Amy, *Thomas Woolner, R.A., Sculptor and Poet: His Life in Letters*, Chapman and Hall, London, 1917.

Magazines and Periodicals

Chesnau, Ernest, "Peintres anglais contemporains: W. Holman Hunt", *L'Art* LIX 20e année, tome IV, 1894. (p. 280-299.)

Davies, Randall, "G. P. Boyce with extracts from G. P. Boyce's Diaries, 1851–1875", Old Water-Colour Society's Nineteenth Annual Volume, London, 1941.

Glynn Grylls, Rosalie, "The Correspondence of F. G. Stephens", *Times Literary Supplement*, Number 2875, 5 April, 1957. (p.

Glynn Grylls, Rosalie, "The Pre-Raphaelite Brotherhood", *Times Literary Supplement*, Number 2876, 12 April, 1957, (p. 232.)

Holman Hunt, William, "Pre-Raphaelitism: A Fight for Art", *Contemporary Review*, April, May and June, 1886.

Holman Hunt, William, "Painting The Scapegoat", *Contemporary Review*, 1887.

Hunt, Violet, "Stunners", *Artwork* VI, Summer 1930. (p. 77-87.)

Manson, Flora, "Holman Hunt and the Story of a Butterfly", *Cornhill Magazine*, CII, n.s. XXIX, November 1910. (p. 641-647.)

Meynell, Alice, and Farrar, F. W., "Life and Works of William Holman Hunt", *The Art Annual* (Special Number), 1893.

Ormond, Leonée, "A Legend of Camelot", *Apollo*, January 1967.

Rossetti, William M., "Reminiscences of Holman Hunt", *Contemporary Review*, XCVIII, October 1910. (p. 385-395.)

Stephens, F. G., "The Triumph of the Innocents", *Portfolio* XVI, April 1885. (p. 80-83.)

Waugh, Evelyn, "The Only Pre-Raphaelite", *Spectator*, 14 October, 1960.

Catalogues

Bennett, Mary, *William Holman Hunt*, Catalogue Raisonné, The Walker Art Gallery in conjunction with the Arts Council of Great Britain, 1969.

National Portrait Gallery, "William Holman Hunt", Second Series, Cassell, London, 1876.

INDEX

Acland, Dr Henry W., 173
Acton, William, 63, 64, 68
After the Ball (Hunt), 237
Afterglow, The (Hunt), 130
Allen, Grant, 17, 184
Allingham, William, 65, 171, 254
Andrews, Georgina, 88, 95, 127
Annunciation (Rossetti), 71
April Love (Hughes), 59
Artists' Rifle Corps, 211
Awakening Conscience, The (Hunt),
104, 107, 113, 115, 124, 133-4, 144,
145, 203, 248

Beerbohm, Sir Max, 295
Bennett, Mr (uncle of Mrs Combe),
58, 74-5
Bethlehem, 143, 266-7
Bianca (Hunt), 262
Birthday, The (Hunt), 261
Blanchard, Auguste, 257-9
Borradaile, Mrs, 264
Boyce, George Price, 60, 85, 97, 138,
167, 171, 184, 189, 199, 203-5,
209-10, 217
Bradley, John, 262, 268, 269, 273, 276,
278, 279-80
Bradshaw, Mrs (landlady), 62, 81,
188, 194, 195, 216
Bradshaw, Sarah, 62, 98, 113, 135, 188
Bramah, Mrs ('educator' of Annie
Miller), 97, 98-9, 113, 135-6, 153,
166, 173, 175, 195-7, 216, 217, 220,
238, 239, 247
Brodie (painter), 118
Brough, Robert, 84, 192, 214
Brown, Emma Madox, 69, 110, 144,
167, 171, 183
Brown, Ford Madox, 43, 46, 49, 52,
53, 57-8, 64, 69-70, 77, 84, 89, 96,
110, 114, 132, 138, 144, 149, 152,
153, 167, 170-1, 182-3, 186, 278, 283,
286-91
Brown, Oliver Madox, 167
Browning, Elizabeth Barrett, 170, 231
Browning, Robert, 170, 230
Brussels, 56-7
Burden, Jane, 187
Burne-Jones, Sir Edward, 58n, 60, 152,
171-2, 183, 186, 278, 286-7, 290
Burne-Jones, Georgina, 183
Burt, Mrs Elizabeth, 111, 191n
Burton, Sir Richard, 215
Burton, Isabella, 162
Bush, Mrs (milliner), 208, 218, 219,
220, 222, 223

Cairo, 119-20, 128-31, 141
Campden Hill, Tor Villa at, 173, 175,
180, 181-2, 185, 187, 196, 199-200,
204-6, 216, 264
Canning, Lady, 105
Carlyle, Thomas, 77, 105-6, 107
Carlyle, Jane Welsh, 106, 234
Carpenter's Shop, The (Millais), 71
Charles, Mme, 55, 118
Childs, Henry, 84n, 135n, 167, 200
Christ Disputing with the Doctors
(Da Vinci), 106, 107
Christ at the Door (later *Light of
the World*, q.v.) (Hunt), 82-3, 84,
85, 91, 93, 94, 104
Christ in the House of His Parents
(Millais), 71
Christ in the Temple (Hunt)—*see
Finding of Christ in the Temple*
Christ and the Two Marys (Hunt),
44
Claudio and Isabella (Hunt), 72, 93

Cobden, Richard, 34
Collins, Charles, 47, 58-9, 64, 73, 74, 76, 82-3, 90, 91-2, 93, 101, 103, 107, 108, 109, 115, 117, 124, 150, 151, 152, 153, 167, 174, 182, 186, 189, 214
Collins, Mrs Harriet, 60, 82, 91, 101, 102
Collins, Wilkie, 47, 59, 83, 117, 167, 174, 190, 212
Collinson, James, 48, 49, 50, 55, 63n, 73, 90, 145
Combe, Thomas, 58, 73-5, 83, 84, 87-8, 89, 92, 94, 97, 101, 105, 107, 113, 114, 127, 144, 169, 186-7, 201, 214, 237, 244, 262, 275
Combe, Mrs Thomas (Pat), 58, 73, 75, 83, 87-8, 94, 95, 101, 108, 127, 186-7, 201, 205, 233
Convent Thoughts (Collins), 83
Converted British Family Sheltering a Christian Missionary from the Persecution of the Druids, A (Hunt), 54, 71, 73, 74-5
Cosmopolitan Club, 91, 213
Craik, Dinah, 284
Creswick, Thomas, 72
Crystal Palace Alhambra, 169, 179
Cyclographic Club, 41, 42

Damascus, 162
Damietta, 141
Dante's Dream (Rossetti), 271
Dead Sea, 155-62
Delacroix, Eugène, 57
Deluge, The (Millais), 124
Deverell, Walter, 63, 65, 89, 110, 111, 123, 127, 170, 173
Dickens, Charles, 22, 59, 71, 94, 190-4, 212, 213, 226
Dickens, Kate (Mrs Charles Collins), 214
Dickinson, Lowes, 77, 167
Digby, Jane, 162-3
Diplock, Tom, 97, 98, 99, 138-9, 150, 167, 173, 187, 196, 216
Dolce Far Niente (Hunt), 203, 205, 237, 245
Doughty, Oswald, 171, 248
Dyce, William, 72

Eastlake, Sir Charles, 149
Eastlake, Lady, 132, 149

Egg, Augustus, 53, 54, 56, 72, 93, 94, 96, 97, 111, 124, 181, 185, 189, 294
Ellenborough, Lady (Jane Digby), 162-3
Eve of St Agnes, The (Hunt), 42, 44, 51
Ewell, 33, 40, 79-83, 91, 185, 190
Ezaak (model for Christ), 268

Fairbairn, Sir Thomas, 104, 134
Fairlight, 80, 87, 207, 208, 209
Falling Rocket, The (Whistler), 136n
Festival of St Swithin, The (E. Hunt), 245
Finding of Christ in the Temple, The (Hunt), 24, 107, 141, 146-7, 169, 179, 187, 198, 200, 209, 211-14, 240
Florence, 250-7, 261-5, 273, 280
Found (Rossetti), 144
Fox, Caroline, 214-15
Frith, W. P., 128
Fryston Hall, 215

Gabriel (Hunt's Cairo servant), 121, 128
Gambart, Ernest, 169-70, 212-13, 214, 260
Gaunt, William, 50, 65n
Germ, The (PRB magazine), 65, 70-71
Gibbs, Superintendent, 195, 197, 216
Giotto, 43
Girl in the Pink Bonnet, The (Millais), 132
Girlhood of the Virgin (Rossetti), 51, 53, 54, 115
Gissing, A. C., 79, 206n, 246
Gladstone, W. E., 96, 181
Glyn, Rev. Sir George Lewen, 79n, 81
Gobat, Dr (Bishop of Jerusalem), 150, 192, 193
Graham, James, 148, 162, 266
Gull, Sir William, 173

Halliday, Michael, 97, 123, 124, 127, 132, 133, 138, 144, 150-1, 157, 164, 165, 168, 169, 173, 174, 182, 185, 199, 205, 207
Hancock, John, 64
Helen of Troy (Rossetti), 132
Herbert, Mrs Sidney, 216, 219
Hireling Shepherd, The (Hunt), 22, 79, 81, 82, 83-4, 87, 105, 190
Hobman family, 31, 33, 83

Hobman, William, 83, 175, 185, 190, 207, 282

Holman-Hunt, Gladys (Hunt's daughter), 111, 191*n*, 284*n*

Household Words, 71, 190-194, 214

Howitt, Mary, 137, 232-3

Hueffer, Francis, 57

Hughes, Arthur, 59, 64, 153, 186, 189

Hughes, Edward, 59

Hughes, John, 67, 180, 187, 216

Hunt, Cyril Benone (Hunt's son), 18, 246, 250*n*, 251-2, 257, 259, 260, 261-2, 263, 264-5, 266, 270-1, 272-3, 276-7, 282, 283, 284, 294

Hunt, Edith Waugh, Mrs Holman (Hunt's second wife and author's grandmother)—*see* Waugh, Edith

Hunt, Edward Henry (brother), 31*n*, 34, 36, 37

Hunt, Elizabeth Ann (sister), 31*n*

Hunt, Emily (sister), 31*n*, 40, 44, 124, 175, 182, 185, 188, 199, 200, 207, 245, 252, 282

Hunt, Fanny Waugh, Mrs Holman (first wife)—*see* Waugh, Fanny

Hunt, Hilary Holman (son), 295

Hunt, Maria (later Peagrim) (sister), 31*n*, 44, 92, 252*n*

Hunt, Sarah (later Wilson) (sister), 31*n*, 36-7, 40, 41, 44, 92, 113, 282

Hunt, Sarah Hobman (mother), 31, 36, 44, 46, 79, 282

Hunt, Violet, 133, 169, 184

Hunt, William (father), 31-3, 34-5, 36-7, 41-2, 53, 106, 145, 149, 150, 169, 175

Hunt, William Holman: ancestry and birth, 31-2; childhood and education, 32-3; fascinated by New Testament stories, 32; determined to be painter, 33; father's opposition, 33, 34, 36, 37; becomes clerk with estate agent James, 33-4; encouraged by him to paint, 34; takes painting lessons from Henry Rogers, 34, 35; again finds sympathetic employer, 34-5, 36-7; discovers Keats, 35, 40; spends free time copying at British Museum, 36; first hears of Millais, 36-7; admitted to Royal Academy lectures, 37; first sees Millais at 1843 prizegiving, 37-8; accepted as Academy student, 39; first meeting and friendship with Millais, 39-42; contrasting family lives, 39-40, 42; rebels against artistic conventions, 40, 43; father's changed attitude, 41-2; his *Eve of St Agnes* hung, 42; bewitched by Rossetti, 42-6; tells him of his and Millais' ideas for reform, 23; gets 'Mad' nickname, 44; meets Woolner, 47; finds 'Pre-Raphaelite' affair getting out of hand, 48; conciliates Millais, 48-9, 50; and 'inaugural' meeting of Brotherhood, 49-50; shares studio with Rossetti, 51-2; paints *Rienzi*, 51; manic depression and fear of Devil, 52, 118, 156-7, 267; Rossetti's defection over Academy exhibition, 52-3; sells *Rienzi*, 53-4; reconciled with Rossetti, 54; their continental tour, 54, 55-7; increasing circle, 58-60; meets Combe of Oxford, 58; appearance, 60-1, 214, 244; moves to Chelsea studio, 62; model-hunting, 62-3, 65-6; finds Annie Miller, 66, 69; financial distress after press attacks, 71-3; cleans Rigaud paintings at Trinity House, 72; sells *Christians and Druids* to Combe, 74-5; at Knole to paint background to *Valentine and Sylvia*, 75-6; becomes Annie's protector, 76; considers emigrating to Australia, 77; loan from Millais family, 77, 86, 87; finds champion in Ruskin, 77-8; paints *Hireling Shepherd* background at Ewell, 79-83; uses Emma Watkins as shepherdess model, 81, 83-4; begins *Light of the World*, 82-3, 84-6; interest in boxing, 85, 191; sells *Hireling Shepherd*, 87; visits Combes at Oxford, 87-9, 92; decides not to emigrate, 89; uses Christina Rossetti and Lizzie Siddal as models for Christ's face, 89-90; anxious to visit Holy Land, 90, 93, 94-5; social success, 93, 104-5; torn between two ideals of marriage, 94-6; decides to educate Annie with view to marriage, 96-9; uses Stephens as go-between, 97, 98-9, 113, 126, 149, 150, 153-4, 173, 175-9, 183-4, 187-8, 194, 195-9,

Hunt, William Holman—*cont.*
200, 203-4, 207-9, 216-28, 245-7; lectures Annie on wages of sin, 98; increasing obsession with her, 101-2; and Millais' dilemma over Effie Ruskin, 103; begins *Awakening Conscience* with Annie as model, 104-5, 113; impressed by Carlyle's denunciation of *Light of the World*, 105-6; determines to study authentic backgrounds in Syria, 106; friends' reluctance for him to go, 107-12; dissuades Millais and Rossetti from accompanying him, 114-15; departure, 116; amorous encounter on train, 117; in Cairo, 119-32; camps near Sphinx, 120-3; problem of models, 128-31; puts new face in *Awakening Conscience*, 134; sails up Nile to Damietta, 141-2; in Jerusalem, 143-55; feels 'increasing need of a wife', 144; hears of hostile reaction to Academy pictures, 145; encounters with brigands, 145-6, 149; begins *Christ in the Temple*, 146-7; camps on Dead Sea shore to paint *Scapegoat*, 148, 155-62; hears of Ruskin's defence of him, 149; urged by friends to return, 150-1; news of their marriages, 151-3; proposes to Annie, 153-4, 175; encounters with natives and sheikhs, 157-61; 'engraves' imaginary Russian secret weapons, 162; has malaria, 163-4, 170; returns to London, 167; shares 'crib' with Halliday and Martineau, 168-9; 'still besotted on Annie', 169; mixed reception for *Scapegoat*, 169-70; ignorant of Rossetti's affair with Annie, 171-2; fails to be elected A.R.A., 173, 182; ill-health, 173; moves to Tor Villa, Campden Hill, 173; warned by Millais against Annie, 174; in no hurry to marry, 174-5; death of father, 175; wishes Annie to continue education, 175-80; increasing social life, 180-1, 185; begins collection of furniture, 181-2; project of artists' colony, 182-3; hears of Annie's relations with Rossetti, 183-4; reconciled, 184-5;

visits Oxford, 186-7; enabled to finish *Christ in Temple* by loan from Combe, 187; moves Annie to Bridge Row, Pimlico, 188-9; prepares friends for his marriage, 189; and *Household Words* satirical account of himself and Emma Watkins, 190-4; quarrel with Annie, 195-200; promises to marry her, 200; woos Miss Strong while awaiting Annie's decision, 201-2, 205; renewed quarrel, 203-5; his drawings of Annie, 205; hears of her liaison with Ranelagh, 206-7; persecution mania, 207-8; determined to dismiss her from mind, 209-10; finishes *Christ in Temple*, 211; mental and physical exhaustion, 211-12; sells it for 5500 guineas, 212-13; worldly and social success, 213-15; Annie's attempts to blackmail, 215-28, 245-9; meets the Waughs, 231-2; courts Fanny Waugh, 232-3, 238-9; anxious to get rid of Annie, 233-4; cannot make up his mind on marriage, 235-7; officially engaged, 240; marriage, 243-4; buys his love-letters from Annie, 245-6; sets out for East again, 249; settles in Florence, 250; birth of son Cyril, 251; death of Fanny, 252; interest in spiritualism, 253-4; designs monument to Fanny, 254; in Paris, 257-9; Cyril's illness, 257, 259, 260; return to London, 260; paints Edith Waugh, 261; realizes her love for him, 261; return to Florence, 261-5; interest in Miss Lydiard, 262, 274; meets Ruskin in Venice, 265-6; in Jerusalem again, 266-75; works on *Shadow of Death*, 266, 267; wishes Cyril to come out East, 272-3; thoughts of re-marriage, 273-5; returns to England, 275; reunion with Cyril, 276-7; non-committal over Edith's confession of love, 277-8; not in love, 278, 279-80; Waugh opposition to their decision to marry, 279; Edith's refusal, 279-80; decision to marry, 282; his growing love for her, 282-3, 284; marriage, 284

Inchbold, John William, 128
Ingres, J. A. D., 57
Isabella and the Pot of Basil (Hlnt), 254, 260, 264
James, Mr (estate agent), 33-4
Jenkins, Rev. John, 88
Jerusalem, 143-55, 266, 267-75, 284

Kingsley, Charles, 77, 94
Knole Park, 75-6

Lady Godiva (Hunt), 205
Lady of Shalott, The (Hunt), 59n, 205
Landseer, Sir Edwin, 148n
Last of England, The (Brown), 110
Last Night in the Old Home, The (Martineau), 59
Laver, James, 139-40
Layard, G. S., 91, 94, 95, 131, 205
Layard, Sir Henry, 86
Lear, Edward, 14, 45, 59, 101, 201, 215, 235, 262, 283
Leatherhead, 230, 232, 261
Leech, John, 125, 127, 152
Leonardo da Vinci, 106, 107
Leslie, Lady Constance, 181
Lewis, Arthur, 180
Light of the World, The (formerly Christ at the Door, q.v.) (Hunt), 59n, 104, 105-7, 108, 113, 131, 145, 149
London Bridge on the Night of the Marriage of the Prince and Princess of Wales (Hunt), 237
Lorenzo and Isabella (Millais), 52
Louise, Princess, 281
Luard, Captain, 266, 268
Luard, John Dalbiac, 151
Lucy, Charles, 70
Lydiard, Miss, 262, 274, 280

Macaulay, Lord, 77
McCracken, Francis, 78
Maclise, Daniel, 127
Marcus, Steven, 64
Martineau, Robert, 59, 167, 168, 169, 173, 182, 185, 189, 199, 205, 207, 208, 209, 237
Mayhew, Henry, 140
Millais, Sir John Everett, 15, 19, 22, 54, 57, 60, 77, 89, 95, 98, 173-4, 181,
182, 188, 205, 213, 277; Hunt hears of, 36; first sight of, 38; physical beauty, 38, 63, 80, 100-1, 126; first meeting and growing friendship, 39-41; rebels against artistic conventions, 40, 43, 46, 56; Academy picture rejected, 42, 49; disturbed by Hunt's extension of group, 48-9; 'inaugural' PRB meeting, 50; first meeting with Rossetti, 50; furious at Rossetti's desertion, 52-3, 55; paints backgrounds at Oxford, 53, 73-4, 76; a bon vivant, 58; disgusted at Rossetti's revealing PRB secret, 71-2; introduces Hunt to Combes, 74-5; at Ewell, 79-83; model-hunting, 79-82; deplores Hunt's absence, 90-2, 93; paints Effie Ruskin, 91; friendship with Ruskins, 93-4, 102-4; in Scotland, 93-4, 100-104; concern for profile, 101; increasing regard for Effie, 102-3, 107-9, 131, 149; Ruskin's bewilderment with him, 103-4, 111-12; dreads Hunt's departure for Syria, 107, 108-9, 110-12, 116, 117; depression, 110-112, 115, 124, 150; Hunt's correspondence with, 117-18, 121-8, 144, 151, 168, 174, 200, 254, 255, 272, 282; friendship with Leech and 'manly' sports, 125-6, 127; abandons idea of joining Hunt in East, 131; grows whiskers, 132, 168; his pictures of Annie Miller, 132; marriage to Effie, 151-3, 168; considers matrimony 'healthy, manly and right', 168; birth of son, 174; disapproves of Ruskin and Rossetti, 186-7; increasing social life, 215; on Fanny Hunt's death, 254; persuades Hunt to return to England, 275; lets him use studio, 277
Millais, William, 93, 100, 101, 102, 125
Miller, Annie, 17, 22, 70, 78, 102, 237; discovered by Hunt, 66, 68, 69; humble background, 66-8, 99; Hunt becomes her protector, 75, 76, 86; at Sevenoaks, 76; her education paid for by Hunt, 97-9, 113-14, 135-6, 149, 173, 174-5, 185; sits for Awakening Conscience, 98,

Miller, Annie—cont.
99, 115, 133-4; sits for Millais and Rossetti, 127, 132, 133; engagement to Hunt 'practically acknowledged', 133, 145, success as model, 133, 137; liaison with Rossetti, 136-8, 139, 144-5, 167, 170-1; other beaux, 138, 175; Hunt proposes to, 153-4, 175; Stephens' susceptibility to, 154, 242; mistress of Lord Ranelagh, 165, 166-7, 175, 180, 188, 195, 202, 206; Hunt still besotted with, 169, 174; Hunt warned by Millais against, 174; resents continued education without prospect of marriage, 175-80; agrees to be day pupil only, 180; forced to admit relations with Rossetti, 183-4, 198; reconciled with Hunt, 184-5; at Oxford, 187; moves to Lupus Street, 188-9; entertains lovers there, 189, 196-7; quarrel with Hunt over money and other troubles, 195-200; temporary truce, 202-3; renewed quarrel, 203-5; Hunt's drawings of, 205; her Ranelagh liaison revealed to Hunt, 206-7; poverty, 208-9; renews favours to Boyce and Rossetti, 209-210; death of father, 211; attempt to blackmail Hunt, 215-28, 245-9; falls in love with Thomas R. Thomson, 224; marries him, 228-9, 245, 247; the Waughs told of her, 238, 239; birth of daughter, 251

Miller, Bess, 66-7, 68, 153, 175, 187, 215

Miller, George, 66-7

Miller, Harriett (later Childs), 66, 67, 84n, 135n, 153, 167, 188, 200, 215, 229

Miller, Henry, 66-7, 68, 98, 166, 175, 211

Miller, John, 78

Milnes, Richard Monckton (later Lord Houghton), 215, 286, 287-9

Miriam (housekeeper and model for Virgin), 269-70

Modern Painters (Ruskin), 265

Moody, Francis, 176, 188, 247

Moody, Miss, 247

Moreau, Gustave, 69

Morning Prayer (Hunt), 205

Morris, William, 58n, 171, 182, 183, 186

Morris, Jane (Burden), 20, 187

Moxon, Edward, 169

Muloch, Tom, 284n

Neufchâtel, 284

Oosdoom (now Uzdum), 158, 163

Ophelia (Millais), 79, 80, 81, 83

Order of Release, The (Millais), 57, 91

Oxford, 58, 73-5, 87-9, 92, 95, 169, 186-7, 201

Palgrave, Francis T., 211-12, 236

Paris, 55-6, 118, 257-9

Parting (Hunt), 205

Patmore, Coventry, 65, 77, 125

Patmore, Thomas, 127

Peagrim, William, 44, 92, 252n

Phillips, Watts, 60

Portrait of a Lady (Hunt), 261

Pre-Raphaelite Brotherhood, origin of, 43, 44-51, 187

Pre-Raphaelitism and the Pre-Raphaelite Brotherhood (Hunt), 27

Price, John Blount, 44, 51

Prinsep, Mrs, 180-1, 186

Prinsep, Val, 186

Prout, Miss (retired schoolmistress), 113, 188, 189, 194, 197, 198, 199, 202, 203, 208, 217, 223, 224

Ranelagh, 7th Viscount, 165-7, 175, 180, 188, 195, 198, 202, 206, 211, 223, 224-5, 226, 264, 271-2

Ranelagh, Caroline Louisa, Lady, 165, 202

Raphael, 43, 50, 71, 105

Reynolds, Graham, 169n

Reynolds, Sir Joshua, 40, 188

Rienzi (Hunt), 42, 51, 53, 65

Robertson, W. Graham, 27, 271

Rogers, Henry, 34-5

Rome, 266

Ross, Janet, 214-15

Rossetti, Christina, 45, 48, 89-90, 97n, 145

Rossetti, Dante Gabriel, 14, 17, 58, 83, 92, 102, 104-5, 152, 153, 169, 215, 271; Hunt's first meeting with, 42-3; anxiety to join Hunt's and Millais' group, 43, 46; Hunt's first

Rossetti, Dante Gabriel—*cont.*
visit to, 44-6; pleads with Hunt to take him as pupil, 46; introduces him to Woolner, 46-7; encourages others to 'secret society', 47-8, 49-50, 55; Millais' first impression of, 50; Hunt shares 'crib' with, 51; trials of living with, 51-2; deserts Hunt and Millais, 52-3; reconciled, 54, 55; continental tour with Hunt, 54, 55-7, 118; frequent caller at Hunt's Chelsea studio, 62, 65; model-hunting, 62-3; and Lizzie Siddal, 65, 69, 90, 97, 109, 132, 137-8, 139, 167, 183-4; cynical attitude to models, 69; betrays secret of PRB, 71-2; at Sevenoaks with Hunt, 75-6; dreads Hunt's departure for East, 109-10, 114-15; sends him a souvenir, 115; intends to join him, 126, 133; his pictures of Annie, 132; betrayal of Hunt with Annie, 136-8, 139, 144-5, 168, 170-1; renewed intimacy with Hunt, 171-2, 182-3; end of friendship, 183-4, 265; alleged procuration of abortions, 184, 286-91; decorates Oxford Union Club, 186-7; employs Annie again, 210

Rossetti, Maria, 45
Rossetti, William M., 45, 46, 47, 48, 50-51, 53, 55, 56, 65, 66, 71, 73, 76, 85, 89, 90, 92, 93, 117, 125, 138, 153, 184, 233, 244, 262, 272, 294
Royal Academy, 36, 39, 41, 42, 49, 52-3, 71, 76-8, 84, 87, 93, 127-8, 131, 133-4, 170, 173; Schools, 37-8, 39, 42, 47
Ruskin, Effie (later Millais), 91, 93-4, 101, 102-4, 107-9, 114, 117, 126, 131, 132, 133, 149, 151-2, 167, 174, 181, 275
Ruskin, John, 40, 43, 77-8, 85, 93, 101, 102-4, 109, 110, 111-12, 117, 124, 127, 128, 131, 132, 133, 136n, 149, 151, 186-7, 265-6, 288, 295

Sanneman, Dr, 138, 139, 173, 187, 216
Scapegoat, The (Hunt), 24, 147-8, 155, 158, 161-2, 163, 169-70

Scott, William Bell, 45, 85-6, 206n, 268, 275
Seddon, Thomas, 64, 90, 102, 109, 120-1, 122, 123, 128, 132, 141-3, 147, 148, 149-50, 175, 266
Sevenoaks, 75-6
Shadow of Death, The (Hunt), 266, 267, 277, 280, 284, 295
Siddal, Lizzie, 65, 66, 67, 70, 71, 76, 83, 90, 92, 97, 114, 132, 137-8, 139, 145, 170, 183, 198, 214, 254, 288, 290
Siloam, Pool of, 145-6
Sim (Jerusalem surgeon), 146, 147, 148, 162, 164, 266
Smith, Bernard, 64
Solomon, Simeon, 253, 293
Spartali, Marie, 271
Spirit of the Rainbow, The (Rossetti), 25
Stephens, Mrs Clara, 240, 241, 250, 263, 264, 270, 271, 272, 281, 284
Stephens, Frederic G., 46, 47-8, 49-50, 58, 70, 72, 73, 75, 76, 80, 81, 85, 87, 89, 90, 125, 133, 138, 144, 151, 152, 167, 189, 201, 213, 234, 235, 238-43, 244, 250-1, 252-3, 254, 262, 263-4, 270-2, 273, 278, 279, 281-2, 283; as go-between for Hunt and Annie, 97, 98-9, 113, 126, 149, 150, 153-4, 173, 175-9, 183-4, 187-8, 194, 195-9, 200, 203-4, 206, 207-9, 216-28, 245-7
Stephens, Holman ('Holly'), 263, 272
Stillman, William James, 271
Stone, Frank, 145
Stratford, Mrs (Annie's landlady), 188, 189, 194-7, 202, 203, 208, 209, 215, 216, 217, 218, 222-3, 224, 225-6, 247-8
Strayed Sheep, The (Hunt), 87, 105, 207
Strong, Miss (of Oxford), 201-2, 207
Surtees, Virginia, 248
Swinburne, Algernon C., 132, 171, 186, 253n, 286-91

Taine, Hippolyte, 136
Taylor, Tom, 261
Tennyson, Alfred, 58, 65, 71, 90, 92, 169, 230
Tennyson, Mrs, 230, 237, 239

Terry, Ellen, 181n, 233
Thackeray, W. M., 91, 94, 213
Thomson, Annie Helen, 249, 251
Thomson, Thomas James, 249n
Thomson, Thomas Jones, 165, 166, 202, 224, 228
Thomson, Thomas Ranelagh Jones, 166, 202, 223-4, 225, 228-9, 248, 249n
Time Was (W. Graham Robertson), 27
Transfiguration (Raphael), 43, 105
Triumph of the Innocents, The (Hunt), 268
Troxell, Mrs Janet, 248-9
Tupper, George, 64, 70
Tupper, John, 58-9, 64, 76, 85, 113
Turner, J. M. W., 38

Valentine and Sylvia (Hunt), 75-8
Varley, William Fleetwood, 41
Venice, 265-6, 284
Victoria, Queen, 281, 284
Vision of Fiametta, A (Rossetti), 271

Waiting (Millais), 132
Warton, Mrs (model), 70
Waterford, Marchioness of, 105
Watkins, Emma, 22, 81, 83-4, 86, 96, 190, 194, 239
Watts, G. F., 91, 180-1, 233
Waugh, Alec, 13, 14
Waugh, Dr Alexander, 24, 27
Waugh, Alice (later Woolner), 14, 17, 20, 23, 59, 231-2, 234, 236, 237, 238, 249, 270, 278
Waugh, Arthur, 13, 14
Waugh, Edith (Mrs Holman Hunt), 17-20, 22-3, 24, 25-6, 27, 37, 57, 59, 80-81, 191n, 231-2, 237, 249-50, 252,

260, 261-3, 264-5, 270-1, 273, 276, 277-9, 281-5, 292, 293, 294
Waugh, Emily, 23
Waugh, Eve, 23
Waugh, Evelyn, 13-17, 20-26, 27-8, 79n, 233n, 292-5
Waugh, Fanny (Mrs Holman Hunt), 17, 19, 20, 23, 80, 230-44, 245, 249-54, 255, 262, 266, 285
Waugh, Dr George, 24, 25-6, 27, 139, 232, 234, 236, 238, 239, 243, 244, 245, 249, 250, 260, 261, 279
Waugh, Mrs George, 245, 250, 251, 260, 261, 262, 272, 273, 276, 278, 279, 282
Waugh, George, 15, 23, 270
Waugh, Isabelle, 23
Waugh, Laura, 13, 20, 24-6, 28
Westmacott, Sir Richard, 37
Whistler, J. M., 85, 135n, 136n
White, Mrs Mary, 26-7
Wilson (upholsterer, husband of Sarah Hunt), 41, 44, 92, 282
Windus, B. G., 170
Winkworth, Catherine, 134
Woman Taken in Adultery, A (Rembrandt), 41
Woodforde, John, 186
Woodman's Daughter, The (Millais), 51
Woodward, John, 20
Woolner, Alice—see Waugh, Alice
Woolner, Amy, 283
Woolner, Thomas, 13, 15, 17, 38, 46-7, 48, 49, 55, 63, 64-5, 69, 71, 73, 77, 89, 90, 92, 96, 110, 128, 150, 180, 214, 215, 230-2, 234, 236, 237, 238, 249, 254, 272, 279